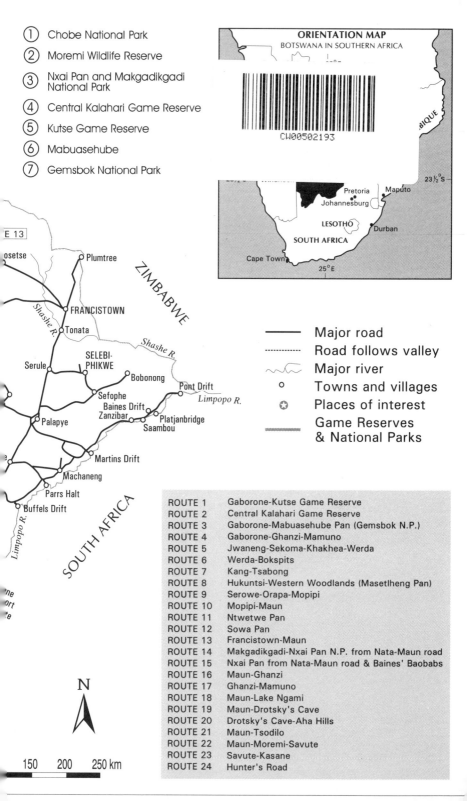

1. Chobe National Park
2. Moremi Wildlife Reserve
3. Nxai Pan and Makgadikgadi National Park
4. Central Kalahari Game Reserve
5. Kutse Game Reserve
6. Mabuasehube
7. Gemsbok National Park

ORIENTATION MAP
BOTSWANA IN SOUTHERN AFRICA

MOÇAMBIQUE

23½°S

Pretoria Maputo
Johannesburg

LESOTHO Durban

SOUTH AFRICA

Cape Town

25°E

E 13

Plumtree
osetse

ZIMBABWE

Shashe R.

FRANCISTOWN
Tonata

Shashe R.

SELEBI-PHIKWE

Serule

Bobonong

Pont Drift

Limpopo R.

Sefophe
Baines Drift
Zanzibar   Platjanbridge
Saambou

Palapye

Martins Drift

Machaneng

Parrs Halt

Buffels Drift

Limpopo R.

SOUTH AFRICA

N

150   200   250 km

—————— Major road
------------- Road follows valley
∼∼∼ Major river
  o   Towns and villages
  ✪   Places of interest
▓▓▓▓▓ Game Reserves & National Parks

ROUTE 1	Gaborone-Kutse Game Reserve
ROUTE 2	Central Kalahari Game Reserve
ROUTE 3	Gaborone-Mabuasehube Pan (Gemsbok N.P.)
ROUTE 4	Gaborone-Ghanzi-Mamuno
ROUTE 5	Jwaneng-Sekoma-Khakhea-Werda
ROUTE 6	Werda-Bokspits
ROUTE 7	Kang-Tsabong
ROUTE 8	Hukuntsi-Western Woodlands (Masetlheng Pan)
ROUTE 9	Serowe-Orapa-Mopipi
ROUTE 10	Mopipi-Maun
ROUTE 11	Ntwetwe Pan
ROUTE 12	Sowa Pan
ROUTE 13	Francistown-Maun
ROUTE 14	Makgadikgadi-Nxai Pan N.P. from Nata-Maun road
ROUTE 15	Nxai Pan from Nata-Maun road & Baines' Baobabs
ROUTE 16	Maun-Ghanzi
ROUTE 17	Ghanzi-Mamuno
ROUTE 18	Maun-Lake Ngami
ROUTE 19	Maun-Drotsky's Cave
ROUTE 20	Drotsky's Cave-Aha Hills
ROUTE 21	Maun-Tsodilo
ROUTE 22	Maun-Moremi-Savute
ROUTE 23	Savute-Kasane
ROUTE 24	Hunter's Road

VISITORS' GUIDE TO BOTSWANA

VISITORS' GUIDE TO BOTSWANA

HOW TO GET THERE · WHAT TO SEE · WHERE TO STAY

Mike Main

SOUTHERN
BOOK PUBLISHERS

ISBN 1 86812 657 9

First edition, first impression 1987
First edition, second impression 1988
Second edition, first impression 1993
Second edition, second impression 1994
Second edition, third impression 1994
Third edition, first impression 1996

Published by
Southern Book Publishers (Pty) Ltd
PO Box 3103, Halfway House, 1685, South Africa

While the author and publisher have endeavoured to
verify all facts, they will not be held responsible for any
inconvenience that may result from possible
inaccuracies in this book.

Cover design by Insight Graphics
Maps by Carto Com, Pretoria
Set in 10 on 11½ pt Palatino
by Kohler Carton & Print, Pinetown
Printed and bound by Kohler Carton & Print, Pinetown

PREFACE TO THE THIRD EDITION

John and Sandra Fowkes, who co-authored the previous editions of the *Visitors' Guide to Botswana*, have been sucked into the maw of a busy world of consulting and no longer have the opportunity to travel the wild ways of Botswana as once they did. Mike Main still lives in Botswana and now carries this particular torch alone.

This book has grown to maturity through the author's many years of residence and travel in Botswana, delighting in the pristine and unspoilt environment, the people and the ambience of the country. It needs to be stressed, however, that despite its title, this is not really a guide to Botswana. It is a guide for those with their own vehicle, usually a four-wheel-drive, who are keen to explore some of the more interesting places in Botswana's wilderness. It is not, and does not pretend to be, a guide to the history, politics, economy and society of Botswana.

In the decade and a half of my time here I have seen significant changes, many of them a source of concern. Fuelled by diamond wealth, the country is rapidly hauling itself out of the 18th century and into the 20th with all the social, economic and political difficulties associated with such a traumatic shift. For a people who traditionally see wild animals only as a food resource, the aesthetic value of game is presently of marginal concern. Due to a combination of factors such as veterinary fences, devastating drought, poorly controlled hunting and, above all, man's steady encroachment into the Kalahari, wildlife numbers have plummeted and animals are now largely confined to reserved areas. It is unlikely that populations will ever recover to former levels.

However, it is not solely (or even principally) because of wild animals that people visit Botswana. The country is unlike any of its neighbours in that most of the land is tribally owned, undeveloped and, most importantly, unfenced. There are still huge areas of true wilderness, where any wayside stopping place is a campsite. Bureaucracy and regulations, like elsewhere, understandably blanket the national parks and game reserves but there is as much to enjoy outside these places as there is within. The Okavango, Makgadikgadi, the vastness of the Kalahari, Tsodilo Hills, Gcwihaba Caves, the Hunter's Road, fossil rivers, ancient dune-fields and remote and beautiful woodlands all await you. Botswana remains special because its wilderness is still seductive; it still whispers the call to excitement, adventure, challenge and self-discovery.

In closing, may I make this point. The very fact that there is a guidebook to the wild lands of Botswana may mean that they will soon no longer be the isolated places they once were. Kubu is going this way, Tsodilo looks set to follow and I suspect Gcwihaba will not be far behind.

In the words of Sandra Fowkes, who co-authored earlier editions of this guide: 'Of those who consult this book, those who seek the soul solace of earth untrammelled by city man, I ask only this: Be thoughtful of your actions that you might not so selfishly enjoy and use the wild areas that you destroy or change them for those who will follow you.'

Mike Main
Gaborone
Botswana

ACKNOWLEDGEMENTS

It is difficult to look back over 15 years and three editions to select particular individuals from the many who, in countless ways, have made this work possible. One, however, certainly stands out above all others. To Alec Campbell: friend, mentor and guide, I offer a humble and sincere 'thank you' for years of patience, thoughtfulness and an endless outpouring of fascinating knowledge. It would be wrong, too, to fail to acknowledge the continued support and assistance of Philip Welch, who still works magic with the mysterious innards of the internal combustion engine and its four driving wheels. I would also like to acknowledge the contribution of Geoff Tucker who wrote long pages of very useful comments, most of which have been included in this new edition. Finally, a special thank you to Mrs Lalage Jackson who slaved over the minutiae and saved me a great deal of of time, for which I shall always be grateful.

As I emphasise elsewhere, I really do encourage comments, criticisms, updates and suggestions. You can post, fax or phone them to:

Mike Main
Box 2265
Gaborone
Tel & Fax (267) 37 5433

ACKNOWLEDGMENTS

CONTENTS

LIST OF MAPS

INTRODUCTION

Botswana is a very special place, rightly renowned for its wildlife. It is the big animals that immediately come to mind and on a visit to the national parks of Moremi and Chobe, for example, you are likely to see many different kinds of antelope, elephant and hippo, giraffe, lion, jackal and hyena, monkeys and baboons. With luck you could see leopard and cheetah. If you delight in birds you won't be disappointed, and you will keep your companions entertained as they witness your dilemma in choosing between picking up binoculars to get a better look at a new bird, a camera to photograph another and a bird book to try to find out what both are!

If your wildlife interests are even more specialised, Botswana offers a great diversity of plants, insects and reptiles. Some are as yet unnamed — and could even bear your name if you introduce them to science.

Add to this array of plants and animals a unique geographical feature, the Okavango Delta, where a river runs into a semi-desert, spills its contents over a surface area of 13 000 km² of waterways and then quietly disappears under the thirsty sands, and you have another reason to explore Botswana.

Although the Okavango Delta is perhaps the most popular area, Botswana has a great deal more to offer. The Kalahari Desert that finally swallows the waters of the Okavango River holds a strong attraction and the diverse people of the country are another good reason to visit it.

Contrast and new experiences must be two of the main reasons for travel. You will not find many countries on the African continent that contrast so strongly with the urban environment of the average American or European traveller than does Botswana.

HOW TO USE THIS GUIDE

This book grew out of the author's experience in answering people's questions on how to get to Botswana and what to do when they got there.

It is written primarily for the person who is travelling in a private party, not with a tour operator, although there is a section in Chapter 8 on the operators who take tours through Botswana.

Before planning your trip, turn to Chapter 2. This covers the places to visit and the routes that can be used to get there. Then work out the time you have available, decide on the way you want to travel (i.e. with your own two-wheel-drive or four-wheel-drive vehicle, or with an operator) and the things that interest you most. Please pay special attention to the note in the map section on how to use the route maps.

This information will give your trip a shape. Now you can decide where on your route you would like to stay.

Finally, there are plenty of useful tips on what to carry with you, what you can expect at the border posts and ways of communicating with the Batswana.

DISTANCES AND TIMES

Times and distances given in the text are only approximate and cannot be otherwise. I have driven one route in two hours and a year later taken 4,5 hours over the same journey. Many variables affect one's time over a given distance of sand or dirt road. Is it wet or dry? What season is it? Is it morning or night, when the sand is cool and firm, or 3 pm when it's hot and loose? Are you heavily laden or carrying a light load? Did the vehicle stop for a break? Everything makes a difference. Driving to Xade in the Central Kalahari Game Reserve I once followed some wide-track four-wheel-drive water tankers. They had so churned up the road that what should have taken five or six hours took nearly two days!

Estimates given in the text are what I think the ordinary driver will take if he or she is not in a frantic hurry and conditions are pretty much as they were when I last went that way.

Distances are also something of a problem. They sometimes vary from map to map, and don't always match the distance you record on your odometer.

I've come to learn that a bit of wheel-spin here and there does not seem to make a great deal of difference over long journeys. A much more significant contributory factor is the variation in odometers themselves. A 1 or 1,5 per cent error does not sound like much, but it can be significant if you are lost because you've missed a vital turnoff because your distances are out.

I believe that tyre pressure, air temperature, road conditions and equipment error all contribute to differences in distance covered. I have checked everything included here as carefully as I can. There are, as far as I know, no major errors (but remember bush tracks are constantly changing).

FEEDBACK

Occasionally readers contact me through the publishers and I am always happy to supply extra information wherever possible. I can be contacted at the following address:

Mike Main, P O Box 2265, Gaborone, Botswana, Tel & Fax (267) 37 5433 (home, office, day and night)

Botswana is a large country and I cannot keep up to date with every route and change of track so, if you have any new information, any new routes or corrections or alterations to existing information I shall be very happy to have it. It will be incorporated in future revisions, with an acknowledgement. If you supply a GPS position, please remember to let me have the datum your machine is set on.

I look forward to hearing from you.

1. BOTSWANA: AN OVERVIEW

Botswana is a landlocked country in the centre of southern Africa, bordered by Zimbabwe, South Africa, Namibia and Zambia. It is relatively flat with an average elevation of about 1 000 m (3 000 feet) above sea level. The Tropic of Capricorn crosses the lower third of the country.

Basically Botswana is formed of two main drainage systems, one towards the north, the other to the south, separated by a slightly elevated ridge that runs from Lobatse north-west towards Ghanzi and Namibia. Another ridge of somewhat hilly country in the east separates these great basins from the watershed of the Limpopo River. The Okavango River flows from the highlands of Angola into the northern basin. Much of this huge quantity of water evaporates, but a trickle sometimes escapes to make its way via the Boteti River to the great ancient lake bed of the Makgadikgadi Pans, which dominate the northern part of Botswana.

The south is largely waterless but the drainage lines that do exist all lead southwards towards the Molopo River, which once flowed south into the Orange River and the cold Atlantic in the far west.

Despite its considerable size (slightly smaller than the state of Texas and a little larger than France) Botswana has no standing water except in the Okavango Delta in the north-west, along the Chobe/Zambezi in the north and the Limpopo River in the east. In addition the evaporation rate is extremely high, averaging just under 2 m per year from an open water surface. As a matter of interest, nowhere in the country does the amount of rainfall exceed the amount lost by evaporation! These factors make Botswana an extremely dry country and this is reflected not only in the fascinating adaptations of the flora and fauna but also in the way its inhabitants have modified their lifestyles to suit the climate.

The rainy season is from November to April when impressive thunderstorms, sometimes accompanied by hail, are quite common, especially in the earlier part of the season. The dry period extends from May to the end of October but periodic droughts are common. In summer temperatures can reach 45 °C. The coldest month is July. Frost occurs then, especially in the southern part of Botswana, and there have been rare reports of isolated snowfalls.

Bechuanaland, as it was originally called, came into formal existence in several stages. The first occurred early in 1884 when missionary John

Mackenzie declared a protectorate over an area south of the Molopo River (Botswana's present southern border). This was not recognised initially but in January the following year the region proclaimed by Mackenzie did come under formal British protection. At the same time, administrative jurisdiction was extended, for whites only, to Latitude 22 south (which included the lower third of modern Botswana).

In September 1885 the area south of the Molopo was upgraded from Protectorate status and declared British Territory. It thus became a colony, and was named British Bechuanaland. The area north of the river, formerly only 'within the British sphere', was now declared a Protectorate. One of the effects of this was to cut in half the lands of the Ngwato people.

For six years no further changes took place but in May 1891 two more steps were taken in the establishment of modern Botswana. British Bechuanaland, the colony to the south of the Molopo, ceased to exist as it was incorporated into the Cape Colony.

The Protectorate, that is the portion north of the Molopo to Latitude 22, was extended northwards to the Chobe River but excluded the Tati Concession. This was the area around modern Francistown where gold had been found. An exclusive mining concession covering this area had been granted to the Northern Light Company by Lobengula, the Matabele king.

The boundaries of the newly expanded Protectorate were also deliberately vague about the area known as the 'Disputed Territory'. This was land between the Shashe and Motloutse rivers which was claimed by both Lobengula and Khama, ruler of the Ngwato. However, in September 1892 both these areas were included in the Protectorate and in 1899 the final boundary between Bechuanaland and Rhodesia was decided.

During those early years and right up to 1965, in fact, Bechuanaland was administered from outside its borders: surely the only country in the world to have an external capital!

Initially the administrative capital was at Vryburg in the Cape Colony but, on the incorporation of British Bechuanaland into that Colony, it moved to the town of Mafeking, 35 km beyond the Protectorate's borders but still part of the Cape. (Note: this town is now known as Mafikeng.)

The capital city of Gaborone was practically built from scratch to house the new government that took over the country following independence on 30 September 1966.

At the time of independence Botswana was among the ten poorest nations on earth. No one could have predicted then that great deposits of diamonds would be discovered in the late 1960s and 1970s.

This wealth has turned Botswana into the third largest producer of diamonds in the world and one of the wealthiest countries in Africa, and has provided her with a growth rate and economic buoyancy seldom paralleled elsewhere. Although this appears to have peaked for the moment Botswana is a unified, peaceful and democratic nation with a successful modern economy supported by an efficient infrastructure of roads, railways, telephones, water and electricity.

Diamonds are, of course, the biggest single earner of foreign currency (accounting for more than 40%). Botswana is a large producer of copper and nickel-matt and so copper and other minerals are the second biggest source of foreign earnings. Beef exports follow with tourism in fourth place. As it is unwilling to depend so heavily upon a single commodity, the government is wisely encouraging diversification in the economy and sees tourism as a major area for growth. This realisation is relatively new and much needs still to be done in this field.

Botswana has some 1,5 million inhabitants and the population is growing at the rate of approximately 3,6 per cent per year. Considerable problems are associated with this rapid birthrate and, as is common elsewhere, the gap between rich and poor appears to be growing alarmingly.

Whilst the country is known as Botswana, residents are properly referred to as *Batswana* (singular: *Motswana*) and the language is *Setswana*. Although Setswana is the national language and English the official language, the former is not the home tongue of all people. Indeed, the population is made up of a surprisingly wide number of tribal groupings of which Setswana speakers include the BaNgwato, BaNgwaketse, BaKwena, BaKgatla, BaRolong, BaHurutse, BaTawana, BaTlokwa and BaLete, to mention a few. Although Setswana has become the effective *lingua franca* there are many groups with other home languages, including the Hambukushu, BaYei, BaSubiya, Ovaherero, BaKalanga, BaKgalakgadi and BaSarwa (the San or Bushmen).

Politically, Botswana is a multi-party parliamentary democracy. The National Assembly, as parliament is called, consists of the President (currently Sir Kethumile Masire) and an Assembly of 34 constituency members and four specially elected members. There is also the normal cabinet system with 11 ministers and four assistant ministers.

Botswana is a country in transition. In 1966, when independence was obtained, it was exceedingly under-developed. With a population of

just 543 100 people, it had no government secondary schools, no industry or economy to speak of and only 8 km of tarred road! Its achieve-
ments since then have been quite remarkable, but there has been a high
price to pay. The cultural life of the people has been severely battered by
the demands of a 20th century existence and the fight for a place in the
world economy. Traditions are disappearing overnight, family structures are under enormous pressure, urban drift has become an
unstoppable flood, population growth is exponential and the generation
gap has become a gulf separating father and son, mother and daughter.
Botswana has accepted this, perhaps the greatest challenge it has ever
faced, and is bent on stepping forward with determination into the 21st
century. Given the successes of the recent past and the willingness of its
people, there is every hope it will succeed, despite the pain and frustra-
tions that can be expected on the journey.

2. PLACES TO VISIT

Botswana offers the visitor some remarkable and interesting places. Some are scenically beautiful, some are of cultural or historical interest. Many are well known, others less so. Whatever your reason for visiting the country, whether it be the game or the birdlife, to find out what the Kalahari is really like, or to experience the freedom of total isolation, you can be sure that your trip will be memorable and worthwhile. This list does not pretend to describe every place of interest. Botswana is sufficiently little known for you to be able to make your own discoveries — a factor that adds to its many attractions.

AHA HILLS (Routes 19 and 20)

Of all the places of interest in Botswana, the Aha Hills are probably the most remote and difficult to get to. However, their isolation and their incongruous existence in the very centre of a vast dune-field lend a certain fascination. Straddling the border with Namibia, the Aha Hills consist almost entirely of limestone, dolomite and marble and form a low plateau some 245 km² in extent. The rocks are approximately 700 million years old. It is said that the hills' name comes from the onomatopoeic San word for the barking gecko which is so abundant in the area.

In addition to magnificent views of real Kalahari country, the hills offer the excitement of a largely unexplored area. The hills are only 50 km from Drotsky's Cave in the Gcwihaba Hills and are made of the same material, but it is not known to what extent similar cave formations exist at Aha. However, recent discoveries in the region strongly reinforce the belief that there are more caves to be discovered in these hills and elsewhere in the area.

The exploration that has taken place has shown the existence of two sink-holes, about 15 km apart but apparently unrelated to each other. Both holes are vertical and dangerous and both have been fully explored. One is approximately 45 m deep and the other about 75 m deep; neither leads to caves although there is a small chamber at the bottom of the shallower of the two. Visitors without experience or proper equipment are strongly advised not to investigate them.

About 15 km south of Aha is the village of Caecae, and approximately 60 km to the north those of Dobe and Qangwa, all inhabited mostly by San and a small percentage of Herero. In the 1960s teams from Harvard University did a great deal of research among the San residents of Dobe, and their findings were later published in many authoritative works. Early, Middle and Late Stone Age sites have been located in the Qangwadum Valley and, as at Drotsky's Cave, there is abundant evidence of previous climatic regimes.

Only the most limited range of commodities is available at the stores in Caecae and other villages along the way. There is no standing water at Aha although the wells and boreholes of the villagers may be relied upon. The nearest petrol, after Maun, is at Etsha-6, Shakawe Fishing Camp and Andara in the Caprivi Strip. Visitors must be entirely self-sufficient. Some traffic does use the main roads but vehicles are very infrequent, so it is advisable to be prepared for any eventuality.

Further information regarding the location of Aha's sink-holes can be obtained from the offices of the Botswana Society, National Museum, Gaborone, in whose publication *Botswana Notes and Records* (Vol 6, 1974) more details can be found.

BOKSPITS (Routes 4, 5 and 6)

The unusual name of this small village, set in the most south-westerly corner of Botswana, comes simply from being the place where a man called Bok once sank a well. It occupies a position at the confluence of two great rivers: the Molopo, which runs mostly westward along Botswana's southern border and here turns south, and the Nossob which drains from the north and north-west through the famous Kalahari Gemsbok National Park. Neither river flows very often nowadays, even after rain, but major floods have been recorded in both. Today Bokspits is a struggling centre of declining karakul production. Petrol and diesel are available here and there is a police station, clinic and a well stocked store.

Few would disagree that 'Mr Bokspits', the unofficial mayor, is Klaas van der Westhuizen and if anybody needs help or assistance, Klaas (or his son Franz) is the man to see. He will willingly introduce you to local farmers if you would like to know more about the karakul industry in the area. In addition, he'll demonstrate his remarkable powers of water-divining!

There are large, red, mobile sand dunes in the vicinity of Bokspits, which make fascinating subjects for photographers. Approximately 20 km to the east is Rappel's Pan, which provides an excellent opportunity to investigate these curious features of the southern Kalahari. Provided one stays on the main roads there is no need for a four-wheel-drive vehicle.

There are many interesting sights to look out for in this region, among them the remarkable nests of social weavers. These massive structures of woven grass stems may be home to several hundred of the small com-munal birds. The huge nests also provide a residence for other creatures such as snakes, scorpions, a great array of parasites and other birds in-cluding owls and falcons. A magnificent sight, common along the Kuruman and Molopo rivers are the striking groves of *Acacia erioloba* or camelthorn acacia. These large trees are specially adapted for this diffi-cult environment. Their seed pods in particular are a vital source of pro-tein for stock and wild animals, especially at the time of year when other food is more difficult to come by.

A road leads to the north-west along the Botswana side of the Nossob to the Gemsbok National Park. It is also possible to enter South Africa at this point, follow the other side of the same river and enter the park through Twee Rivieren.

CENTRAL KALAHARI GAME RESERVE (Routes 2 and 10A & B)

Established in 1961 exclusively as a reserve for Botswana's San popula-tion, the CKGR was not open to the general public until quite recently. This has changed and a remarkable tract of Africa is now open to those who have the resources to make the journey.

There are three entrances to the reserve: from the west at Xade (some 185 km from Ghanzi; the 'x' is a click sound so the word is pronounced 'click'-ade), the south-east at Kutse and the north-east through Rakops and Matswere. Each offers a different experience of the Kalahari. (But note comments regarding veterinary fences and cut-lines on page 43.)

Kutse is described elsewhere (see page 21). The challenging drive from Kutse to Xade is for those who want to see the Kalahari in all its forms. Game is infrequent and pan features are few, so the attraction is the immense changefulness of the vegetation and landscape. This is African wilderness in every sense. Even when it wears its drab winter dress, the late afternoon or morning sun brightens the muted autumnal colours so that the dark greens of the *Boscia* and the bright yellows of the stunted *Lonchocarpus* merge with reds, fawns and gold to make a memorable picture. In the wet, the range of greens is staggering, especially against the inevitable backdrop of blue-black storm clouds.

The drive from Kutse to Xade is long and tiring (271 km), especially if the wide wheel-base water tankers are still churning up the sand tracks and making them almost impassable. However, there are some compensations to having completed the journey, not least of which is the sense of achievement at the journey's end.

As if challenging the Kalahari were not enough, there is the added bonus of a visit to Xade, a large and growing formal San settlement. Departing north-eastward from Xade, one is in a position to enjoy one of the most fascinating journeys in Botswana.

To a person accustomed to the variety of the Central Kalahari Game Reserve, very little changes in the first 50 km north from Xade, but at that point the first of an almost unending series of pans is encountered. As elsewhere in the Kalahari, game tends to congregate in vast numbers around these pans.

Giraffe, gemsbok, springbok and wildebeest are common; jackal hide in the shelter of the tiniest shrubs on the open plains and birds in profusion can be seen in the numerous 'tree islands' that dot the great pans.

Evocative names such as Piper's Pan, Letiahau and Deception Valley dot the maps. Discrete but artificial waterholes abound and a dozen secret tracks slip off towards some enticing group of acacias where a cool and open spot can be found.

Mark and Delia Owens brought this spectacular area to the notice of the public with their popular book *Cry of the Kalahari*, and since reading it many people have wanted to visit it. (You'll find the Owens' famous campsite easily but note that the photograph in the book has been reversed!)

What makes a visit all the more fascinating is that these pans (which, on a 1:250 000 scale map, clearly form continuous lines), are not wind-formed pans as are their cousins in the south and south-west Kalahari. They are the remnants of a once-vast river system that drained into the former palaeo-lake Makgadikgadi which lies further to the east.

Perhaps 14 000 to 17 000 years ago the climate was very different from today; rainfall was higher, evaporation lower and surface water common in this region. At least two major rivers brought water from the then moist west and south-west (the present day semi-arid Ghanzi region and beyond) and delivered it to the dying super-lake. Modern maps indicate these fossil river systems as the Letiahau (of which Deception Valley is a lower part) and the Passarge Valley. A massive delta must have existed somewhere in the area, which caused the great rivers to back up and fill the wide valleys we see today.

In those times it must have been a paradise for wild animals, brimming with life of every kind. For a sense of what it must have been like, stand on the track at Letiahau and look at the prominent but distant riverbanks to the left and right of the road. Imagine how much water that vast system must once have held. Is it any wonder that, even in the present arid conditions, this remains one of the most beautiful places in Botswana?

Not only does the north-eastern CKGR display evidence of much wetter times, it also reveals abundant clues to the era of the great desert. The journey from Deception Pan to Sunday Pan crosses a north-south fossil dune-field before the track turns off to the north-west. The regular pattern of dune crest and inter-dune valley speaks eloquently of ancient sand dunes now trapped in place beneath a mantle of trees, grass and shrubs.

Winter or summer, the north-east Central Kalahari offers stunning vistas as well as the most remarkable and visible reminders of ancient deserts and flooding deltas. It should not be missed.

CHOBE NATIONAL PARK (River front and Nogatsha)

Served by the tarred road from Francistown, the Kasane/Chobe area is becoming increasingly popular with motorists. This has both disadvantages and attractions. On one hand it is easier to get there — the whole journey can be completed in a standard vehicle. On the other hand the park's facilities are often overcrowded, especially during school holidays, and cannot easily be enjoyed in any vehicle except a four-wheel-drive. The only alternative at the moment, for those without four-wheelers, is to take a place on one of the many game or boat drives organised by local safari operators. The overcrowding is being addressed by two approaches. Firstly, a booking system has been introduced and one can only hope that an effort will be made to upgrade the roads for normal cars. A second effort to reduce overcrowding is the intended closure of Serondela campsite and the construction of a replacement at Ihaha, on the river but about 15 km further west.

Perhaps the greatest attraction of the Chobe River area is the elephants which are almost always seen there. Their late afternoon visits to the water's edge offer hours of fascinating viewing and wonderful opportunities for the photographer. It is wise, however, to be extremely cautious with Chobe's elephants. Often the herds consist mainly of females with young. The cows are sensitive to interference and more than one incident has been recorded where a vehicle has been damaged after an imprudent approach.

The drier months are the best time to visit Chobe, when the animals are driven back to the river through lack of water in the hinterland. Huge numbers will be seen, particularly of elephant and buffalo. You can also expect to see tsessebe, waterbuck, roan, eland, kudu, impala, sable, giraffe, lion and, if you are lucky, one of the rare puku. The floodplains of the river make an ideal viewing area, with mixed patches of open grassland, thickets of bush and riverine forest. In the river itself you should see hippo, crocodile and, with patient watching, the wonderful otters.

The floodplains are, however, not the only parts of Chobe worth visiting. A programme of waterhole development is under way with old water points being upgraded, repaired and properly maintained, as well as new ones being constructed. As a result, the Nogatsha region is now a must at any time of year with water widely available. Boreholes and watering points at Savute have had the same effect of keeping game in the area, even though the famous channel itself is dry (see Savute, page 31).

Birders will find the river front particularly rewarding but a still richer area for birds is the Kasane Rapids, a beautiful stretch of rock-filled river immediately downstream of Mowana Safari Lodge for which protection status is currently being sought. Here, with luck, you'll find the African finfoot, half-collared kingfishers, the whitebacked night heron and rock pratincoles nesting out on the rocks during low water. Richard Randall, a well-known southern African birder and expert on the area, lives and works at Mowana Lodge. He is most approachable and can often be induced to part with advice and help — especially in finding those elusive birds! He is also an official recorder for the area and is building up a vital record of 'new' sightings and species. He will appreciate your help too.

DECEPTION VALLEY

(See Central Kalahari Game Reserve, above, and Routes 2 and 10A & B.)

DROTSKY'S CAVE (PROPERLY: GCWIHABA CAVERNS) (Route 19)

In western Botswana, not far from the Namibian border, is a remarkable series of caves, shown by the San to Martinus Drotsky in 1934.

Perhaps not as extensive as the better known Cango Caves in South Africa, Drotsky's can certainly equal any with the truly breathtaking splendour of its stalagmites, stalactites, flowstones, caverns and passages. It has, for some, an additional attraction in that it is quite unspoilt and undeveloped. Apart from their scenic attraction, the caves are of great interest to geomorphologists and palaeo-climatologists because of the abundant evidence they provide of former climates.

As is so often the case in Botswana, the approach and surroundings leave one quite unprepared for the splendour to come. Set in an apparently endless dune-field of rolling, arid country, the low outcrop of dolomite barely protrudes above the ubiquitous sand on the banks of the now dry Gcwihaba River. Yet once this river flowed, and flowed strongly. There was sufficient water to dissolve the rock itself, to carve out the great winding passages and caverns. At other, slightly drier times, falling rain percolated through the dolomite, forming and shaping striking displays of white flowstone or cave sinter.

The age of the caves is not known. There is, however, evidence for a very wet period between 17 000 and 14 000 years ago, during which the old passages were flooded and re-excavated. Drier times returned and some of the flowstones were deposited, to be partly eroded during a subsequent wet period about 4 500 years ago. A succession of wet and dry periods followed, including at least one especially wet period when the most recent of the cave sinters were deposited, between 2 000 and 1 500 years ago.

There are two entrances to the cave. The track will lead you to one which is 300 m from the right-hand bank of the river, on the slopes of the low hill. Beside it is a large information board, erected by the National Museum. The second entrance is 200 m away from the first in a direction at right angles to the river valley and further from it.

There are no facilities at Drotsky's. There are no people living in the immediate vicinity. The nearest village (Caecae) is 36 km and 1,5 hours drive away. There is no water at all, not even in the caves themselves. Take care, therefore, to be entirely self-sufficient. The nearest reliable fuel is at Maun or Etsha-6, but you may find petrol at Gumare (where a licence has been applied for). A minimum of two full days is recommended to explore the area properly. Because of the lack of water game is seasonally rare and the chance of encountering any large predators is remote. Bats are almost always found but, in drier times, are restricted to the inner portions of the cave and will have to be sought out rather than avoided.

For years there has been speculation about the possible existence of other caves, both at Gcwihaba and at the Koanaka Hills (some 20 km to the south-west and close to the Namibian border fence). Within the last few years enthusiastic exploration has discovered four. One new system is at Gcwihaba itself and three more have been located at Koanaka Hills. In all four cases, these remarkable caves contain material of vital importance to paleontological studies and so, for the moment, their exact location is not being disclosed to the general public. However, to avid 'cavers' and seriously interested parties, directions are available from Conservation International (P O Box 448 Maun, Tel & Fax [267] 66 0017, open five days a week and Saturday morning). In order to prevent bats from entering one of the new caves through an entrance which had to be created, a steel door has been installed. The key may be obtained on request from Conservation International.

The caves can be dangerous. There is, of course, no lighting so you must take your own. Gas lamps are useful and torches are essential. You will make constant use of your lights, so ensure that you have plenty of spare gas and batteries. Never enter the caves without a secondary, emergency light supply on you, such as matches or a small torch. This precaution is absolutely essential. If you put a light down and it goes out, a very serious situation could develop.

Previous explorers of the cave have left strings marking the main routes. Some sections have been removed but the remainder serve as a guide. It is possible to go in one entrance and out the other but only if you know the system well.

Photographers are advised to equip themselves with more than one flash, preferably slave units mounted on tripods. Three standard flashes will provide sufficient light. Dust within the caves is a major problem. It hangs in the air for long periods and special care should be taken to protect sensitive equipment.

Plans of the cave are available from the Botswana Society, National Museum, Gaborone, in whose journal *Botswana Notes and Records* (Vol 6, 1974) they can be found.

GHANZI (Routes 3 and 4)

The frontier town of Ghanzi in the west of Botswana consists of a small and thriving community. Today it is the centre of a substantial cattle ranching industry. Deep in the Kalahari, it owes its unlikely success to the limestone ridge on which it is situated, providing as it does an abundant supply of groundwater for most of the 190 farms that now exist there.

Originally the home of the San, Ghanzi has seen many people come and go. The first white inhabitant was the extraordinary Hendrik van Zyl, who took up permanent residence in 1874 on what is today Ghanzi Farm Number One. Tales of his exploits and lifestyle abound — his double-storey house with its French furniture and stained glass windows, his murder of 33 San, and the slaughter of 103 elephants in a single afternoon. A feature known as Van Zyl's Cutting is attributed to him but its purpose is uncertain. Cut 3 m deep into solid rock and nearly 12 m long, some people today believe it was a reservoir to catch rainwater. By this means, it is thought, Van Zyl was able to extend his hunting in the area, sure of a dependable water supply. It is difficult now to separate fact from fancy but Van Zyl certainly seems to have been a law unto himself.

The ill-fated Dorsland Trekkers reached Ghanzi in late 1875 but soon moved on to their sad future in Namibia and Angola. Next to arrive were Rhodes's Trekkers, the first of whom reached the area in October 1898. Ten years later all but one family had left. The descendants of that family, and others who drifted into the struggling settlement in those early years, remain in Ghanzi today where they form the strong Afrikaans- and English-speaking communities.

Today Ghanzi is prosperous. Land prices have improved, as has the quality of the herd and management practices. The town is a busy administrative centre but, more importantly, it is a pleasing testimony to the ability of widely disparate and strongly independent peoples to live together equably and in harmony.

The ruins of Van Zyl's house can still be found on Dick Eaton's farm, Ghanzi One. Van Zyl's Cutting is on Dagga Camp farm, about 60 km from Ghanzi, owned by the Vosloos. Owners must be contacted for permission to enter the farms. The management at the Kalahari Arms Hotel in Ghanzi will assist in organising this. Ghanzi can provide all basic necessities and has a hospital, as well as telephone contact with the rest of the country.

An interesting place to visit is the San community established at D'Kar, 35 km north-east of Ghanzi on the Maun road, run by the Dutch Reformed Church. Here, under the determined and courageous leadership of Braam Le Roux and with the assistance of Case Otto, The Kuru Development Trust (Tel [267] 59 6285) has created a community of artists and craftsmen. There is an excellent craft and leather shop as well as a small art gallery. There have been several exhibitions of San art from this establishment at the art gallery and museum in Gaborone as well as at a number of international venues where the work has attracted a great deal of interest. D'Kar is a remarkable venture, successful and worthy of your support. Camping facilities are available and are being constantly upgraded. A game farm is planned for the future.

Note that the main road across the Kalahari to Ghanzi is being tarred and re-aligned so check the route before embarking on a journey there.

HUNTER'S ROAD (Route 24)

Hunter's Road is the name given to a wagon road used extensively in the latter half of the 19th century to move trade goods and supplies over the northern part of what is now Botswana from Ramokgwebane to the banks of the Zambezi at Kazungula. It is part of a network of such routes that early explorers in this part of Africa developed to help them penetrate the hinterland.

Shoshong, the Ngwato capital, was a major centre and it was from there that the road to Bulawayo in the north started. It passed through Tati to Marula.

Livingstone's early explorations created interest in the Zambezi and, by the 1860s, traders and explorers were visiting it in greater numbers. Usually they took the road to Bulawayo and turned north-west at Ramokgwebane to follow the watershed in that direction until the great river was reached. In 1870 or 1871 an English trader by the name of George Westbeech began trading with the Lozi in Barotseland and found it convenient to follow the route from Ramokgwebane to the north-west. Eventually, he established a residence and a trading store at Mpandamatenga, and stores at both Leshomo and Kazungula, and be-

gan to improve the wagon trail from the south-east. In the next 20 year:
the trail was extensively used and became known as the Hunter's Road

In addition to being a vital trade artery to the heart of central Africa
the Hunter's Road was also the first major tourist route. Mpandamateng;
was situated in a cool, well-watered area and was at the southern limi
of the tsetse fly. Visitors to the Victoria Falls, who came in ever-increas
ing numbers as the years passed by, typically left their horses and oxel
in Westbeech's care at Mpandamatenga before setting off on foot to visi
that remarkable site.

Eventually, when political demands of the 20th century dictated th(
need for defined international borders, the commissioners responsibl(
could find no more expedient method for deciding the demarcation lin(
than to declare the wagon trail itself to be the boundary between Rhode
sia and Bechuanaland. And so it has been to this day!

Inevitably, a shortcut from Shoshong was developed. Instead of pass
ing through Tati and Ramokgwebane, some travellers went directly nortl
through Tlhabala and along the eastern edge of Sowa Pan to Nata. Fron
here the trail went north-west and north to the watershed, intersectin{
the Hunter's Road at Ngwahla Pan. This shortcut came to be known a:
the Western Old Lake Route and has yet to be re-discovered. Modell
roads and fences have made the route from Shoshong and Tlhabala t(
Nata difficult to find, and so the route described here begins at Nata anc
uses existing roads to get you to the border and Ngwahla Pan.

Progress along the watershed follows the border tracks, one on eacl
side of the actual border line (there is no fence, except for a few kilome
tres when you reach Ngwahla). The big attraction of the route is the fac
that you pass by a series of pans which often hold water for three or fou1
months after the rains, attracting game from elephant, leopard and lioı
downwards — not surprising when you consider the game reserves o:
hunting concessions that lie on either side of the route.

As you make the journey to the Zambezi, you can hear the pages o·
history turn. It was along here, after having spent a year as the 'guest' o·
the Lozi King of Barotseland, that George Westbeech returned with ;
wagonload of ivory in 1872 worth, it is said, over £12 000! It was thi:
successful expedition that prompted Westbeech to set himself up a
Mpandamatenga.

The pan names tell something of the history of this area. Stoffel's Par
was named after one Christoffel Schinderhutte, an employee of West
beech. He left for the south from Mpandamatenga in July 1875 but hi:

wagon broke down. He got drunk on 'Cape smoke' (brandy) and set off again whilst out of his senses, knocked a servant off the wagon and crushed him to death beneath the wheels. Running amok, Schinderhutte then shot some of his oxen and one of his teamsters before rushing off into the bush, never to be seen again. The only traces ever found were his veldskoens and part of his beard, which were taken to Shoshong and identified. How he met his death has never been established. Hendrick's Vlei is named after a servant who killed a giraffe there, and Jolley's Pan for another of Westbeech's men who died from the fever at Mpandamatenga. Cream of Tartar Pan was well known for the tree with a cross carved into its bark by Jesuit priests. The cross was still visible in the 1970s but, alas, the tree itself is now no more.

The route is scenically spectacular. The first part of the journey north from Ngwahla is somewhat trying with a lot of stunted mopane to cope with, but this is followed by stretches of beautiful broad-leaved woodland and pans frequented by game. As you approach the Deka River and Mpandamatenga and reach the high basalt landscape there are majestic views of vast tracts of country. The hilltops are well wooded and the wide meandering valleys lined with swathes of tall grass through which streams make their way. This wild countryside still looks the same as it did to those who travelled through it 150 years ago. Just south of Mpandamatenga is an astonishing grove of giant acacia (*Acacia polyacantha*) so tall they resemble a hilltop looming blue-black on the distant horizon as you approach.

North of Mpandamatenga is the extraordinary Kazuma Pan, which straddles the border. There are water points within sight of the track and this sea of golden grass is an exhilarating sight that must not be missed. Animals can almost always be spotted on this great plain.

There is much to see besides the spectacular scenery on this route: Stone Age sites, mislaid 19th century artifacts, strange initials carved on isolated trees, wagon wheel scars on rocks, game, birds, and even the odd hippo at Mpandamatenga.

KALAHARI GEMSBOK NATIONAL PARK AND GEMSBOK NATIONAL PARK (Routes 4, 5 and 6)

The standard point of entry to this park is through South Africa, via Bokspits and Twee Rivieren. There is, however, a road north from Bokspits with a gate into the park on the Botswana side of the border and Botswana's Department of Wildlife and National Parks now has a warden and staff stationed within the Gemsbok Park. Access is now possible from either the Botswana or South African side. There is a border fence running from Twee Rivieren to Bokspits, so the 'decision point' for which side to enter is at the latter small town.

It should be noted that there is no exit from the park at Union's End.

A visit to the Kalahari Gemsbok does not require a four-wheel-drive vehicle. The park is open all the year round.

From Bokspits, where the border post is open from 8 am to 4 pm, take either of the dirt roads north for 55 km to the park entrances at Twee Rivieren Camp, where entrance formalities are completed. On the South African side there is a shop selling a wide range of essentials and fuel, and there are camping and residential facilities at the camp. Visitors entering on the Botswana side may make use of these facilities once entry formalities are complete.

There are three main sand roads in the park. All are maintained in first-rate condition. One extends for 157 km up the Nossob River to Nossob Camp and then 128 km beyond it, on the same river, to Union's End. A second road runs beside the Aoub River for 118 km to the camp at Mata Mata. (Note: this former entrance from Namibia has been closed since that country gained independence.) A link road of 68 km joins the two river roads and affords excellent views of the drier Kalahari with its typical stabilised, red dunes. Fuel and basic essentials are also sold at both Mata Mata and Nossob camps.

The park has a fluctuating population of game but a visit is always well rewarded. The best time is thought to be between February and April. At least two days are recommended, during which you can expect to see gemsbok, wildebeest, eland, hartebeest and springbok, as well as lion, cheetah, hyena and jackal.

Plans are in hand to develop Botswana's side of the park (the Gemsbok National Park) but it is too soon to know what form this will take. The much more arid reaches of the Kalahari found in this sector of the park are stunningly beautiful, especially in early and late light.

Pans in the Gemsbok Park tend to take a parallel form, possibly reflecting ancient north-south drainage lines emptying into the Nossob River. Opalescent and elongated, they nestle between long low dunes and almost always have game animals sampling the salt and trace elements that these features so conveniently collect and concentrate.

Somewhere in this vast wilderness lie the traces of a fierce battle fought on 16 March 1908. German and Hottentot forces under Simon Cooper (alias Kopper) clashed in circumstances blending tragedy, excitement, adventure and mystery. The Germans boasted a force of 710 specially trained camels, 23 officers leading 373 riflemen and four Maxim machine guns. There are indications that there was a mutiny, and the German commander was suspiciously killed by the first shot fired. Sixty-six others died in the battle. Clues to the site are steadily being discovered but the precise location of the encounter has yet to be found. (More details of this fascinating incident can be found in *Botswana Notes and Records* (Vol. 24, 1992, pp. 1-11).)

KUTSE GAME RESERVE (Route 1)

This relatively small game reserve (2 500 km^2) is the closest reserve to Gaborone (excluding the small Mokolodi and Gaborone reserves in or near the city). Set in typical pan country of undulating savanna, it abuts the vast Central Kalahari Game Reserve to the north.

Most of the larger arid-adapted herbivores can be found in Kutse Reserve, together with the more common predators, including lion, leopard and cheetah. Game is usually seen on or near the pans (of which there are more than 60, large and small), but it is seasonal. Its presence will depend largely on where and when the rain last fell, and it is difficult to predict. If there has been a drought game may be very scarce, if not completely absent. In the absence of larger animals there is an abundance of smaller creatures and Kutse is renowned for its birdlife. There is, of course, the special atmosphere of the countryside itself. The Kalahari is unique and a visit to Kutse allows the visitor to savour its silence and fascinating immensity.

An entry fee is charged for each vehicle and its passengers. Campsites have been laid out and there are presently 26 of these. Although water is available at the gate, it is fairly salty and visitors are advised to bring their own. A guide can be taken on but it is not really necessary to do so. The road layout is a simple circular drive (see Map 1). Starting at the gate, it forks at Kutse II Pan after 13,6 km. The left-hand road extends 53 km to Moreswe Pan and Mabuakolobe Pan; the right-hand side continues for 12 km where it forks again. The south fork completes the circle to Moreswe Pan; the right-hand fork continues to the distant San settlement of Xade. Map availability at the gate is unreliable and so it is wise to make a hand-drawn copy of the one on display.

LAKE NGAMI (Route 18)

A four-wheel-drive vehicle is not essential for a visit to Lake Ngami but it is strongly recommended. There are no facilities beyond the limited range of goods available in the occasional small general dealer's store.

Lake Ngami has spawned a host of myths and it remains something of an enigma. This was the mysterious inland lake that drew explorers into the heart of the continent. It was the lake that lured David Livingstone across the Kalahari and launched him on his career of discovery in Africa.

Today Lake Ngami has no exit and survives on infrequent overflow from the Okavango Delta via the Kunyere and the Nchabe (Boteti or Lake) rivers alone. This flood of water has not arrived for ten years or more and so Ngami is now completely dry. In the past, water entered Ngami from both the Nchabe (north-east) and the Thaoge (north-west), and so the Nchabe played the unusual role of both supply and exit, depending on the flow from the Thaoge and relative water levels in the delta itself. There is good evidence that lake levels were once much higher, and covered a huge area of 1 800 km^2. When Livingstone reached it on 1 August 1849, it had already lost its former glory and it is unlikely to have been more than 810 km^2 in extent. He described it as 'a fine looking sheet of water' and estimated the circumference at 120 km. As the years passed, the supply of water diminished and the levels fluctuated around a much lower mean. Often it was quite dry for long periods. In the last 100 years Ngami has been a faint shadow of its former self, barely exceeding 250 km^2 in area.

The dynamics of Ngami's inflows are now better understood and it seems clear that the gradual drying up of the Thaoge River is the main reason for its diminution in size since Livingstone's day. The reasons for the Thaoge's demise are more controversial. However, the weight of opinion now seems to favour a change in the levels of the tectonically unstable Okavango Delta. Like a giant tabletop, it may have tipped slowly in a different direction, altering the flow pattern of the waters spread across its surface.

Lake Ngami remains the centre of an important cattle raising area for the Tawana and Herero people. Estimates of the total number of cattle supported by the lake flats and surrounding areas vary from 30 000 to 70 000 head, but some consider this far too high a figure, and it is true that there are dramatic collapses in the cattle population when drought occurs.

MABUASEHUBE PAN (PART OF AND NOW CALLED GEMSBOK NATIONAL PARK) (Route 3)

Across the southern third of Botswana, from east to west, runs a ridge of land marginally higher than that to the north or south. Siegfried Passarge, a German geologist and explorer, called it the Bakalahari Schwelle (*Die Kalahari*, 1904) and, indeed, it is a gigantic watershed. Characteristically, it is dotted with many thousands of pans.

These features vary in shape but most are oval or circular. Typically there is a high sand dune, or series of dunes, on the south or south-west side, attesting to its wind-formed origins. Some dunes are 20 or 30 m high. If rain has fallen most of the pans will hold water for three or four months. When not full their covering ranges from bare, salty clay to light grass. They play a vital role in the ecology of the area and have also played an important part in man's invasion of the Kalahari, providing him (by means of shallow, hand-dug wells, usually near the edge of the pan) with access to water and grazing for his animals. It was partly recognition of these facts that led to the establishment of Mabuasehube Game Reserve in the south of the country.

Remote and costly in terms of time and fuel, the reserve is nevertheless well worth a visit. The simple beauty of the stark pans, the extraordinary colour changes that occur as the day progresses, and the often abundant game will make it a unique and memorable visit. It is a good place for seeing brown hyena.

Mabuasehube is not fenced but an entrance fee is required. Bookings will probably have to be made for overnight camping facilities here in future but, at the time of writing, this was not the case. It would be wise to check by phoning the Department of Wildlife (Tel [267] 37 1405) before proceeding, however.

There are six major pans or pan clusters within the reserve as well as many smaller ones. During the rainy season, from October to April, wildebeest, gemsbok, springbok, hartebeest and eland, with their associated predators, especially lion, usually abound. There are now three watering points situated at Lesholoago, Mabuasehube and Mpaathutlwa pans respectively. These do much to retain a game population in the area throughout the long dry months.

Water is available, but there are no other facilities of any kind in the reserve and the visitor must be entirely self-sufficient. The nearest fuel is at Tsabong, 110 km away. On the approach, the last fuel stops are at

Jwaneng or Werda. Both centres have limited shopping facilities and there is a small store at Khakhea.

At least two full days should be allowed for a visit to the reserve to enable you to appreciate all that it has to offer.

MAKGADIKGADI NATIONAL PARK (Route 14)

Now part of the Nxai Pan and Makgadikgadi National Park, this reserve is a vast unfenced area (3 900 km²) of open plain and bush country to the south of the main Francistown-Maun road, about halfway between the two centres. It is informally serviced by a series of un-signposted tracks, mapped on the notice boards at the north and north-west entrances. Depending upon the time of year, a four-wheel-drive vehicle is not necessary but is becoming increasingly advisable.

From November or December, when the first rains have fallen, to about May, innumerable game will be encountered — herds of zebra, springbok and wildebeest that seem to stretch from horizon to horizon. Each draws in its wake lion and other predators, including cheetah.

It is not only the game which is the attraction here, however, but the simple beauty of the area itself. The rolling grasslands seem endless. Early morning mirages build clear and distant mountain ranges which dissipate as the sun edges higher. Over the centuries shallow depressions in the plain have accumulated deep deposits of clay and detritus. In these reservoirs of richer soil trees have taken root so that the plain is dotted with widely separated islands of vegetation. These islands create micro-habitats as unique and varied as their ocean counterparts. If you are prepared to sit quietly for an hour or so on one of these islands, you will soon be accepted by the animals and can enjoy the rare privilege of watching them go about their daily business, undisturbed and at close quarters.

Two places in the game reserve are particularly worth visiting as they both make memorable campsites. One is Njuca Hills, the other is Xhumaga on the Boteti River.

Njuca is an ancient dune of especially large proportions. A track leads up to two good campsites with magnificent views, each equipped with its own 'whistle and thud' toilet.

On the east or left bank of the Boteti River, opposite a village called Xhumaga, game scouts have a second camp and near it, under a group of shady acacias in a large sandy area overlooking the river, a new public campsite has been built. Here (with luck) you will find cold showers and flush toilets. There is an adjacent stand-pipe which delivers fresh water and also a convenient pit for dumping rubbish.

The site itself is remarkable for its position in the ecotone between riverine woodland and the grasslands of Makgadikgadi. The birdlife is prolific and the scenery unusual, for the Boteti is a river flowing to nowhere. Its waters simply soak away into the sand. In recent years the Boteti has not always flowed and it is wise to check with the Department of Wildlife (Tel [267] 37 1405) that there is water there.

Visitors must be entirely self-sufficient in food and fuel. In addition they must collect and carry their own firewood, which is singularly scarce at Njuca although supplies may be available at the Xhumaga campsite. It is advisable to bring wood from further afield, thus reducing the impact on the immediate area.

MOREMI WILDLIFE RESERVE (Route 22)

This wildlife reserve was declared by the Tawana people in 1963, an act which was described at the time as a shining mark in African tribal history. Administered today by the Department of Wildlife and National Parks, it is a rich and fascinating area.

Located on an extensive sandveld island, known as Chief's Island, in the north-eastern Okavango Delta, it encompasses several different types of ecological zones, adding greatly to its interest.

Entry is controlled by two gates, one in the north and another in the south. An entrance fee is required and booking for campsites is essential (see page 130). A system of roads provides what is essentially a circular drive that allows the visitor to experience the ecological diversity of the reserve. It passes through dense mopane woodland, forests of giant acacia trees and in places skirts the edge of the Okavango with magnificent views of floodplains, reed banks and open lagoons. Animals and birds are prolific throughout the year but the drier months, from May to November, are best for viewing. At both entrances and at various locations along the road are designated campsites and it is well worth spending at least a night in this reserve. Note, however, that campsites must be booked and paid for in advance (see page 130). Mekoro (singular: *mokoro*) are not available for hire in Moremi.

You can expect to see most game animals in Moremi, including lion, leopard, elephant, eland, kudu and roan antelope, as well as buffalo, zebra, lechwe and impala.

NTWETWE PAN (Route 11)

This enormous and fascinating area, the twin in many ways of its east-erly neighbour Sowa Pan, has been receiving more and more attention from visitors. This is as it should be, for it is a gloriously free and open part of the country — ethereally beautiful and still almost completely unspoilt.

There are innumerable tracks and means of access to this area and it would be impractical to try and list them all. Besides, this spoils the fun for intrepid explorers! In the section on routes, you will find a description of one major north-south track and another that enters the area from the south-east and establishes a link with Sowa Pan and the island of Kubu.

The region abounds with places of great interest and I would like to highlight a few of them to encourage the exploration of this fascinating region.

The north-south track links Orapa mine with the village of Gweta. It is highly probable that David Livingstone used this very track on his journeys to Linyanti and the Caprivi Strip.

By means of this track it is possible to visit two famous baobab trees. The first, known as Green's Baobab (*GPS 20 25 29S 25 13 53E u/k*), lies immediately beside the route. The tree is scarred with initials from a century or more ago, one of the earliest being those of trader and ex-plorer Frederick Joseph Green.

Green had been hunting along the Boteti River as early as 1851 but in 1858/9, when his initials were carved into the bark of the tree, he, with his brother and a large group of wagons, was exploring the vicinity of Makgadikgadi whilst on their way to western Matabeleland.

The initials of H Van Zyl, the notorious explorer, hunter and murderer from what is now the Ghanzi District, are among those to be found on this tree by the sharp-eyed and persistent. If you look carefully you will also see the initials of P Viljoen, son of Jan Viljoen. Jan was a well-known hunter and trader and an early visitor to Lake Ngami (getting there about 18 months after Livingstone). He was accused by the missionary of 'buy-ing several African boys'.

Within 300 m of the tree, to its south-west, you will find Gutsa Pan. It is mostly dry now but does hold water for months after rain. Over 100 years ago there were reports of hippo here! When full, it is particularly beautiful with rich birdlife and waving palm trees. Even when it's dry there is a lot to see; Stone Age artifacts abound and the hunting blinds (used initially by the San to ambush game) are still visible. Look for an especially well preserved one under a tree on the west side.

Another equally famous though less visited tree, Chapman's Baobab, lies south-east of Green's tree (see Map 10 on page 216). This tree is visible from great distances across the pan and is worth seeing if only because of its size and photogenic qualities. It was certainly a landmark for early explorers of the region, including one, if not more, of the Chapmans. Although it has yet to be systematically scrutinised for interesting signatures, even a casual examination will reveal those of James Chapman, members of the ill-fated Helmore-Price expedition and other well-known travellers. The large cavity between the main trunks is reported to have been used as a post office box by travellers from both north and south.

This colossal, six-stemmed specimen measures 24,82 m in girth at approximately 1,5 m above ground level. (The largest known baobab, found in north-eastern South Africa, measures 33,4 m.)

To the west of the north-south road is what I call the 'land of a thousand islands'. Reflecting a chaotic climatic past, these numerous islands are in fact sand dunes stranded on the surface of the ancient lake bed, and they comprise one of the most weirdly fascinating landscapes in Botswana.

The dunes are evidence of much more arid times when the lake temporarily dried up and barchan dunes began to advance across its baked and bare surface. Eventually a wetter era returned, the lake flooded again and the dunes were trapped, islands in an ancient sea. Climatic change did not stop, however, and the lake level fell once more, but slowly this time, almost as if the water was struggling against the elemental forces that wished to banish it forever.

Proof of this struggle will be seen if you look carefully at the island profiles. Many of them show distinct steps and lines of vegetation, revealing clearly where the fall in lake levels was momentarily arrested for long enough to leave permanent evidence in the shape of ancient shorelines.

Driving through this area is a unique experience. The pan surface is hard and unyielding and, in my experience, very much safer than elsewhere on Makgadikgadi.

A good map is essential, and navigation is made very much easier if you sit on the roof of your vehicle to get a good view. The experience is very much like sailing a galleon through unknown seas with islands beckoning from all sides. It is both exhilarating and wildly exciting.

Careful navigation will lead you to a waterhole known as Mgobe wa Takhu in the north-west of the area which contains water for much of the year. To the north of the waterhole a little-known track will, in turn, deliver you to a group of palm trees known as Makolwane a ga Wateka, 10,6 km east of Njuca Hills (described under Route 14, p. 75).

To the west of the south-north track that crosses Ntwetwe Pan, and approximately midway between opposite shores, is the island of Gabasadi. An unusually large barchan dune, it is bare of vegetation but it is worth climbing to the (low) crest for the wonderful view of Ntwetwe that can be had, especially in early or late light. This remarkable spot, so remote and apparently inhospitable, is a place of great archaeological interest. If you look carefully you will find pottery shards and stone tools there.

It was here that Prince Charles, on a visit to Botswana, sat and painted his last picture before returning to England. He commented that it was so hot his watercolours kept drying before he could spread them onto the paper!

Along the west shore of Ntwetwe that reaches down from the Nata-Maun road there are, as elsewhere on this pan, numerous Stone Age sites and among them, in a hidden cleft along the shore, is a secret waterhole that seldom dries up. There are cattle at this particular place but game is also found there sometimes.

Around the hole are hunting blinds built of calcrete blocks that were used in the past by the San, who hid there to ambush game as it came down to drink. Along the approach to this waterhole you can see stands of glorious aloes (*Aloe littoralis*) that bloom in winter and add a splash of unforgettable colour to the landscape.

This whole region can provide days of fascination for those with a penchant for 'beach walking', for exploring and for quietly encountering the 'non-game' wilderness at its unexploited best.

NXAI PAN NATIONAL PARK (Route 15)

A four-wheel-drive vehicle is necessary to get to this national park, which lies north of the Francistown-Maun road and is 36 km from it.

Nxai Pan National Park, recently enlarged to include Baines' Baobabs and the Kudiakam Pans, is set on the northern fringe of the Makgadikgadi basin and includes Nxai Pan itself, part of an ancient lake bed. There is a manned entrance gate and a fee for vehicle and passengers is required. There is no accommodation other than two campsites, one of which has an ablution block. Note that booking and payment in advance are required. Visitors are expected to be entirely self-sufficient, although water can usually be relied upon. Game scouts will direct you to the campsites, which are both within 10 km of the entrance.

About 15 km to the east of the entrance, inside the park, is a large, unnamed pan complex. Kgama-Kgama Pan lies a further 9 km northeast of this. The pans themselves are the only parts to which there is ready access. A road map is sometimes displayed at the entrance gate and a few minutes spent studying this will prove rewarding.

At certain times of the year, notably December to early April, if rains have fallen, game can be prolific and viewing spectacular. The area is a breeding ground for large herds of zebra, wildebeest, gemsbok, springbok and eland. It is one of the few places in Botswana where impala and springbok occur together.

In the south of the national park is another complex of pans, the largest of which is Kudiakam. On a site overlooking this pan is a group of very large and impressive baobab trees, a picture of which was painted by Thomas Baines on 22 May 1862. Photographs taken in July 1967 scarcely show any changes. These trees are known today as Baines' Baobabs (also the Seven Sisters and the Sleeping Sisters) and were, until recently, a very popular camping spot. Human pressure has, however, proved too destructive and camping there is no longer permitted. A game scout's camp will be found about 200 m to the east of the trees and an official there will issue the necessary permit and direct you to a nearby camping site.

OKAVANGO DELTA

The Okavango Delta must be one of Africa's most enchanted places. A swirl of lushness in a desert of Kalahari sand, the delta is a remarkable phenomenon. It owes its origins to the emergence of a rift valley across the course of the Okavango River. When exactly this occurred is not certain but, geologically speaking, it is likely to have been relatively recent, possibly between two and four million years ago. Certainly, the process is still developing and constant movement in the earth's crust may well explain the shifts in water distribution that are such a feature of this remarkable area. In the aeons that have followed since the rift valley was formed, windblown sand and sediment delivered by the river have filled it and its original floor now lies as much as 300 m below the fan-shaped delta that we see today.

A characteristic of the delta is its yearly flood. The Okavango rises in Angola and is filled by heavy rains there. When it flows into Botswana the swollen river breaches its low-water banks and begins the annual inundation of its floodplains. No two floods are ever the same but one can say that the permanent delta is some 6 000 km² in extent, whilst a big flood may seasonally cover as much as 13 000 km². In general, at Mohembo, where the Okavango enters Botswana, the flood begins as water levels rise from November onwards, but the peak is not reached until February or March. It can take six months to work its way through the labyrinth of channels and lagoons to reach Maun and re-fill the Thamalakane River which drains the area and leads the remainder to the Boteti and Lake rivers. It is an extraordinary fact that more than 95 per cent of the Okavango's water evaporates before it reaches Maun.

Flooding in the Okavango is not a violent process. The waters spread gently down the channels and across the plains. The total fall in height from one end of the delta to the other is only 62 m, and that over a distance of some 250 km! The slow movement of water means a low sediment load and hence the incredible clarity and purity of the Okavango's water, for which it is justly renowned.

One of the world's few inland deltas, the Okavango adds enormously to the variety of experiences open to the visitor. Fishing is an obvious attraction, but game-viewing is also possible, if not always on the same scale as in Chobe and Savute. In addition, one can take to the waters of this magic world of islands and lagoons by dugout canoe (*mokoro*) or powerboat. Aircraft can be hired and a flight across the delta is a memorable experience. So too is a helicopter flight — if you can afford it. I am told that the best way to view the delta and its game is from the back of one of Randall Moore's trained African elephants at Abu's Camp. But once again, this experience is strictly for the better-off tourist.

It is, however, difficult to enjoy the Okavango to the full without using the services of professional safari people. There are a number of reasons for this. Although the delta is mapped, no practical map can hope to show the intricacies of the myriad channels. Indeed, many channels cannot be seen easily at all as they are overgrown with reeds. In order to find your way around successfully you need a guide who knows the area well. Also, you require some kind of boat, and it is a major undertaking to haul your own boat to the Okavango for a short visit. All the services you require can be arranged by any of the numerous safari camps and businesses found in Maun and elsewhere in the delta, and it is best to make the necessary arrangements through them. These services include flights, hotels, camping, equipment hire, fishing, game-viewing, boat hire and mokoro trips. A list of recommended operators is given in Chapter 8.

SAVUTE AND MABABE (Route 22)

In the north of Botswana, well within the Chobe National Park, Savute is perhaps one of the best known game-viewing areas in the country. Under ideal conditions the number and variety of animals seen can be quite staggering. Someone once described it as 'wall-to-wall game'!

Savute is particularly well known for its elephant and it seems to be an area preferred by lone bulls. More docile than the cow, these gentle giants are quite at home among the parked cars and campsites — they have been seen stepping delicately between guy-ropes without touching them or damaging the tents! Be warned, though. Docility does not prevent these animals from seeking a little variety in their diet. One visitor had the boot of his car destroyed when a bull used his tusks as a tin-opener to get at the oranges he could smell inside. Do not feed the elephants under any circumstances.

Savute's elephants are only one of its many attractions. Game-viewing is at its best from November to May, but the provision of artificial waterholes has helped keep a wide variety of animals in the area and improved year-round game-viewing.

The Mababe Depression (that immense ancient lake bed to the east of the Gubatsha Hills) stretches endlessly to the horizon as a flat and apparently featureless plain but, when it has received its first rain and has turned to a carpet of green, hundreds of thousands of animals are drawn to it. Zebra, impala, hartebeest, wildebeest, kudu, warthog, buffalo, lion, leopard, hyena, wild dog and jackal are but a few of the bewildering variety of animals to be seen. It is the experience of a lifetime.

As you drive into Savute from the south you will see, on your left-hand side, a low sandy ridge. This is the Magwikhwe Sand Ridge, an old barrier beach more than 100 km long that may once have defined the western boundary of the great lake. Beyond it, to the west, is a chaotic pattern of ancient sand dunes which may have been an area of lagoons and mud flats lying beyond the sand ridge.

There is much speculation as to how this once massive lake received its waters. The most popular explanation is that once the upper Zambezi, the Chobe and the Okavango rivers flowed together, across the north of Botswana and down to the sea via the Motloutse and Limpopo. A gentle warping of the earth's crust dammed this flow to create a vast lake. In time, however, further crustal movement caused these rivers to find a new route to the sea. Their direction changed by faulting, the upper Zambezi and the Chobe turned to the north-east and, after plunging over the Victoria Falls, joined what is now the middle Zambezi. Trapped by an emerging rift valley, the Okavango bled its waters into vast accumulations of sand, to create the delta we see today. Condemned by a changing climate which reduced rainfall and brought a return of almost desert-like conditions, this super-lake dried up and vanished, leaving only the evidence of its form in the shape of Makgadikgadi Pans.

Signs of the lake's existence are still abundant, however. Apart from the obvious feature of the sand ridge, you will notice the nearly sheer north-eastern faces of the Gubatsha Hills. These were cut into cliffs by the crashing force of the waves which once pounded against them. In the lee of the hills you will find accumulations of rounded gravel — pebbles that were ground to their oval shape by ceaseless rolling on the shores of the lake.

One of the great mysteries and fascinations of Savute is its famous channel. It covers a distance of 100 km from the Chobe River through a gap in the sand ridge to the Mababe Depression. Falling only 20 cm for each kilometre of distance covered, this channel can bring water from the Chobe to Mababe, creating a small marsh where it enters the depression. It is this channel and its water which explains the fantastic abundance of game that has been seen at Savute. However, the channel has not flowed since 1981 and even before that flow regimes were always erratic and unpredictable.

We know from accounts of early explorers that the channel was flowing in the 1850s and until about 1880. At that time it ceased to flow and remained dry until the mid-1950s when, without explanation, it began to flow again. Since then, it has 'switched' on and off several times. It is this quixotic flow that explains the dead trees you will see in the channel. They established themselves during the long dry period of this century and were killed off by renewed flooding. No really convincing explanation for this paradoxical flow pattern has been put forward. For me, the most likely candidates include tectonic instability of the region, which may be tilting surfaces first in one direction and then in another, or the coincidence of high flood levels in both the Chobe River and the Zambezi (which backs up along the Chobe).

There is San rock art at several places within the Gubatsha Hills and any of the national park staff are likely to be able to point these out to you.

Even without water from the Chobe, Savute remains a place of enchantment and singular beauty, and still boasts one of the greatest concentrations of animals in southern Africa. It certainly should not be missed on a visit to Botswana.

SOWA PAN (Route 12)

Sowa Pan can be explored, with care, experience and common sense, in an ordinary vehicle, but a four-wheel-drive vehicle is recommended. Heavy loads must be carried as the whole area is quite isolated and offers no facilities whatsoever. You will need to provide your own water, food and fuel.

Sowa and its companion pan Ntwetwe, to the west, form the great Makgadikgadi Pans. These pans are all that is left of a once-great lake that covered most of northern Botswana.

The complete history of the lake is not yet known. It is unlikely to be older than two or three million years and may have held substantial quantities of water up to quite recent times. The most prolonged wet period for which there is good evidence was from 17 000 to 14 000 years ago. There were other such periods between 4 000 and 2 000 years ago. It is not known precisely how high the lake levels were during these wetter periods. The most recent evidence suggests that the old lake bed might have been substantially flooded as recently as 1 500 years ago. It is certain, however, that levels have been as high as 40 m above the present lake bed. Even today good rains will bring floods of water into the northeast and south-west of Sowa. When this happens waterbirds congregate in their millions and flamingos breed in the shallow waters. Tim Liversedge has recorded one of these events in his remarkable video *Year of the Flame Bird*, available in Maun and elsewhere.

There are places of indescribable beauty along the shores of these pans. Perhaps only a poet could really convey the feeling of tranquillity, space and freedom engendered by the immensity of these silvered pans and adjacent grasslands. Many such places remain to be discovered in this remote and enchanting wilderness, but those that are known are well worth visiting. One is Kubu Island.

The name of this small rocky island is derived from the Setswana word 'Lekhubung', meaning a rocky ridge. Studded with grotesque yet appealing baobabs, it has a unique atmosphere. Its isolation and the starkness of its setting against the vast, featureless pan give it a magical quality, and few who visit Kubu come away untouched by this magic. Near the survey beacon which marks its low summit, and set about it like a tonsure, lies a ring of rolled pebbles, which marks an old lake shoreline. At 919 m above sea level, it is one of the lower, and probably more recent, levels.

To reach Kubu, find the turnoff described in Route 12B. The island is 19 km from that point. The track heads roughly north-east. You will be guided mostly by previous vehicle tracks. Some claim that finding the island is easy and that often there is a 'highway' of tracks to follow. This may be true, but the tracks do get washed away after the rains. In their absence, you will have to thread your way through the tussocked grass. Place a lookout on the roof to watch for the low hillock that is Kubu. When you sight it, do not drive directly towards it across the open pan unless you are following vehicle tracks. The surface can be very treacherous, especially during or after the rainy season, and it is difficult to extricate a vehicle that has sunk in deeply. Instead, like a churchmouse, work your way around the edge of open spaces, staying close to the grass. It will take a little longer to get there but at least you will arrive! On the open pan it is safest to keep your vehicle in four-wheel-drive.

Apart from its remarkable beauty and extraordinary aura, Kubu is notable for its archaeological remains. Most obvious of these is a semi-circular stone wall on the south end of the island. The wall, with its deliberately constructed 'loopholes', is associated with the former Khami Empire, an early African state centred at Khami near Bulawayo. The wall dates to the late 17th or 18th century. Also on the island are more than 400 distinct circular stone cairns, each a metre or so across and up to 30 or 40 cm high, constructed of easily lifted stones. It is not known precisely what these were for, but current thinking suggests that they mark initiation ceremonies. To the north end of Kubu, among the giant boulders of a granite outcrop there, is the remains of an Early Iron Age village. The pottery and ostrich egg-shell beads are still abundant. All such remains are the property of the government of Botswana, and should not be disturbed in any way.

To the south of Kubu, and within sight if you look carefully, are two smaller islands, 10 km away on the horizon. They suggest, even more eloquently than Kubu, the splendour and isolation of Sowa Pan. It is not wise to approach these islands directly, unless you are certain of the surface conditions. Again, the 'churchmouse' technique is recommended. As it is, large expanses of bare pan must be crossed to reach them. I've noted that, sometimes, large areas of a darker colour in the pan surface may indicate patches of dampness lethal to vehicles. But this is not a reliable indicator; there is no sure-fire way of determining what the surface ahead may be.

If at any stage while driving on the pan surface you feel the vehicle sinking in, you can take steps to avert disaster. Do not do anything suddenly. Don't swing the steering wheel wildly, brake violently or accelerate harshly. A soft patch will create a distinct drag on the wheels. Collapse is heralded by the drag increasing to the point where the surface suddenly gives. Try and move away from the softer areas when drag is felt. Two tips are offered for driving on this pan: get into four-wheel drive well in advance (you will have no time to change if you really need it!) and drop tyre pressure down to about 0,8 or 1,0 bars. It's a nuisance to inflate them again afterwards but far less trouble than digging yourself out!

To the south-east of Sowa is the lesser known island of Kokonje or Kokoro. Directions to this island can be found in Route 12A. From the turnoff indicated you will see the island about 3 km from the shore. It is possible to drive across to it by following the fence out from the eastern shore. The shortest approach is from the north, where the island is much closer to the mainland. You can drive around to this point, either by crossing the grassland or by 'churchmousing' round the edge. There is a shelf-beach in this area, and you can drive up it to a campsite which offers a magnificent view. Kokoro is a beautiful island, gentler than Kubu but also set about with fossil beaches. It also has Late Stone Age sites. Like Kubu, Kokonje is still used as a rain-making shrine.

If you should approach either of these islands from the south and pass Mosu, it is worth turning into this village. There, set among tall palm trees, is a remarkable spring from which gushes clear, fresh water. Behind Mosu rises a towering escarpment, once the precipitous southern shore of the great lake. Now eddies of hot, dry wind swirl dust against the banks where once cool waves washed.

In recent years important Iron Age archaeological sites have been found in many places along this escarpment crest. It appears that although it is arid now, about 1 000 years ago this region supported large numbers of villages and, probably, a higher population than it does today. Evidence of long-distance trade has also been found. There are signs that goods from Persia and the Far East found their way, through a network of villages and from hand to hand, to these ancient village sites at the south end of Sowa Pan. Local goods in turn travelled to Zaïre and the west coast and down the old trade routes to the Indian Ocean and the Orient. Evidence for this comes from exotic sea shells and tiny blue or green glass beads of Eastern origin, recovered at the sites.

In the north-east of Sowa Pan is the delta of the Nata River. Flowing from Zimbabwe, in a good wet season it may flood large areas to a shallow depth. When this happens the birdlife is breathtaking and the area becomes a paradise for canoeing, boating and board sailing. In the dry part of the year the grasslands invite you to explore. There is no game here; it is cattle country, as are all the grasslands around Sowa. The cattle do not detract at all, however, from the feeling of openness and freedom as you walk. And always, to the west, lies the limitless expanse of Sowa with its kaleidoscope of muted pastel colours, ever changing to reflect the passage of the sun.

Near the delta is Nata Sanctuary, created in 1988 largely thanks to the efforts of Nigel and Liz Ashby from Nata Lodge and the Kalahari Conservation Society. The sanctuary comprises an area of grassland abutting the shore that was given up to tourism by local tribesmen and fenced to keep cattle out. Representatives from four nearby villages, including Nata, are members of a Board of Trustees. Surplus revenues from the project are directed by the trustees to fund capital expenditure in the villages concerned. There are toilet, ablution and camping facilities and rates are reasonable. The sanctuary is 230 km^2 in extent, of which 55 per cent is grassland and the remainder pan surface. This part of the pan is filled only when the Nata River is in flood (it drains part of southern Matabeleland in Zimbabwe) but, when that happens, the huge sheet of water attracts thousands of birds, including summer migrants, to nest and breed. This type of sanctuary, in which local residents are part of the scheme and benefit directly from it, is an encouraging development and one way of ensuring that wildlife will survive in the long term.

Sowa or Sua means salt, and a major project to extract salt and soda ash is located on the eastern side of Sua Pan on Sua Spit. Wells pump brine from an underground aquifer through an 82 km pipeline network to solar evaporation ponds covering an area of 25 km^2. Salt is scraped mechanically from the ponds but a further stage is needed to recover the soda ash via a chemical extraction process. At the time of writing this huge investment was on the brink of insolvency. New owners were being sought and big losses will have to be carried by the Botswana government. It is likely, however, that the project will continue in one form or another. Despite the size and complexity of the project, it is interesting to note that modern man was not the first to think of mining salt from Sowa Pan. There are historic San and Kalanga salt extraction pits in Nata Sanctuary which, I am told, were still in use until 1990!

TSHANE/HUKUNTSI CLUSTER OF VILLAGES (Routes 4 and 7)

Almost in the very centre of Botswana's Kalahari, four villages over 100 km from the nearest town cluster together as if for protection and mutual support. Remote as they are, they are of interest to the visitor because so much of the country's early history is represented here. The area may be reached via the Kang-Tsabong routes.

Tshane is one of the four villages and is located on high ground overlooking the magnificent Tshane Pan. (Note the wind-created dunes on the south and south-west sides of the pan.) Watering of animals from hand-dug wells on the pan's edge still takes place and provides a fascinating insight into the traditional way of performing this task, which has remained unchanged for 150 years or more.

Lokhwabe (which means 'stony pan' in Setswana), is 11 km from Tshane to the south-west. It is the home of, among others, Khoikhoi descendants of Simon Cooper, who fought the Germans of South West Africa during the 1906-8 rebellion. Cooper also confronted German forces after their epic campaign through what is now the Gemsbok National Park (see Kalahari Gemsbok National Park, p. 19). After that battle Cooper and his followers sought the protection of Britain and were allowed to settle at Lokhwabe. Simon Cooper is buried at the village.

About the same distance north from Tshane is the settlement of Lehututu. Those who are familiar with early explorers of the Kalahari will have heard of this village. Unlikely as it may seem now, it was once a busy commercial centre. Although times have passed it by, the old store is still standing and remains open for business. When the inventive Mr Farini traversed this portion of the Kalahari in 1885 he reported (and his son photographed) 'King Mampaar and his wife'. This is a clear allusion to the Moapare family, chiefs of the area, who live there still (though now they have moved to Hukuntsi). 'Lehututu' is an onomatopoeic Setswana name for the ground hornbill.

Hukuntsi, the fourth village in the group, is the administrative headquarters for the area and the one to which the main road leads. Its name means 'four points of the compass'. Petrol and diesel are sold here and there are several well-stocked stores.

TSODILO HILLS (Route 21)

The Tsodilo Hills, located in Botswana's remote north-west, are among the most rewarding of destinations for adventurous visitors. Brought to world attention by Laurens van der Post in his book *Lost World of the Kalahari*, they are surrounded by myth and mystery and the magic of the place is almost tangible. This is perhaps partly because of their setting.

The hills, formed of micaceous quartzite schists, rise abruptly through rolling sand dune country. The dunes, long since stabilised and held in place by abundant vegetation, might at first escape your eye, but, as you approach the hills over a sandy track from a distance, you will gradually become accustomed to the gentle climb to the 20 m wooded crest and the descent to the flat, grass-covered valley before the next crest.

Four hills, set roughly in a line, make up the group. The most southerly, and the largest, is bare rock rising 400 m above the plain. Immediately to the north is a group of scattered summits, and beyond that two small, separate hills. The San call the largest the Male, his companion the Female and the nearest of the small hills the Child. There is no name for the fourth and smallest hill. It is the Male that is first seen on the approach, its summit looming blue-black above the trees.

As you approach, the road will take you to a permanent settlement of Hambukushu, a Bantu-speaking people, near the Male hill. About 1,5 km away is a small Zhu San village. The Bantu have been settled in and around Tsodilo for at least 1 000 years and the San are likely to have made use of it for very much longer.

Ongoing archaeological studies have revealed occupation by humans for at least 100 000 years. That Tsodilo is a place of special significance to the San is suggested not only by the existence of a number of secret and permanent springs among the hills, but by the profusion of rock art in the area. There are over 4 000 separate paintings, some of outstanding impact, on more than 370 individual sites. The majority are on the Female hill and most are to be found around the base on the west and along the side of major drainage lines.

In recent years a lot of research has been carried out at the hills. The National Museum and Art Gallery has completed the task of photographing every known painting. This exercise was of vital archival importance and also helped locate more sites and an additional 500-odd depictions. Without question though, more are still to be found. Alec Campbell of Gaborone and Larry Robbins, a colleague from Michigan State University in America, have been excavating various shelters at the hills and now have evidence of human habitation going back at least 100 000 years. In addition, other workers have identified shorelines of a small lake that once stood to the west of the Male and Female hills. Among the rare and precious artifacts found here are bone fishhooks dating back 20 000 years, no doubt used by the local inhabitants to catch fish in the lake.

Perhaps the most dramatic and exciting of recent discoveries has been the location of 18 mines among the hills. Some of these were known in the past but were not recognised for what they were. Nevertheless, it is clear that, between approximately AD 800 and 1100, people at Tsodilo were engaged in a busy industry. Evidence suggests that they were mining black haematite and possibly mica and trading it far and wide through the extensive trade networks of Africa. Their technique appears to have used fire to heat the rock causing it, on cooling, to spall off the face.

With all these discoveries and ever-growing interest in Tsodilo Hills, visitor impact has inevitably increased and, sadly, steps have now been taken to control access.

The hills are a national monument and, as such, are in the custody of the National Museum. The museum maintains an airstrip near the Male Hill which is suitable for single-engined aircraft only. A fence runs westward from the south end of the Male Hill to keep cattle out of the immediate vicinity. All roads leading to the hills now approach the same gate in this fence, close to the Hambukushu village. Visitors will be met there and directed to the museum's field offices about 5 km away, on the west side of the Female Hill, within site of the Van der Post Panel. At the office, visitors will be directed either to one of four campsites in the immediate vicinity or to one of three more distant sites. The latter have no facilities besides a fireplace. Sites near the office already have access to piped fresh water and will eventually be provided with showers and toilets. It is also expected that a site museum will be erected and this will help further explain the magic of these extraordinary hills. When all the new facilities are in place and working, an entrance fee will be charged. Nothing is set at the moment but the fee will probably be about P10 per adult except for residents and citizens, who will pay a lesser amount.

There are six trails of varying length that wind their way through and among the hills. Three are clearly cut paths, three are not and will require local guides, either San or Hambukushu, who are available through the museum office. Those that are cut are marked with painted signs and brochures describing each numbered viewing point are currently being produced. Written by Alec Campbell, a man who has done a great deal of exploration here, they should make fascinating reading.

Apart from water and campsites, there are no facilities at Tsodilo. Food and fuel must be taken with you. The nearest fuel is obtainable from Barrie Pryce at Shakawe Fishing Camp, 50 km away. Beyond that, petrol should be found at Etsha-6 village to the south and at Andara in Caprivi to the north. An airstrip at Tsodilo is maintained by the museum but is not manned. You will need to stay a minimum of two nights to explore the hills fully.

WESTERN WOODLANDS (MASETLHENG PAN) (Route 8 from routes 4 and 7)

This incredibly beautiful part of Botswana was shown to me by that grand adventurer and man of the bush, Izak Barnard. If you want a first class tour of the area, travel with him but, if you wish to visit independently, I thoroughly recommend a visit.

The pan of Masetlheng lies just 90 km west of Hukuntsi and it is remarkable for a number of good reasons. The journey there takes you through a series of striking pans and gives a very good feel of what these features look like (notice the build-up of wind-created dunes on the south or south-west sides of all these pans). On the way you pass through and have the opportunity of visiting relatively new San villages. This is an illuminating, if somewhat depressing, experience.

Some years ago, with the assistance of the Canadian government, Botswana had a deep exploratory borehole drilled within a kilometre or two of Masetlheng Pan. This hole, which was part of the (unsuccessful) search for oil, penetrated to the remarkable depth of 4,2 km! However, the project spawned a maze of existing tracks and cut-lines which one can explore. No maps of these are available as they were created quite recently and the information, the private property of a now-defunct exploration company, is difficult to retrieve. The deep hole lies beside the main north-south cut-line. Southwards one can travel towards the Kalahari Gemsbok National Park boundary and thence either west to the Namibia border or south-east along it to Mabuasehube. Alternatively one can drive north, rejoin the road from Hukuntsi and travel northwest towards Ncojane Farms and, ultimately, the border with Namibia at Mamuno. I have not personally completed this journey but I look forward to doing so for, along the way, lies Ukwi Pan, said to be among the largest in Botswana.

By far the greatest attraction of Masetlheng, however, is the acacia woodland that is to be found just 10 km beyond it. The vast stand of large acacias extends across a swathe of countryside, varying from 3 to 5 km in width and stretching for some 40 km in length.

The dominant trees are *Acacia luderitzii* and *A. erioloba*. There are no young trees and no scrub and so the impression of a carefully mani-cured and maintained parkland is quite overwhelming. In the late evening with the sun low and long shadows creeping across the grass between golden trees, the sight is striking and unforgettable. It is one of the most beautiful places I have seen in Botswana.

3. GETTING AROUND

This section is intended to help you plan your route once you have decided which areas in Botswana you wish to visit. A number of routes are described in great detail. Inevitably, some of the information concerning the quality of road surfaces will be out of date by the time you use this book. Roads in Botswana change with the seasons, with the amount and type of traffic using them, and depending on how recently a grader has passed over them. The roads department does the best it can to maintain the roads but its task is monumental and it simply cannot maintain the thousands of kilometres of gravel and sand roads as well as it might wish to do.

A second problem with describing road surfaces is that what one person considers a fair surface may very well be considered execrable by another. There is no standard by which a convenient measurement can be made. Descriptions used in the following section reflect, as far as possible, the general opinion at the time the road was used.

Similar problems apply to indications of the length of time required for certain journeys. Many factors influence the speed at which one travels and no two people will do the same journey in the same time. Statements of road quality and time should therefore be regarded as approximations only.

If you pride yourself on your ability to get from A to B using maps, making logical deductions and following instructions to the letter, you are in for a new experience in Botswana.

Direction-finding in the remoter areas requires boldness, common sense, perseverance and more than a little faith. Even if there were accurate maps, there is absolutely no guarantee that the roads would be the same as they were when the maps were drawn. This is understandable, when you think about it: a herd of elephants passes by, doing its work of tree demolition. One of the trees falls onto the road and the next vehicle to arrive finds its own way around the obstacle, creating a new road that may only rejoin the previous track many kilometres further on.

Then there are the dreaded sand ridges. Your speed drops, the whine of the engine rises higher and higher as it strains with greater and greater effort. As a last resort, you swing out of the track, hoping to get better purchase on the vegetation alongside. A new road is created.

These facts pose certain problems for the writers of guidebooks who are trying to furnish helpful, clear and concise directions. My approach is to give you a general description of the lie of the land and approximate direction and distance. You can use the 'decision-point' approach, i.e. calculate how long it should take to reach your destination, knowing how fast you travel and get a feeling for the direction. Drive in that direction for that length of time, keeping a note of times and landmarks. If you haven't arrived at your destination in the time you have allowed, then it is time for a reassessment and maybe a cup of tea or coffee!

VETERINARY FENCES

One of the country's top earners of foreign exchange is its beef exports, the bulk of which go to the European Community. To do everything possible to control outbreaks of foot-and-mouth disease Botswana's state veterinary department has used fences to divide the country into a number of huge 'paddocks'. Movement of stock, meat (and pets) across fences is strictly controlled.

The fences are popularly referred to as 'vet fences'. They are mentioned here because they provide a comprehensive highway system that provides access to remote areas.

For example, the cut-line that demarcates the boundary of the Central Kalahari Game Reserve can be accessed from main roads via the Kuke Fence, the Makalamabedi Fence or the Makoba Fence.

The fences are almost always in pairs, roughly 100 m apart. They are four- or five-stranded and nearly 1,5 m high. There is usually a track on the outer sides of both fences which, although infrequently maintained, is generally of perfectly adequate standard.

When I last counted there were over 2 500 km of fences in Botswana — a considerable highway system indeed, well over half of it remote wilderness areas! Gates are infrequent but they are all in sensible and logical places. It is, however, important to know exactly where they are. The map included in this edition is too small to illustrate such detail and so I strongly recommend you purchase the latest map of Botswana Foot and Mouth Veterinary Control Fences from the Department of Surveys and Mapping, Private Bag 0037, Gaborone (Tel 35 3251), before venturing forth.

For those with a penchant for exploring the unusual and the little known, I do heartily recommend that you use the vet fence system. But remember that if you wish to move pets or large quantities of raw meat through these fences you will require a permit.

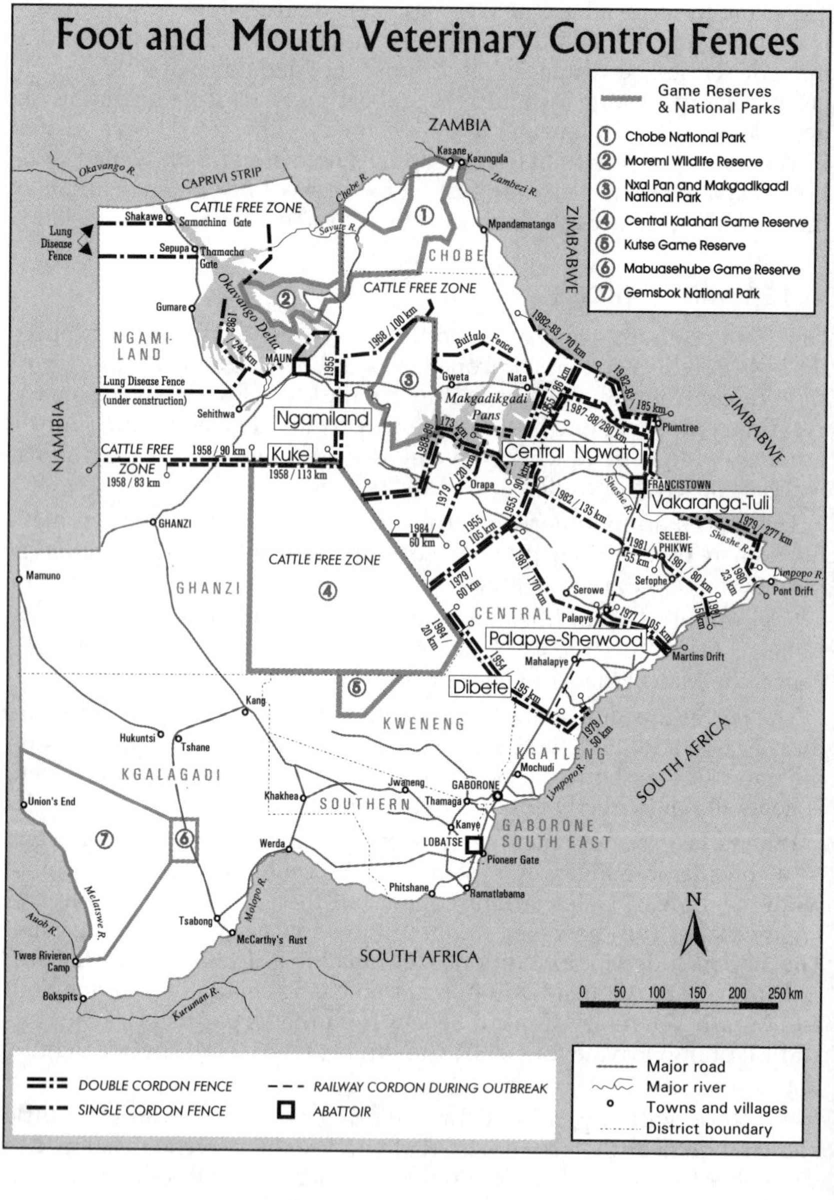
Foot and Mouth Veterinary Control Fences
Game Reserves & National Parks
① Chobe National Park
② Moremi Wildlife Reserve
③ Nxai Pan and Makgadikgadi National Park
④ Central Kalahari Game Reserve
⑤ Kutse Game Reserve
⑥ Mabuasehube Game Reserve
⑦ Gemsbok National Park
ZAMBIA
ZIMBABWE
NAMIBIA
SOUTH AFRICA
CAPRIVI STRIP
CATTLE FREE ZONE
Lung Disease Fence
Lung Disease Fence (under construction)
NGAMI-LAND
CHOBE
GHANZI
CENTRAL
KWENENG
KGATLENG
KGALAGADI
SOUTHERN
GABORONE
SOUTH EAST
Ngamiland
Kuke
Central Ngwato
Vakaranga-Tuli
Palapye-Sherwood
Dibete
Buffalo Fence
Makgadikgadi Pans
Okavango Delta
1958 / 90 km
1958 / 83 km
1958 / 113 km
1968 / 100 km
1982 / 242 km
1982-83 / 70 km
1982-83 / 185 km
1987-88 / 280 km
1982 / 135 km
1979 / 277 km
1981 / 55 km
1981 / 80 km
1980 / 23 km
1981 / 15 km
1977 / 105 km
1954 / 195 km
1979 / 50 km
1984 / 20 km
1979 / 60 km
1955 / 105 km
1984 / 60 km
1979 / 120 km
1981 / 170 km
1955
Kasane
Kazungula
Mpandamatanga
Shakawe
Samachina Gate
Sepupa
Thamacha Gate
Gumare
MAUN
Sehithwa
Gweta
Nata
Orapa
Plumtree
FRANCISTOWN
SELEBI-PHIKWE
Sefophe
Serowe
Palapye
Mahalapye
Martins Drift
Pont Drift
GHANZI
Mamuno
Kang
Hukuntsi
Tshane
Union's End
Khakhea
Jwaneng
Thamaga
Mochudi
Kanye
LOBATSE
Pioneer Gate
Werda
Phitshane
Ramatlabama
Tsabong
McCarthy's Rust
Twee Rivieren Camp
Bokspits
Okavango R.
Chobe R.
Zambezi R.
Savute R.
Shashe R.
Limpopo R.
Molopo R.
Melatswe R.
Auob R.
Kuruman R.
N
0 50 100 150 200 250 km
DOUBLE CORDON FENCE
SINGLE CORDON FENCE
RAILWAY CORDON DURING OUTBREAK
ABATTOIR
Major road
Major river
Towns and villages
District boundary

GLOBAL POSITIONING SYSTEM (GPS)

The Global Positioning System (GPS) is a satellite-based navigation system that gives a position on the earth's surface with remarkable accuracy. There is a Russian as well as an American system. The latter is the one used mostly in the West and in southern Africa.

A GPS is a (usually) hand-held instrument that makes contact with orbiting satellites and, within minutes, displays its geographical position. It was developed for military purposes and can be accurate to within metres, but civilian channels are not as precise. Despite this, most GPSs today will give a 'fix' to within 50-100 m.

Five years ago GPSs were extremely expensive. Today their price is a fraction of what it was and is still falling. In future more and more travellers will own a GPS and use it routinely for their wilderness travel. It is for this reason that GPS references have been included in this book.

(If you have any new routes, roads or positions of interest to report to the author (see Feedback, p. 3) GPS references will be very much appreciated. When supplying these, please indicate what datum was used; see next paragraph.)

It is important to note that different countries use different datums on which their topographical maps are constructed. Most GPSs allow the user to select the datum of the country in which they will be operating. The default datum is a standard known as WGS 84. The datum for southern Africa (including Botswana) is Clark 1880. The differences in final position between these two datums can be considerable. For this reason, it is important to know which datum was used for the GPS reading. If it is Clark 1880 the fix, when transposed to a map, will be as accurate as the technology allows; if the datum is WGS 84, an error of up to 300 m may occur.

However, such errors are minuscule compared to the distances involved in travelling in Botswana and are hardly relevant. Nevertheless, the user needs to be aware of them and to be a little more forgiving if small discrepancies do occur.

Note: All GPS positions given in this book are followed by the words (1880), (WGS 84) or (u/k).

CUT-LINES

This term describes straight lines cleared of vegetation which penetrate through the bush, sometimes for hundreds of kilometres.

Most were created by prospectors and survey departments who used cut-lines to carve vast tracts of wilderness into manageable portions within which it was possible to find one's way without getting lost. Almost invariably, cut-lines carried the prospector's vehicular traffic.

Once their purpose is served, cut-lines are left to fall victim to encroaching bush; but the process takes many years and it often happens that others find a use for the makeshift 'road'.

Old cut-lines have opened up huge portions of Botswana to the casual traveller. An excellent example is the Central Kalahari Game Reserve, where it would be impossible to travel widely without cut-lines, but there are many, many others.

Cut-lines do not always appear on government maps, however, as there is no centralised record of them. Nevertheless they are invaluable aids to getting around Botswana. The relevant ones that I know of are mentioned here. Many others exist, and the adventurous will want to use them to travel ever further into Botswana's wilderness areas. Here are some basic facts about cut-lines that might assist such hardy spirits.

Cut-lines are always absolutely straight (they are 'cut' with the help of a compass and follow a compass bearing). They do not necessarily go anywhere, and can simply end abruptly. Those in current use will have well-used vehicle tracks down the middle. If the tracks are overgrown, it may be risky to follow the line. A sure indication of a cut-line is the distant vertical 'notch' you'll see in the tree line on the horizon. (The Kalahari traverse cut-line viewed from Deception Pan is an excellent example of this.) Cut-lines invariably (but not always) run east-west or north-south and mostly on magnetic as opposed to true bearings.

SOME COMMON ROUTES FOR TWO- AND FOUR-WHEEL-DRIVE VEHICLES

The route you choose is usually determined by the type of vehicle you are using and the amount of time available to you.

Two-wheel-drive vehicles

It is now possible for ordinary vehicles to penetrate and enjoy large parts of Botswana. At the last count the state department of roads was responsible for maintaining 4 114 km of tar, 2 006 km of gravel and 2 632 km of earth and sand. On top of this there are 9 377 km of tracks of various kinds within the nine district council areas that are not maintained at all.

(Many up-to-date road maps are available, and these should be used when planning routes.) In spite of the ever-growing number of tarmac kilometres, there remain some limitations, of course. Kombis have been known to penetrate successfully the heart of the rough country, but for less intrepid explorers routes such as that between Maun and Kasane, through the Moremi Wildlife Reserve via Savute, are not possible except in a four-wheel-drive.

It is possible to travel on tarmac from Maun all the way up the western side of the Okavango Delta to the border gate at Mohembo, beyond Shakawe, and along the south-eastern side to Shorobe. Maun itself is connected by tar to Nata whilst the Nata-Kasane section has been tarred for some years. The main road from Gaborone to Ghanzi is under construction and the tar shortcut from Gaborone through Thamaga to Kanye considerably reduces the time and distance to Jwaneng on the Ghanzi route. From the village of Sekoma a narrow (but excellent) tar road runs through Werda to Tsabong, helping make Mabuasehube more easily and rapidly accessible; just as the tarmac road to Letlhakeng did for Kutse Game Reserve and the Central Kalahari.

These changes make it possible to see much that Botswana has to offer: the arid southern Kalahari, the Central Kalahari and the game-filled northern regions. The water world of the Okavango is much more accessible whilst the northern parts of Chobe National Park are within most people's reach.

For example: drive Francistown-Nata-Maun. Leave your vehicle in Maun and fly into the delta. Once there you have a number of options. You can select from a wide range of experiences — from the ultra-luxurious to the basic (and infinitely cheaper) camp and canoe (mokoro). You can find out what is available through local travel agents in Maun and refer to Chapter 8 in this guide.

From Maun, drive back to Nata and from there head north on the tarmac road to Kasane. This is the gateway to the big game world (although you cannot enter Chobe National Park in saloon cars and must arrange to do a game drive with one of the local safari companies). You can either camp in the Chobe National Park or stay outside the park at Chobe Safari Lodge or Kubu Lodge.

From here you can plan an overnight excursion into Zimbabwe and take the excellent tar road to Victoria Falls. You can continue through Hwange National Park to Bulawayo, then turn south via Beit Bridge. The alternative is to return to Botswana and head south to Francistown.

Four-wheel-drive vehicles (a two-week trip)

If you are approaching the Okavango Delta from the south or east, the best route for those short of time is to push through to Maun as quickly as possible. Spend the night there, then refuel, stock up and head north-wards to Moremi South Gate. Spend four nights in the Moremi Wildlife Reserve, dividing your time between Third Bridge and Cakanaca camp-sites (remember, you have to book in advance now). Then drive north to Savute and spend a couple of nights there. Head north again to Serondela campsite in Chobe National Park (after 1996 this campsite will close and there will be a new campsite at Ihaha, approximately 15 km further west along the river). The final two nights before the journey home can be spent at Victoria Falls.

Once in Maun you will probably be eager to be 'up and at' the big game country and may be reluctant to waste an afternoon wandering among the water lilies and taking in the phenomenal birdlife of the wa-terways around Maun. Do take the time, though, to hire a mokoro (dug-out canoe) and let your poler take you into this peaceful watery world. It is well worth it.

Four-wheel-drive vehicles (a three-week trip)

With more time to spend, all kinds of possibilities are open to the visitor with a four-wheel-drive vehicle. Visits to the Nxai Pan and Makgadikgadi National Park are a must, especially if your visit coincides with the game migration.

You can leave your vehicle in Maun and fly into the Okavango Delta for two or three days' camping and canoeing. Remember that Maun is the last place where you can hire a mokoro if you follow the Moremi-Savute-Chobe route.

Begin by taking the standard route through Moremi to Savute, but thereafter head north to the campsite on the Linyanti River. Alterna-tively, stop at Tjinga or Nogatsha, both pleasing but less well-known campsites in the Chobe National Park on the route to Serondela (note comment above regarding the closure of this campsite and its replace-ment by Ihaha).

Caprivi route: Kasane-Ngoma Bridge-Katima Mulilo-Popa Falls-Mohembo
Gate-Shakawe

Nothing in life is all good or all bad. Even war sometimes has a silver lining, and in this case it is the road which runs through the Caprivi

Strip. This excellent road can be used to travel speedily and smoothly from one side of the Okavango Delta to the other. The route will be described as though travelling from east to west.

As this route takes you out of Botswana and into Namibia you will have to clear immigration. This is done at Ngoma Bridge.

Unless you want to do some last-minute game-viewing along the river bank, take the more southerly main road that leads to Kachikau. It travels along the higher land and then drops down to the river floodplain where the Ngoma Bridge is clearly visible. The bridge will take you across the Botswana/Namibia border. The distance from Kasane to Ngoma Bridge is 64 km and the trip takes about an hour.

Your next destination is Katima Mulilo where, after 67 km from the Ngoma Bridge border post, you are clearly in a different country. It is a bustling centre and a good place for picking up any spare parts needed or stocking up with excellent Windhoek beer! Note that Namibia has its own currency — the Namibian dollar — but at the time of writing the South African rand was still used and South African credit cards were valid. If it's likely to be important for you, it would be a good idea to check ahead of time.

From Katima Mulilo to the Kwando River is a run of 120 km on a tar road and then there is a good quality dirt road for the remaining 212 km to the Popa Falls campsite. This appealing campsite is run by Namibia's department of nature conservation.

You can buy petrol at Andara — at the junction, not very far up the road from Popa Falls — or you can rely on Barrie Pryce having some at Shakawe Fishing Camp, 65 km away in Botswana. Apart from these two sources, the nearest supply will be at Etsha.

At the Popa Falls campsite you can walk and 'boulder-hop' your way to the main body of water. Looking across its width of about half a kilometre, it is quite sobering to think that this water feeds the whole of the magical Okavango Delta, 13 000 km^2 of unique wetland paradise.

At the Andara junction, take the road to Botswana. This will take you through the Mhlango Game Reserve to the Mohembo Gate, which is the border between Botswana and Namibia, where you can clear customs and immigration. The distance from the junction to the border is about 85 km.

DETAILED ROUTES

ROUTE 1: Gaborone-Kutse Game Reserve (Map 1, page 207)

Total distance: 220 km. Time: 3,5-4,5 hours.

To reach the Kutse Game Reserve from Gaborone, take the tarmac road via Molepolole (signposted turnoff at 58,6 km) to Letlhakeng (a further 61,5 km and end of tar). About 46 km from Molepolole it is worth looking out on the northern side of the road for a deep, striking river gorge. The river no longer flows but the incised nature of the valley and its precipitous cliffs indicate the huge volumes of water it must have carried.

Petrol is available at Letlhakeng from a hand-operated pump 100 m along on your right-hand side after you turn left at the traffic circle. To continue to Kutse, return to the traffic circle and turn left (thus continuing in your original direction).

From Letlhakeng the road is poorly signposted. It is 24 km to Khudumelapye on a reasonable sand surface. Signs in this village guide you left along a shallow river bed and past a small store called 'Faroul Trading Store'. The track is often difficult to follow but pass to the right of this store (as you face it) and you will soon find the main road again. The road deteriorates from here on and becomes extremely sandy. It is 32,6 km to Salajwe and, beyond that, a further 43 km to the Kutse gate.

For travel in Kutse Game Reserve, refer to Map 1 (which includes GPS waypoints) in this book. For further maps obtain either Botswana 1:250 000 *Kutse Sheet No SF.35.13* or Botswana 1:500 000 *Sheet 7*. Neither of these is essential but the enthusiast will appreciate them.

ROUTE 2: Central Kalahari Game Reserve (CKGR)

There are three official ways into this game reserve, which has recently opened to the public. They are through Xade in the west, Kutse in the south-east and Matswere Camp in the north-east.

The Kutse entrance is reached from Gaborone (see Route 1, above).

Xade can be reached from Ghanzi (see Route 4), but note this road is currently being tarred and will be substantially re-aligned near Ghanzi. At the time of writing the turnoff for Xade was approximately 33 km south-east of Ghanzi. From that point Xade was a further 142 km. As this will most certainly change you are strongly advised to ask for directions to Xade from the Ghanzi road.

Rakops is to the west of Orapa and Mopipi and will be found on any map of the country.

Warning: The northern half of the CKGR is well served by good tracks and is frequently visited. A number of tracks can be driven in an ordinary car (at least in the dry season). In the event of a breakdown, help is not likely to be too far away.

The southern part of the CKGR is quite another matter. The tracks are very sandy — some of the worst sand I have seen in 15 years' travel in Botswana. There are many remote cut-lines along which vehicles can travel. However, travellers are infrequent and if you break down it is unlikely that anyone will come along for some time.

I do not intend to deter individuals from visiting this part; I wish only to sound a strong warning. Do not venture into the southern CKGR unless you have adequate supplies of food and water, a map, a good vehicle and are a competent 'bush' mechanic, are in the company of a second vehicle and have ensured that friends and the game reserve staff know where you have gone and when you expect to be out again. Do not treat this area lightly. Unprepared travellers have died in the remoteness of the Central Kalahari.

Total distances:	Times:
Gaborone-Kutse Gate 220 km	3,5-4,5 hours
Kutse Gate-Xade 272 km	1 day (if you are lucky!)
Xade-Deception Valley 172 km	4 hours minimum
Deception Valley-Rakops 86 km	2 hours

See Maps 2 and 3 at pages 208 and 209 (which include GPS waypoints) and also the following Republic of Botswana maps: 1:500 000 *Sheets 3,4,6* and 7 1:250 000 *Sheets SF.34.4* (Toteng), *34.8* (Letiahau), *34.12* (Okwa), *34.16* (Kang) and *SF35.1* (Bushman Pits), *35.5* (Lake Xau), *35.9* (Metseamonong), *35.13* (Kutse).

I believe it would be foolhardy to venture into the more remote areas without being properly prepared; and this includes having good maps.

This route will be dealt with in two parts: Kutse to Xade and Rakops to Xade.

Route 2A: Kutse to Xade (Map 2, page 208)

Total distance: 272 km. Time: about a day or two! Four-wheel-drive is essential.

A hundred metres or so west of Kutse Gate you will see a well-used track leading to the north. It is marked 'Heavy vehicles to Gope'. Although you can drive to Xade via Gope, it takes longer and apparently the detour adds little to the experience.

Turn right after 13,6 km and right again after an additional 12 km. After a total of 46,8 km while travelling a little west of north, you will cross a heavily used east-west cut-line. This links with the Gope road. Ignore it and continue north-west. After 7 km you'll pass the village of Kukamme, which may be abandoned. It is extremely difficult to find the track out of this village but it will eventually be found if you continue to the north-west and keep your eyes open.

There is a critical junction 10,5 km from the village. Here the track you are on turns due north onto a clear north-south cut-line that is as well used to the south as it is to the north. A track also continues to the west. It leads to Kikao village. Turn right (north) here.

Some 87 km from the gate is a sign: 'Xade 184'. From 91 km on, for the next 3 km are a series of San settlements culminating at the borehole at Motlhomelwa. The road is extremely sandy here, and the going is heavy.

At 113 km you will notice the abandoned De Beers base camp, Bape, on the east side. The ten diesel storage tanks are empty! Four kilometres further on is a second crucial turning point: a T-junction to the west. It is indicated by two clear confirmers. Firstly, if you look to the west you will see within a few kilometres the shape of a valley cut by a north-east flowing river. Secondly, if you continue north for 400 m you will see a cut-line joining your original route from the east. The east and west lines appear to have 'missed' each other by this amount. Turn west here. The track improves, you can shift into high-ratio drive and cruise up to 30 km/h.

Your route turns abruptly north after 33,5 km although a faint track will be observed continuing west. Still the track is good and high range can be enjoyed. The final westward turn occurs after another 31,8 km and you face the last 35 km of easy driving. At 33,3 km you cross a tributary of the Okwa and a little further on a turning north to Molapo settlement. For Xade, of course, you continue west.

At the time of my last visit, drought had forced the Ghanzi District Council to deliver water to remote San settlements. Big Mercedes tankers with a wide wheel-base were being used and these vehicles inevitably caused considerable damage to the sand track. Lesser vehicles were forced to cut new tracks through the soft sand, crawling in first gear low-range, for hour after hour. At the best of times this stretch to Xade is bad; under these conditions it is appalling.

After 34 km of miserable driving from the Molapo turnoff, the track splits. The cut-line continues west but a new track angles off to the north-west. Follow this 20 km to Xade. The Department of Wildlife office is on your right as you enter, the clinic and primary school on your left.

Route 2B: Rakops to Xade (via Deception Valley) (Map 3, page 209)

Total distances:

Mopipi-Rakops	68 km, tar
Rakops-Deception 85,5 km	average 45 km/h
Rakops-Xade 257,6 km	average 35 km/h

See Map 3 at page 209 (which includes GPS waypoints) and also the following Republic of Botswana maps: 1:500 000 *Sheets 3,4,6* and *7* 1:250 000 *Sheets SF.34.4* (Toteng), *34.8* (Letiahau), *34.12* (Okwa), *34.16* (Kang) and *SF35.1* (Bushman Pits), *35.5* (Lake Xau), *35.9* (Metseamonong), *35.13* (Kutse).

A four-wheel-drive vehicle is highly desirable but not essential.

Route 9 takes one from Serowe to Orapa Mine and 10A from Orapa to Rakops. To get to Mopipi, follow the tarmac road west of Orapa, drive around the south side of the mine concession and a further 46 km from the point at which you rejoin the main road, westward to Mopipi.

From the petrol station at Mopipi Village continue to follow the tar and the road signs westward to Xhumo (38 km) then north-west to Rakops, an additional 30 km.

At the time of writing the tar ended abruptly in the centre of Rakops. There is talk of the road north being tarred but no date appears to have been set. In the meantime, from the end of the tar turn sharp left onto the main dirt road and follow this out of the village for 3 km to the north. There you will see the sign to Matswere Camp and the CKGR. The road onwards is excellent.

Twelve kilometres from the turnoff you will notice a rise in the road as it goes up successive sandy levels. This is the old lake shore, dating from a time when the great lake of Makgadikgadi filled the vast spaces around you. Stop and look back at the view: it's worth it. Imagine an immense sea filling the horizon!

Forty-seven kilometres from Rakops brings you to the border of the CKGR and the one-day-to-be-erected Mananga Gate. 'Kuke Corner' is 56 km to the north-west along the boundary cut-line. A further 8,8 km west is Matswere Camp and the present permit office. Some 27,5 km from here is a prominent and well-used east-west cut-line. This was cut as part of a geological survey of the Kalahari in 1973 and is known as the Kalahari Traverse (KT cut-line). It used to be the old way into Deception Valley but now a track has been cut from it to Matswere and beyond to Rakops.

After hitting the KT cut-line, you turn west for 2,2 km and enter Deception Valley. From this point it is possible to drive further west along the KT cut-line to gain access to Sunday Pans (very pretty and about 20 km) or even further to Passarge waterhole (just under 60 km). (Try and have the sun behind you when you travel these sections — it makes the sights and colours spectacular.)

Immediately north of Passarge waterhole there begins a well-defined drainage line, the remnant of a large river system that flows to the north-east. There is no track down this, but you can get a good view of it from spot height BPS 507, approximately 1 km east of Passarge waterhole, just off the KT cut-line (see map). The road north-west to Motopi is only worth following if game scouts have confirmed that the borehole there is working and there is water. Despite what is sometimes said, the KT cut-line does not continue westward to Ghanzi.

The main route to Xade turns south, along Deception Valley and, at 45 km, passes Letiahau waterhole. At 18,7 km beyond that the track turns out of Letiahau Valley (which you entered at Deception). This whole 64 km drive is over hard pan surface between great islands of acacia trees standing shoulder to shoulder, as if for shelter and protection against the silent immensity of the northern Kalahari. It is a stunning drive, with some sort of game almost always in sight!

After leaving the Letiahau Valley, a journey of 37 km brings you to the complex known as Piper Pans. Pan formations are encountered again a further 20 km to the south and continue sporadically for another 30 km. After that, for the last 20,5 km into Xade there is only the vastness, the colours and the fascination of the Central Kalahari to be enjoyed.

Almost all of this road is high-ratio two-wheel-drive and could probably be done in an ordinary car by those disposed to reckless adventure.

ROUTE 3: Gaborone-Mabuasehube Pan in the Gemsbok National Park (Map 4, page 210)

Total distance: 450 km. Time: 7-8 hours.

There are three approaches to this reserve. One is from the south, through Tsabong. A second route is from the north, via Kang and Tshane. (Fo details of these routes see Route 7, Kang-Tsabong.) The third route, which approaches from the east, is considered to be the best and is recommended — the road is better and the distance shorter.

To travel by this route, drive from Gaborone to Khakhea, via Thamaga and Moshupa, Jwaneng and Sekoma (Map 4). After passing through Kumakwane (27 km from Gaborone), one crosses the Kolobeng River. A National Museum signpost on the south side of the road, beyond the bridge, directs you to the remains of Livingstone's last mission station at Kolobeng. It was from here that he left to discover Lake Ngami and, ultimately, for his great trans-African journey. One of his daughters is buried here.

From Khakhea drive south on the main road for 40 km to the small village of Khokhotsa (63 km north of Werda), which is distinguished by a prominent pan on the east side of the road and a microwave tower on the west. To this point, the road has been tarmac from Gaborone. Leading to the west for about 200 m past the base of the tower is a short length of tarmac. Take this and, where it stops, continue west along the cut-line for approximately 100 km. This will take you to Mabuasehube's boundary. At this point you can turn either north or south, picking up other ways into the reserve, or you can continue for a further 10 km. This will deliver you to the pump and borehole at Lesholoago Pan. It is 8 km further west from this point to the main north-south road.

ROUTE 4: Gaborone-Ghanzi-Mamuno (Map 5, page 211)

Total distances:	Times:
Gaborone-Ghanzi ± 676 km	7-8 hours
Gaborone-Mamuno ± 796 km	8-10 hours
All tar	

The road to Ghanzi from eastern Botswana is being tarred. Tar has reached Kang and a start has been made on the next section, which does not go directly to Ghanzi. Instead, there is to be a junction approximately 221 km north-west of Kang. Turning north will lead 45,4 km to Ghanzi. Continuing west will join up with the original road at Tsootsha (or Kalkfontein: it is uncertain which name will be used in future) and will continue on through Karakubis and Forest Hill to the border post at Mamuno. Both sections are expected to be complete by the end of 1997 or early 1998. The tarmac from Windhoek to Mamuno is complete. (Note: there are rock engravings at three sites at or near Mamuno. See *Botswana Notes and Records* (Vol. 7, 1975, p. 19) for details.)

Starting from Gaborone, follow the tar through Thamaga and Moshupa to Jwaneng, the site of one of Botswana's diamond mines, and pass directly over the first traffic circle you come to, which is 86 km to Sekoma. Have a look at Sekoma Pan, just after you have passed the town, noticing the three-peaked dune on the south-west side. Continue straight after Sekoma, and you will arrive at Kang after passing through Mabutsane and Morwamosu. Both villages have small general dealers and bottlestores. Water and telephones are also available there. From Sekoma to Kang is 161 km. Kang is one of the largest villages on the route. There are several stores here, including a butchery and a bottlestore. Fuel is also available, but be warned that the prices are the highest in Botswana. You will be able to get fuel after normal shopping hours in certain circumstances. Just before Kang village, on the south side of the road, are tracks leading to a large and striking pan, which is well worth seeing. The road forks at Kang, the left branch turning south-west to Tshane and Tsabong. Continue straight on.

There are many boreholes along this route, although set back from the road. They are part of the chain that was established for watering cattle being trekked from Ghanzi to the abattoir at Lobatse. None is signposted.

Takatshwaane, about 115 km north-west of Kang, is a village accommodating many San people who have settled in the area. A further 25 km or so beyond Takatshwaane brings you to the crossing of the Okwa River. Flowing only in years of exceptional flood, and then only for short periods, the river is nevertheless of interest. It was once a major tributary of a great lake that covered as much as 110 000 km² of northern Botswana. A glance at the high banks and great width of the river valley is enough to confirm the former size of this now insignificant river.

From Takatshwaane to the new Ghanzi turnoff will be about 58 km. It is then an additional 34 km to Ghanzi. Ghanzi offers a full range of facilities. There is a small hotel, which makes arrangements for campers, and shops supply most general goods. There is also a hospital and telephone contact with the rest of the country.

ROUTE 5: Jwaneng-Sekoma-Khakhea-Werda (Map 4, page 210)

Total distance: 239 km. Time: 2,5 hours, tar.

(For directions to Sekoma see Route 4: Gaborone-Ghanzi.)

A four-wheel-drive vehicle is not necessary as the route is all tarmac. At the time of writing, Jwaneng was the last fuelling station until Werda.

At Sekoma there is a tarmac turnoff to the south. For this surprising and welcome sight we must thank the people of Norway, who paid for 160 km of new road. The completed tar now runs from Sekoma through Khakhea to Werda and then turns south-westward, along the border to the village of Makopong and, beyond it, the administrative centre of Tsabong.

Khakhea, which is notable for the very large pan to its immediate west, has an interesting history. In the 19th century, so the tale goes, two Europeans were discovered wandering around the Kalahari by a group of San. They were exhausted, lost, waterless, close to death. Their rescuers took advantage of a San 'sip well' at this pan and used it until the two travellers had made a full recovery. Later the Europeans returned, dug a well and opened a store at this place.

From Khakhea it is 103 km to Werda, where you may purchase both petrol and diesel. There is a general dealer who stocks most items you are likely to need. It is possible to leave Botswana at this point. To do this, report to the Botswana Police, who serve as immigration authorities. There is no corresponding facility on the South African side and so you are required to travel to Bray, 58 km away, and report to the South African Police Services there. Border facilities are available from 8 am to 4 pm only.

ROUTE 6: Werda-Bokspits (Map 6, page 212)

Total distances:
Werda-Tsabong: 145 km, tar
Tsabong-Bokspits (in Botswana): 245 km,   poor gravel, 3-4 hours
Tsabong-Bokspits (in RSA): 325 km,   good gravel, ± 4 hours

A four-wheel-drive vehicle is not required on this section.

To reach Werda, either enter Botswana from Bray, in the Republic of South Africa, or see Route 4, Gaborone-Ghanzi, and Route 5, Jwaneng-Werda (Map 4).

The distance from Werda to Tsabong is 145 km, all of which is tarmac. Tsabong, which is the administrative centre for Kgalakgadi District, has most basic facilities for the visitor, including fuel.

There are two ways to get to Bokspits from Tsabong. One is within Botswana and the other in South Africa. The former is not recommended.

It is 110 km to Khuis and a further 135 km from there to Bokspits. The road is used daily but its state varies enormously from quite good to very poor. Severe corrugations are likely to be a problem. Progress will be slow and uncomfortable and there is no fuel along this route.

To leave Botswana at this point, it is necessary to report to the immigration authorities (near the police station) at Tsabong before departing. Take the tar south for 26 km to McCarthy's Rust, the South African border post, which is open from 8 am to 4 pm. From McCarthy's Rust to Vanzylsrus is 132 km on excellent gravel roads. There are three different routes to Vanzylsrus but the shortest is to turn off at Elandsvlei and go through Prairie Glen farm. Watch for this turnoff, which is *not* signposted as a route to Vanzylsrus (see Map 6).

Vanzylsrus offers all the usual facilities. From there to Bokspits is a further 168 km on similar, good quality roads.

The country in this region is fascinating. It is still Kalahari but is much more arid. The dunes are more pronounced and the red sand more obvious. In the changing light of day the landscape offers superb photographic opportunities. A feature is the numerous and massive *Acacia erioloba*.

At a point 11 km west of Vanzylsrus, it is worth deviating at a signposted turnoff to the north which takes you to the South African border post of Middelpits 26 km away, and beyond it, in Botswana, to a group of villages on the banks of the Molopo River.

The Molopo, now dry except for occasional and short-lived floods, was a great river in times gone by, as is evidenced by the massive valley and the eroded calcrete walls. Worthy of a visit are the high cliffs just below the village of Khuis (within sight but a little downstream) and the impressive gorge, carved through solid rock, at Kolonkwaneng (a little upstream). Both villages are within 10 km of Middelpits.

Whilst travelling from Vanzylsrus to Bokspits you will follow the Kuruman River, which takes its name from the amazing spring at the town of Kuruman (Kudumane in Setswana). In this area, however, the river seldom flows.

Entry into Bokspits is well signposted. Shortly before the border is a motel at Andriesvale, close to which you will see the turning for South African customs, open only from 8 am until 4 pm. Visitors entering Botswana are required to report their arrival to the police at Bokspits. Fuel and basic supplies for the independent traveller can be purchased in Bokspits.

ROUTE 7: Kang-Tsabong (Map 4, page 210)

Total distance: 355 km. Time: 10-11 hours.

(For directions to Kang from Gaborone see Route 4: Gaborone-Ghanzi, Map 5.)

A four-wheel-drive vehicle is necessary for this journey. The first section consists of 111 km from Kang to Hukuntsi on tar. Fuel is obtainable at Kang and also at Hukuntsi, 11 km from Tshane, also tarred.

Tshane is one of four villages which cluster together in the heart of the Kalahari. (For more detail see Chapter 2: Places to visit – Tshane / Hukuntsi cluster of villages.) It is 240 km from Tshane to Tsabong. (Whether the road to Tsabong can be reached directly from Hukuntsi, now that the tar goes directly there, or whether one still picks it up at Tshane, I do not know. Ask in the vicinity.) Wherever the start, the sand road is very badly corrugated and traffic volume is light. You will be obliged to drive slowly and the journey is uncomfortable, taking up to 8 hours. There are no towns, villages or facilities along the way, although water may be available from the ranger stationed at Mabuasehube in the Gemsbok National Park. His camp will be found high up on the north-eastern side of the only pan you actually drive across, near the 130 km point.

Beyond this pan there are a further 110 km of bad road, which can take up to four hours, before Tsabong is reached.

ROUTE 8: Hukuntsi-Western Woodlands (Masetlheng Pan)
(Map 5, page 211)

Total distance: 100 km. Time: 4-6 hours.

(For directions to Tshane and Hukuntsi, see routes 4 and 7.) A four-wheel-drive vehicle is necessary for this journey.

In Hukuntsi, ask the way to Masetlheng Pan — it will be extremely difficult to find otherwise. The village is a maze of unmarked tracks, and it is essential to get good directions or find a guide. Start asking at the store near Hukuntsi Pan.

Once found, the road is followed out of the village to the west, later swinging north-west. The track will be sandy and difficult. Petro-Canada dragged their massive drilling rigs along this cut-line in 1989/90 when, in search of oil, they drilled a 4,1 km borehole at Masetlheng Pan. You will find this noteworthy point just beyond Masetlheng Pan where a cut-line heads due south from the main track. The borehole is on the west side of the cut-line a kilometre or two to the south at *GPS 23 41 59S* and *20 51 08E (u/k)*.

From Hukuntsi, a pan called Kwakai will be the first feature encountered. This is just before the large Zonye Pan, which is 28-30 km from Hukuntsi. The road is deep, soft sand and the going is extremely slow.

After Zonye Pan, 7 km further on and some 33 to 35 km out of Hukuntsi, is Bohelabatho Pan. A further 3 km beyond that, Bohelabathwana Pan will be encountered.

The scenery then returns to that of the essential Kalahari until 73 km from the start. Here one should cross Ngwaatle Pan. On the far side of this feature and only a kilometre or two from it will be found a San village.

There still remain 28 km to Masetlheng Pan. When the pan is reached, proceed a further 10 km along the track and take your pick of the wonderful campsites that abound in the woodlands to the north-west of the pan.

ROUTE 9: Serowe-Orapa-Mopipi (Map 7, page 213)

Total distances:	Time:
Serowe-Orapa 212 km	2 hours, tar
Serowe-Mopipi 282 km	3 hours, tar

The turnoff at Serowe is a few kilometres before the town centre but is well signposted. There is no petrol along the route, except at Letlhakane, at its northern end. On the journey north, there are several features worth noticing.

Between Serowe and Paje you will see an escarpment to the west. This is the eastern edge of the Kalahari. The flat-topped hills about you are sandstone outliers that have been left behind by the westward-moving effects of erosion. Stretching to the east is the immense Motloutse Valley leading down to the great Limpopo River.

After the sharp left-hand bend at Paje the road begins to climb the escarpment and basalt boulders appear on both sides. This basalt is exactly the same system as that which creates the Drakensberg, underlies the Kalahari sands, outcrops along the Hunter's Road and forms the Victoria Falls. On the edges of the road, as you reach the crest, the familiar red sand of the Kalahari is first seen.

After Paje, once over the crest and on to the Kalahari, you will see on the west side of the road the new Khama Rhino Sanctuary. This sanctuary contains the remainder of Botswana's rhinos, in addition to some recently acquired from South Africa. This project is developing at an amazing rate. It is worth a visit. See 'Small reserves' on page 138 for more details.

The next village is Mmashoro, where you will see a flat-topped hill on either side of the road. You might be surprised to learn that on each summit there are extensive and important Early Iron Age sites that have yielded gold fragments and clear evidence of trading across Africa and down to the coast. Evidently, the Kalahari has not always been seen as inhospitable.

Between Mmashoro and Letlhakane, you will be stopped at the Makoba veterinary fence. (From this point, if you intended to travel up the east side of Sowa Pan, you would proceed north, along the east side of the fence on a good track to Tlalamabele on the Francistown-Orapa road. It is 64 km and takes approximately 1,5 hours, and is usually possible without a four-wheel-drive vehicle.)

As you approach Letlhakane, you will see the massive dump of the mine away to the north. This is DK1, the mine itself, not the village, which you encounter from about 189 km onwards. The mine is said to be the richest gem-quality mine in the world.

The handiest petrol is at 191,5 km among some shops on the left-hand side of the road. At this point there is also a T-junction to the right which eventually leads on 12 km of gravel road to the main Francistown-Orapa road at a point exactly opposite the track to Kubu Island, one of the access routes for Sowa Pan. However, it is actually nicer to drive into Letlhakane and find the Shell service station. There, an able and enterprising Motswana businessman has opened a small restaurant he calls 'Granny's Kitchen'. In addition, he lets out accommodation. The result is a perfect refreshment, meal or rest-over spot, entirely unexpected in so remote a place and always most satisfactory.

For Orapa, do not turn right but continue straight on. The road leads you to the east gate of the mine at 215 km. The diamond-mining town of Orapa is contained within a large security fence. It is private property and permission is needed to enter. Whilst the town has all facilities, they are not automatically available to the general public. A permit may be applied for, in advance, from the head office of Debswana in Gaborone (P O Box 329, Gaborone, Tel 35 1131, Fax 35 2941). Alternatively, you could try to persuade the security personnel at the guarded gates to let you in, but you will not necessarily be successful. Emergencies will, of course, be treated sympathetically. The main road bypasses Orapa to the south (21 km) and leads on from there to Mopipi Reservoir and the Boteti River.

ROUTE 10: Mopipi-Maun (Maps 8 and 9, pages 214 and 215)

Total distance: 355,3 km	Time: 5 hours
Mopipi to Rakops: 69,3 km (tar)	50 minutes
Mopipi to Motopi: 199 km (gravel)	2,5-3 hours
Motopi to Maun: 87 km (tar)	1 hour

Map 7 gets you to Orapa Mine and Mopipi. Distances on Map 8 are counted from the petrol station on the north side of the road in Mopipi. As far as Rakops, the road is tar. Look out for the abrupt and unsignposted right-hand bend just under 3 km west of Mopipi. A dirt track leads on but the tarmac swings right to cross a bridge. It's easy to miss this turning, particularly in the dark. About 19,5 km from the filling station on the north side of the road is a well-used track, marked with a rusty and bent metal sign that sits low on the ground (and is therefore easy to miss!). This is a turnoff that will take you through cattle country and over seemingly endless stretches of fine dust and bone-shaking calcrete until, after about 33 km, one crosses into the most southerly reaches of Makgadikgadi National Park. The rest of the journey to Rakops is straight-forward.

It is perhaps as well to realise, as one drives through this country, that the Boteti River extends for the whole way on your right-hand side (north or east). It is not always easy to recognise it as a river but early in this century and certainly in the last, the river regularly flowed here and the southern end, between Xhumo and Mopipi, was a wetland teeming with birds and aquatic creatures. It's hard to believe that now!

It is more than ten years since the Boteti has reached Mopipi which, I am told, it has done only three times since 1963. In fact, the large, dry pan you see to the south of the village was modified and an arrangement made so that water from the Boteti could be pumped into it, turning it into a huge reservoir. From there it was pumped 50 km to Orapa Mine. The last time I saw water in Mopipi was in 1983.

The Boteti is an overflow from the Okavango Delta and draws its water from the Thamalakane, which flows past Maun. A low earthen embankment (bund) at the Boteti/Nchabe/Thamalakane junction was designed to divide the flow. The Okavango's flood does not reach Maun until July or August and it takes many more months for the water to make its way down the Boteti. Mopipi is the most southerly bridge across the Boteti north of Xhumo, so, if the river has water, getting to the other side is not easy between those points. When the river is dry, however, as it is now, it offers wonderful chances for exploration. There are beautiful acacia woodlands along its banks, calcrete cliffs, birds in remarkable profusion and innumerable attractive rural scenes for the photographer. Nearer villages there will be a maze of tracks leading everywhere, but further away you make your own. Be cautioned, though; the sand can make for slow, heavy driving.

David Livingstone passed this way on both of his visits to Lake Ngami with William Cotton Oswell. They found the sand so heavy and the trees so thick that they abandoned most of their wagons and went on only lightly equipped.

At the time of writing, the tar ended abruptly in the centre of Rakops. There is talk that the road onward to Motopi is to be upgraded but it is not known when it will be completed. The new road is likely to follow the same alignment.

Three kilometres north of Rakops on the west side is the signposted turnoff leading 45 km to the CKGR boundary and, beyond that, 8,8 km to Matswere Camp and permit office.

If you were to take this track, and drive 13 dusty and uncomfortable kilometres west you would arrive at the top of an ancient sand ridge. This, the Gidikwe Ridge, is either a shoreline or an offshore barrier beach of the old palaeo-lake and marks its western margin at one time. Ascend to its summit and look back. If you do this in the afternoon, so that the sun is behind you, the view will be stunning. Even from this relatively low elevation the whole of the old lake bed lies before you. The course of the Boteti is traced out with a dark green ribbon of riverine trees while, in the distance, the waters of the old lake still seem to shimmer and dance in the heat. It is incredible to think how changeable landforms really are and how insignificant a human lifespan is against the immensity of geological time.

The road north presents few difficulties, since it is usually very well maintained gravel (but it can change dramatically, so don't rely on this!). Access to Tsoe is presently unsignposted so you need to ask once you get into the area (work on distances and Map 8 to do this). In the dry, you can cross the Boteti there and drive up the east side of the river in the national park to the game scouts' camp at Xhumaga.

At a point 35,8 km north of the microwave tower at Xhumaga one reaches the place where the Boteti cuts its way through the Gidikwe sand ridge. There is interesting scenery to enjoy here. On the side of the road in that vicinity you will find one of Botswana's most enigmatic and unlikely road signs!

When the river is full, there are beautiful lagoons around Motopi. You can usually find your way up or downstream on the north bank sufficiently far for reasonable privacy. The area is little known as a magical camping spot.

At Motopi one can cross the Boteti, join the main tarmac road to Maun and be there within an hour or less. If there is time, however, one can stay on the south side of the river, drive through the Makalamabedi veterinary fence and either cross the Boteti 10 km further west or go on to Samadupe bridge (Map 9). The further upstream one travels, especially in these drier times, the more likely one is to encounter water in the river — and with it, all the attendant wildlife, including hippo and crocodiles. So beware! In addition, the river flows over long stretches of calcrete, especially in the Samadupe region, and among the rocks you will find hundreds of Early and Middle Stone Age tools. Please remember that these are the property of the state and all of the many sites in this area are protected by law. That should not, however, stop you from seeking out admiring these artifacts. The Middle Stone age ones date back at least 20 000 years and the Early Stone Age ones could be 300 000 years old.

The Makalamabedi vet fence is accessible either from this route or from the Nata-Maun road. Following it south is an interesting drive (Map 9). It leads you to 'Kuke Corner' (the infamous Kuke Fence) and then to the boundary of the CKGR. Game scouts at Matswere camp use the boundary cut-line and the Makalamabedi fence to get to Maun for their monthly shopping.

Route 10A: Mopipi-Lake Xau

Total distance: ± 20-30 km. Time: 1 hour.

Find a track off the road back to Orapa that circles Mopipi Reservoir on its east and south side. (The reservoir is that vast, circular grey, dry and dusty area before you — usually quite empty of any trace of water!) After some 9 km you will reach a junction where a road departs from the 'circular drive' and heads off to the south-west. Take this road.

In the next 30 km you will pass Lake Xau on your right. When it had water wildebeest used to herd here in their tens of thousands, though now it stands as empty and as forlorn as its neighbour Mopipi. For interest's sake, you can drive onwards to the Kedia Hills, past a smaller pan on your right.

ROUTE 11: Ntwetwe Pan
Part 11A: Orapa to Gweta (Map 10, page 216)
Total distance: 134 km. Time: 4-5 hours.

(To get to Orapa see Route 9.) A four-wheel-drive vehicle or LDV is recommended.

You may pass through the mine concession area of Orapa only if you have obtained a permit by prior arrangement with Debswana, P O Box 329, Gaborone. Tel 35 1131, Fax 35 2941. Permits are not lightly granted.

On reaching the east gate, the mine area can be bypassed by following the tar around to the south. A journey of 25 km will bring you, 1,8 km after a veterinary fence, to a T-junction to the north. This in turn takes you to the original Mopipi road and the west gate. Distances are recorded from this point. Seek the mine boundary road that heads directly north from the west gate.

Drive directly north and continue in this direction. To begin with, the mine perimeter fence will be on your right. This fence soon turns abruptly to the east and the road turns to the north-west. After 5 km you will have a veterinary fence on your right. Follow it for a total distance of approximately 34 km from the start.

Having travelled through rather unattractive scrub lands, on roads of very indifferent quality, you will notice the increasing occurrence of open grassy areas interspersed with woodland. When the sun is low, these grasslands with the woodlands beyond are quite breathtaking. Try to time your trip to take advantage of this.

After 34 km you will come to the banks of the Boteti River where it cuts through the base of the great tongue of land that juts into Ntwetwe from the south. North of this point are prairie-like grasslands of great beauty. They, and reaches of accompanying woodlands, extend over a further 36,2 km to the north, which will bring you to a veterinary fence and the edge of Ntwetwe Pan at Tchai gate. This section takes about 1,45 hours from the start.

The next 20 km over the pan is very fast going but care and common sense are required if the surface is wet. If you cannot see the tracks of a vehicle in front of you because of water, do not go on unless you are very sure of what you are doing. This track is heavily used by people commuting from Orapa to Gweta and if there are no tracks you are either in the wrong place or the way is impassable.

Approximately 8,7 km north on the pan will bring you to the island of Gabasadi. It is difficult to recognise for the first time, being nothing more than a low sandy prominence on your left-hand side (west). (Actually, it is a stranded barchan dune. If you climb up it you will see at once the typical horseshoe shape of such dunes.) A further 12,6 km beyond Gabasadi brings you to the Gweta mainland. As you are racing across this exhilarating piece of pan towards the shore, look to the north-east and notice what a remarkable landmark Chapman's Baobab is!

Travelling north, 1,8 km from the edge of the pan you will see a turnoff to the east. After 5,4 km east along this track you will reach Chapman's Baobab. Continuing north past this turnoff for 11,1 km will bring you to Green's Baobab. From this tree to the village of Gweta is 28 km.

Green's Baobab can be difficult to find. You will notice, as you drive north, that the (appalling) track is very braided. Take the wrong 'braid' and you'll miss the tree. The tree is not very large, and is no landmark — so the trick is to keep your eyes open for a tall and obvious clump of vegetable ivory palm trees. These grow on the south side of Gutsha Pan and tower above everything else. Green's tree is about 300 m to the north-east of the palms. When you are that close, the baobab you seek will be obvious.

If you are attempting the journey in the reverse direction and are departing from Gweta, seek the assistance of villagers in that village to get onto the correct track — ask for the Orapa road. A mistake can be enormously frustrating and, in the absence of signs, is easy to make.

Part 11B: The Western Islands

A safe route to the western islands is to turn west at the point where the north-south track reaches the Gweta mainland. Careful observation may show you the tracks of previous travellers in this area, but from this point on a map is best relied upon.

A general, but not very helpful, picture of the region can be obtained from the 1:250 000 'Bushman Pits' monochrome map. However, for navigating through the islands and the areas referred to in this text, you should have the 1:50 000 series maps *2024 D2, D4, 2025 C1, C2, C3* and *2025 A4*.

Some of these are full colour and therefore P8,50 each. Others are black-and-white photographic mosaics and cost P3,50 each. They can be obtained from the Department of Surveys and Mapping, Private Bag 0037, Gaborone, Botswana (Tel 35 3251).

These maps are the minimum you need to navigate successfully. Your own experiences and individual requirements must determine whether you want a wider spread. Any competent geographer will be able to help you plot these maps out onto the 1:250 000 so that you can see those areas covered in detail.

Part 11C: Nata-Maun Road to Gabasadi Island

Total distance: ± 75 km. Time: 2-3 hours.

A different and interesting route into this area is from the Nata-Maun road. At a point 51 km from Nata the north-east 'finger' of Ntwetwe crosses that main road and it is easy to get down onto the pan surface. It is not so easy to drive south-west 'down' the finger. The exercise is fun but requires some directional skill, a lot of common sense and some luck too, for you have to work your way round, between or over areas of tussocked grassland.

More than once I have seen heavily laden vehicles sink through the surface — but escape with relative ease. However, if you drive with care you can avoid these calamities.

Large areas of grass make it difficult to find a clear 'open pan' surface, especially in the northern reaches. Eventually, however, patience is rewarded and an excellent route will be found by staying close to the western shore of the 'finger'. This can be followed round to the south and then west to meet up with the north-south Orapa-Gweta track that passes Gabasadi island.

On the journey along the 'finger', you will encounter a track coming out of the open pan and running from south-east to north-west (see Map 11: You can turn north-west along this track to Gweta, south-east to Kubu Island, or continue south-west along the present shoreline). This approach is a scenic and exciting route into the area.

Part 11D: Kubu Island to Gweta (Map 11, page 217)

Total distance: ± 95 km. Time: 3-4 hours.

From the Kubu turnoff on the north-south track from Mmatshumo to Zoroga and Nata, travel north. After 8,4 km you may notice a small borrow pit (formed by the extraction of road-building material) on the right. After 12,4 km from the turnoff you will reach the pan edge where the bush begins again. There is a turning to the west 1,5 km beyond this with two or three huts in evidence; ignore it. A further 2,3 km north brings you to a crossroads which includes another turning to the west. This crossroads is the start of the track to Gweta. Set your odometer to zero here. You are 16,2 km from the Kubu turnoff, roughly due south of you.

To ensure that you have the correct turnoff, verify that there is a single baobab in sight on the west side of the road and that the track passes between it and a group of huts on the right with an acacia tree growing inside a wooden palisade surrounding the huts.

After following the Gweta track first west and north-west for 9,8 km you arrive at a veterinary fence. Just 3,2 km beyond the fence is a rather spread out cattle post where it is easy to get lost. Find the main track, which continues to the north-west. At about 18 km from the starting point is a crossroads, with open grasslands on the northern side. Some 4 or 5 km further, the grasslands open out on both sides of the track. Three large and beautiful *Acacia tortilis* once stood on the southern margin of this great plain. Regrettably, all are now dead.

The grassland that begins here and stretches to the north is almost too beautiful for words — especially in March when the stands are high and full. Passing through, I once climbed onto the canopy of my vehicle and looked down in wonder at successive waves of wind as they bullied and buffeted the grass. I shot off countless pictures, which turned out to be rather uninteresting studies of somewhat blurry grass. Still cameras just don't capture the thrill of such moments!

After 25 km from the start you will be on the edge of Ntwetwe Pan. Before crossing, take a few minutes to look around. In the exposed sides of the sand features all about you, you will find fossil reeds and mollusc shells. Both testify to the fact that this was a swamp not long ago. Moving on, you will be driving on the surface of Ntwetwe Pan but, after 12,5 km of a relatively high-speed drive, the road returns to the mainland again for 12,8 km before reaching the 'finger' of Ntwetwe at approximately 49 km. The crossing itself is 9,7 km away and then there remain 31,4 km into the village of Gweta.

When starting from the Gweta end the track will be extremely difficult to find. You are best advised to ask for directions and use names such as Kubu, Lekhubung, Thabatshukudu, Tshwagong, Thitaba or Mmatshumo (all of which use this route).

ROUTE 12: Sowa Pan

Part 12A: East of Sowa Pan (Maps 12 and 13, pages 218 and 219)

A four-wheel-drive vehicle is not essential for this route.

There is a little-known track, maintained by Botswana's state veterinary department, that runs near the east side of Sowa Pan and gives excellent access to the area.

The southern end of this track begins on the Francistown-Orapa road at the Tlalamabele veterinary fence (approximately 144 km from Francistown). The fence forms a barrier across the main road which is manned 24 hours a day. Approaching from Francistown, the track you seek begins on your right-hand side, immediately after the barrier.

Once on the track, which follows the double fence (on your right) in a northerly direction, the going, although a little rocky in places, is on a firm, smooth surface. As you drop down off the escarpment you will be driving occasionally on the edge of the pan. This can be slippery when wet. After 20 km and about 45 minutes you will reach Tlhapane gate. This point is a crossroads. The turning east takes you about 3 km to Thapama Hill and the Zimbabwe site on its summit, and beyond that to various cattle posts. If you travel west for 35 km you will reach the village of Mosu.

The Mosu track allows access to the whole fascinating escarpment area of southern Sowa Pan and some rather dramatic camping spots. There have been a large number of new and very exciting archaeological discoveries in this region, but you have to do a lot of climbing and walking to find them. (If you are really interested, contact the author for more details.)

Another 28,6 km north from Tlhapane brings you to a second veterinary fence and a pair of gates. On the way to them, you pass through two rather beautiful stretches of mature mopane woodland, which look like ideal places to camp. Just before the gate, to the west, you'll notice a rather large and very striking baobab. Among others, you'll see the name 'Ker' and a date. This tree was evidently on the 'Western Old Lake Route' used by those travelling north to Mpandamatenga, the Zambezi and Barotseland.

The gate you arrive at is Kwadiba. If you turn west immediately after passing through it you will see a well-worn track leading to Kokonje Island. This island has become quite a popular destination but you can avoid the 'crowd' and sidle your way around the pan's edge until you get to a point due north of it. You'll see a low ridge there, and you have to pick your way through the bush to camp on top of it. The site is fantastic, for the sun sets on your right as you look south and the view, from this slightly elevated position, is spectacular.

To complete the journey to Dukwe, return to Kwadiba gate. From this point it is just under 50 km, on a reasonable track, to the tarred Francistown-Nata road. You emerge at the Dukwe veterinary gate, on the west side, approximately 133 km from Francistown. Note that there are two rather steep stream crossings on this section. If rain has fallen they may prove difficult or impossible to cross (see Map 13).

At 9,5 km towards Nata from the Dukwe gate is a signposted turning to the left labelled SUA. This will take you to what is known as the Sowa Spit — a long tongue of land that juts far out into Sowa Pan. It is approximately 40 km to the base of the spit, Sowa town and the site of Botswana's soda ash project. The road is tarred. An additional 18 km of sand track will take you along the spit to its western extremity.

From the base of the spit you used to be able to find a track going north-east, more or less along the shoreline. But apparently there is a veterinary fence there now and one can no longer get through that way.

Returning to the main Nata road, after 27,2 km in the direction of Nata you will encounter yet another veterinary fence and 3 km beyond this is Nata Sanctuary. The prominent baobab tree to the west of the road that used to mark this spot was blown over some years ago. The tree is still growing, however, with a single finger-like branch still pointing defiantly to the sky, barely reaching above the tree-line!

Part 12B: West of Sowa Pan (Maps 14 and 15, pages 220 and 221)

North to south, Nata to Kubu
Total distance: 120-130 km. Time: 4 hours.

This section can be travelled in a pick-up vehicle but a four-wheel-drive is strongly recommended.

The starting point for this section is at Nata. (For directions to Nata see Route 13, Francistown-Maun, and Map 13 at page 219.)

There are three main routes on the west side of Sowa Pan. All three pass through a single gate in the veterinary fence 9,7 km south of Thabatshukudu. One route follows a series of tracks down the dry and dusty mainland between the two pans; another is on the pan surface itself. The last is along the western shore of the pan, and this is the most beautiful and interesting drive. The start of all these routes is to turn off the Nata-Maun road at various points in the first 20 km.

The most exciting and exhilarating approach is to drive south on the pan surface, but this is a highly risky method. If you get stuck you cannot rely on outside help. Do not take this route lightly. To begin it, go west from Nata on the tar and look out to your left towards the old road. At about 10,6 km there is a track to the south that starts from this old road, opposite a distinctive grass-covered mound on the north side. Get to that point, turn and meander south through the grasslands for 9,7 km. Whenever there is a fork in the road, always choose the southerly alternative. There is a particularly difficult junction to find on a sharp bend. Close to the pan's edge you may pass a few borehole liners which have been lying there rusting for over 20 years.

If you've been lucky and found the right tracks you will find yourself on the pan surface at some spoil dumps I call the Pyramids — a name suggested by the shape of the spoil dumped when the trench was dug. The trench is part of the exploration for what is now the Sowa Pan soda ash project which extracts salt and soda ash from the sub-surface saline brine. Do stop. Note how high the water table is and how saline the water. Swim in it and notice your unusual buoyancy. Carefully examine the strange aquatic life that is growing there, with its grotesque and repulsive forms. But treat it with great respect for it is a scientific wonder: stromatolites, an algal growth mat and one of the most ancient forms of life on earth!

The next section is not for the faint-hearted. From the Pyramids, you must now rely on your sense of direction and common sense. The island of Kubu lies 81 km to the south, across the open pan. Stay close to the shore and hope for the best — it is an exhilarating drive! Regretfully, one cannot now go all the way to the island. A new veterinary fence extends into the pan about 60 km to the south and reaches too far east for vehicles to drive round it safely. When you reach this fence turn west along it until you get to the gate. Thereafter follow the route as shown in Map 14.

For the nicest and safest route, continue westward on the track you selected at the 10,6 km mark, ignoring the Pyramids and the open pan choice. This track will lead you to the route down the mainland between the two pans.

If you miss the 10,6 km track there are others at 16 km and near the 18 km mark. I use one at 17,5 km. Turn south and work your way through the large borrow pit at the very edge of the road (left there by the road builders), and pick up the faint track which quickly strengthens. Within 1,6 km pass a small quarry, half a kilometre to the west of which is a well-used track and a T-junction. One branch heads north, back towards the main road, but ends in a small collection of huts before getting there. Turn south-west at the junction. The object, on this section, is to maintain a southerly direction but make a deliberate error to the east whenever forks or junctions give you a choice. You'll certainly recognise Sowa Pan when you see it! Keep it close on your left.

Gradually the track turns south and soon one finds oneself in an elevated position on top of one of the long, low shorelines that marks the west side of Sowa Pan, immediately overlooking the pan. On a clear day you can see across the pan to the soda ash factory, and if the sun is in the west the wash of colour over the pan and the scenery before you are quite superb. This elevated position is important and the views through the acacia trees characteristic of this route. If you do not seem to be on the right track here, work your way further east until the surroundings fit the above description.

A key point, especially for those using this route from the south, is the blue-green painted 'small general dealer' store at Thabatshukudu. It is important to locate this and take the correct route — otherwise you will end up in Zoroga!

Just under 10 km south of the store is a veterinary fence. If you continue south you will reach Mmatshumo and, ultimately, the Francistown-Orapa road (74 km). To reach Kubu, bear left after 2 km. A further 3,2 km will take you to Kebetseng's cattle post from which, turning left again, it is 14,4 km to Kubu (Map 14 or 15).

The third route south is really not very attractive. It threads its way between the two pans and is out of sight of either. Usually one gets on to it in error, by straying too far west. It is useful, however, for people coming from the Maun direction. They turn south through the village of Zoroga on the main road. The track is firm, but in places exceptionally dusty. It will be impassable in the wet. In the dry it is a fine, black dust which once formed the old lake bed on which you are travelling. The road is excessively braided and, in the absence of any landmarks, it is difficult to know quite where you are. Use the sun to help you keep heading south and rest assured that nothing much can go wrong; you'll either hit a pan on the left, a pan on the right or the veterinary fence in front of you! The village of Thabatshukubu is not signposted, nor does it have any facilities (it is little more than a large cattle post) but it is distinctive in being perched on a very low ridge. If you have come down the central route from Zoroga or thereabouts, it will be from this vicinity that you'll have your first clear view of Sowa Pan to the east.

South to north, Letlhakane to Kubu (Maps 14 and 15, pages 220 and 221)
Total distance: 83 km. Time: 1,5 hours.

This section can be travelled in a pick-up vehicle but a four-wheel-drive is strongly recommended. The starting point is at Letlhakane (For directions to Letlhakane see Route 9 and Map 7 at page 213).

From Letlhakane, take the (usually) good gravel road 12 km northeast to the point where it crosses the Francistown-Orapa main tar road. Directly opposite is another gravel road that leads 22,7 km to Mmatshumo, which has a small general dealer and a bottlestore.

Just over 5 km north of this village the road suddenly becomes very stony and drops steeply. This is the highest and oldest of the great lake's shorelines. If you examine the stones underfoot you will see that they are all smooth and rounded — the remains of a former pebble beach! As you descend further towards the pans, especially if you stop and look back, you'll notice a succession of shorelines which mark progressive reductions in lake levels.

The road surface before you reach the pan leaves something to be desired. Lake bed deposits are particularly fine and deep ruts have been worn in the track. Many alternative tracks have been created and it is wise to make use of them for they avoid the worst places. If you are in an ordinary vehicle, it is here that you will have the most trouble. In any vehicle when this section is wet you can expect to have difficulty. At 15,3 km from Mmatshumo you will come to the edge of the pan, an obvious feature which it is not difficult to spot. A new veterinary fence is 6 km further on.

Once through the fence it is 7,4 km to the Kubu turnoff. This point has not, to date, been marked in any formal manner. Stone cairns come and go, as did a discarded tyre that someone once left there. Beer cans also make the odd appearance and the occasional stick remains standing for some time. The most reliable cue is to watch carefully for vehicle tracks heading out through the patches of grass, into the pan beyond. You have 19,5 km to go for one of the most amazing camping places in the world!

Part 12C: South of Sowa Pan

Mmatshumo is 22,7 km from the main Orapa-Francistown road. The junction is directly opposite the point where a gravel road leads 12 km south to join the Orapa-Serowe road at Letlhakane village (see Route 9 and maps 7 and 15). The intersection is a major one and difficult to miss. It is 14,5 km west to Orapa's East Gate and 216 km from Francistown, all of which is tarred.

For an interesting route, travel east from Mmatshumo for 34 km on a passable dirt road to the village of Mosu. From Mosu it is a further 27 km on a similar road to the veterinary fence on the main Francistown-Orapa road at Tlalamabele. About 3 km to the west of Mosu, on top of a low hill overlooking Sowa Pan, is the small but beautiful and well-preserved Khami ruin known locally as Mmakhama's. Ask for directions, as it is well worth visiting. From Mosu one can gain easy access to the southern end of Sowa pan. On rough tracks it is possible to travel either east or west, meeting up with the areas on maps 12 and 15 respectively. This is really isolated country. You are not likely to meet anyone and you'll find yourself at liberty to wander in perfect freedom.

ROUTE 13: Francistown-Maun (Maps 13 and 16, pages 219 and 222)

Total distance: 497 km. Time: 5 hours, tar all the way.

Starting at Francistown, travel north-west along the main tarred road towards Kazungula. There are two veterinary fences to pass through before reaching Nata at 190 km from Francistown. The first of these, the Dukwe fence, will be found at 132,6 km; the second (a new fence) is at 169,3 km. Nothing is required of you at these fences except to provide information on where you have come from and are going to. Your vehicle registration number will be recorded. If you have a dog with you, you must produce a veterinary permit authorising its movement around the country.

The turnoff to Botswana's soda ash project, at Sowa Pan, is signposted to the west 142 km from Francistown.

Just after the second veterinary fence is Nata Sanctuary (see Route 12A). At 11,3 km beyond the fence is Nata Lodge, a haven for long-distance travellers 181 km from Francistown or 9 km out of Nata. Apart from a welcome pool, a bar and excellent meals, the Ashbys also provide good accommodation in chalets and camping facilities.

It is at Nata that one turns left and begins the 307 km journey to Maun. This is the last petrol station before Gweta, 100 km further west. Nata is also a good place to fill up with water.

The new tarmac road to Maun is a delight to drive on (but at night be on the lookout for vehicles parked without lights on the verges and cattle on the road, especially in winter when the road's warmth attracts them). If you are planning to drive south-west along the 'Ntwetwe Finger' to Gabasadi (Map 10), your turnoff onto the pan is 51 km from Nata. During the Second World War two young pilots landed their aircraft at the northern extremity of this pan. They were on a training flight from Bulawayo and had run out of fuel. They apparently surprised some San who might have been illegally hunting giraffe and were murdered. A number of San were arrested and tried but the evidence was too circumstantial and they got off. Later the plane was flown away.

At the 99 km post is a signposted left turn to Gweta where there is water, petrol, a general dealer, a safari camp and a bottlestore. It is also an access point for the Makgadikgadi Pans and grasslands (Map 10).

An interesting point is to be found 199 km from Nata (Map 16). The road cuts through the Gidikwe Sand Ridge and engineers have built a short offramp which takes you to the crest of the ridge and offers a magnificent view. Do drive to the top and have a look. This gives you a sense of the size of the old lake, for everything to the east of you once lay under water. Get on the roof of your vehicle if you can and look north and south. You can see the ridge of sand, an offshore barrier beach, stretching away in either direction.

At 59 km from Maun you will be stopped at the Makalamabedi veterinary fence, where the gate is manned 24 hours a day.

All facilities are available in Maun — good shops, fresh meat and vegetables, fuel, health services, international communications, hotels and camping grounds (see Chapter 8).

ROUTE 14: Makgadikgadi-Nxai Pan National Park from Nata-Maun road (Maps 8, 16 and 17, pages 214, 222 and 223)

Makgadikgadi grasslands: four-wheel-drive essential in places.

There are three entrances to this section of the now combined national park which consists of the former Makgadikgadi Game Reserve and Nxai Pan National Park (see Map 17). Manned entrances are to be found at Xhumaga in the west and at Makolwane in the north, just off the Nata-Maun road. The third entrance is from the south. It is not official but is likely to be manned in years to come. Visitors using this entrance will be required to obtain the appropriate permit at one of the other gates on exiting.

The most commonly used gate is Makolwane. The turnoff to it is 140,7 km from Nata and 165 from Maun. The permit office itself is 8 km south of the main road. At both entrances is a painted map board, and it is recommended that visitors note the details shown on it (in case no printed maps are available). Remember that campsites have to be booked and paid for in advance. (See national park regulations, p. 129.)

To explore the park, begin at Makolwane game scout camp and enter the reserve there. (A turnoff after a few hundred metres goes a short distance to an artificial waterhole—well worth spending a few hours at.)

Travel 14 km south-west. At that point there is a T-junction (un-signposted) to your left. The road straight ahead will take you to Xhumaga, the Boteti River (check if it has water in it) and its riverine forest. Turn left, and after a further 6,2 km (during which you may have noticed Njuca Hills looming above the scrub to the south-east) you will reach a second T-junction. If you turn left here it is but a short distance to Njuca Hills and the astonishing views to be had from there. The dominant tree on this massive ancient dune is *Albizia anthelmintica*, a species rarely occurring in South Africa but common on the watershed in Zimbabwe. Its bark is known as an anthelmintic (cure for worms) from Namibia to Somalia and Ethiopia.

If you wish to return to the main road from Njuca via a different route, drive east from the hills for 11 km. This will bring you to a distinctive group of palm trees, known as Makolwane a ga Wateka, and what appears to be a T-junction with one track continuing to the east (it goes 40-50 km to Gweta but is not a very good track) and another turning north. After 12 km this track will deliver you to the old main road. Turn left (west) and, after 3,2 km, you will be back at Makolwane game scout camp. As a matter of interest, there used to be a cut-line leading south from these palm trees into the north-west corner of the area I call 'the land of a thousand islands' (see Chapter 2: Places to visit – Ntwetwe Pan). It is not that easy to see from the ground, but worth searching for to gain access to this incredible area.

If you do not wish to visit Njuca, turn right at the T-junction mentioned and travel south-west and south for about 16 km. This will bring you to a third turnoff to the left (south). Take this turnoff and drive due south along the cut-line for 43 km. On the way you will pass Nomad Pan and, if it hasn't been moved now, you will see why it is so named. At the end of that distance will be another turn to the left. Take this and soon you will be out of the park and in cattle country. After some 27-33 km (distance depends on which of the many tracks you follow southward) of rather difficult going you will reach the tarmac between Mopipi and Rakops at the point 19,5 km from Mopipi (see Map 8). Turn left for Mopipi.

Approaching this route from Mopipi and the south one needs to be aware of several sharp right-angle bends, which particularly confound the night-time motorist, encountered when travelling west soon after the petrol station at Mopipi has been left behind. At 19,5 km a track to the right (north) will be discerned. It is not signposted. There is a low, rusty sign on the left-hand side of the turning. It has nothing written or marked on it. You need to look carefully to spot it.

ROUTE 15: Nxai Pan from Nata-Maun road and Baines' Baobabs
(Map 17, page 223)

Four-wheel drive essential.

The turnoff to this park is from the main Nata-Maun road approximately 165 km from Nata or 140 km from Maun. The sandy track that leads 37 km to the national park gate is in an execrable state; it always has been bad but it is now worse than ever. It takes an hour and 20 minutes or more to get to the gate, and it is only that fast because the last 12,5 km are on broken calcrete where speeds of up to 50 or 60 km/h are possible. The rest is mostly low-ratio first-gear work. Be warned! There are apparently plans to build a new access road sometime in the future.

Starting north up the track, you will reach a crossroads at 18,9 km (as a matter of interest, this is one of the original Nata-Maun roads once known as 'the Wenela Road': there have been up to four roads with this name). Going north, the track continues for another, slightly less agonising, 18,4 km to Nxai Pan gate. Remember, you need to book and pay in advance for a campsite in this national park. The staff there will direct you to your campsite. Examine and sketch the map of the park on the wall in the entrance hut.

There is a better way to the park gate that is much quicker for those approaching from the east. This route is longer for those coming from the west but is kinder on the vehicle and takes about the same time. For details of this route see the access to Baines' Baobabs, below.

Access to Baines' Baobabs (See Map 17.)

The area round Baines' Baobabs has become increasingly popular, and while you can camp near the trees it is no longer possible to camp right beside them. The crossroads described above, 18,9 km north along the Nxai Pan track, is the official access route for Baines' Baobabs. As shown in Map 17, turn east here and drive for 0,9 km to a fork in the road. You can go either left or right at this fork but the latter is recommended.

The road leads 11 km directly to the baobabs on a fair surface. The alternative route is longer (17 km, with a right turn after 13,3 km that is hard to find) and less comfortable, but vital for the wet season when the shorter route may be flooded or too wet for safe travel.

The first 18,9 km of this route are notoriously bad. There is a much better route that is also much shorter for those approaching from the east and south (refer to Map 17). Turn north for 19 km along the western boundary of Odiakwe Ranch (132,3 km from Nata). Turn left (west) onto the old Nata-Maun road for 16,3 km. At that point you will see a well-used track turning to the south and Baines' Baobabs 3,7 km away. This route saves easterners a total of 24 km and about an hour in time. Those approaching from the west who use this route will have to travel an extra 40 km, of which 32 km are on tar. However, I suspect they may agree that the longer approach is the better choice. As mentioned above, this is also a way of getting to Nxai Pan itself that will avoid the worst of the present access road.

ROUTE 16: Maun-Ghanzi (Map 18, page 224)

Total distance: 280 km. Time: 4-5 hours.

Much of this section is dirt road of variable standard, but a four-wheel-drive vehicle is not required. There is talk of the road being tarred but this is not likely to happen until 1998 or 1999. From Maun, set off in a southerly direction along the main street. The 65 km of road to Toteng, a continuation of that street, is tarred.

Near the village of Toteng there is a clearly signposted left turn to Ghanzi. From here the road alternates between sand and hard calcrete, which can be very corrugated and deeply potholed. Generally, the surface is adequate and an average speed of 60-80 km/h is possible. There is a veterinary fence at Kuke, 98 km from Toteng. It is manned 24 hours a day but the attendant will ask only for basic information. A permit is required if you have a dog with you.

Once through the Kuke gate you enter the Ghanzi farming area. After 79 km you will come to the small farming village of D'Kar, the home of Kuru Development Trust (see Chapter 2: Places to visit – Ghanzi) and a good place to stop off. There is a well-stocked store and plans are currently being made to sell fuel here too.

Ghanzi is 35 km beyond D'Kar.

ROUTE 17: Ghanzi-Mamuno (Map 5, page 211)

Total distance: 210 km. Time: 2 hours, tar (under construction 1996).

Construction of this section should be complete by the end of 1996 or early 1997. Distances given here are for the new road.

If you are planning to travel between Ghanzi and Windhoek, remember that Namibia's tarmac is expected to reach the Botswana border in 1996 and will be in place before the Ghanzi-Mamuno section. The completion of a trans-Kalahari highway takes hundreds of kilometres off the road journey from Gauteng to Windhoek and it is expected to become a major long-distance truck route.

ROUTE 18: Maun-Lake Ngami (Map 18, page 224)

Total distance: about 230 km. Time: 4-5 hours.

If you are going to explore widely here and do a lot of off-road travel, the heavy sand makes it essential to have four-wheel-drive. Remember that the lake is presently dry and has been so for many years.

There are two approaches to the lake, one from the east and the other from the west. Both involve travelling from Maun to Toteng, a distance of 66,9 km, now tarred. At this village there is a road to the left which crosses the Lake River and turns south-west towards Ghanzi (Route 16). Bypass this turning and continue another 30 km to Sehithwa.

The best way to get onto the lake, I am told, is via a track from the Sehithwa end. You'll still see the 'Three-way Trading Store' at the old crossroads in the village. The track starts to the left and behind the store and can be followed in an easterly direction, right across the lake and out the other side over some very sandy dunes. It eventually links up with the gravel Ghanzi road on the east side of the old lake and will take you back to Toteng and Maun. It's an interesting and enjoyable two-hour drive across the lake.

ROUTE 19: Maun-Drotsky's Cave (Maps 18 and 19, pages 224 and 225)

Total distance: 289 km. Time: 7,5-8,5 hours.

The easiest route to these caves is from Maun, via Sehithwa and Tsau. The whole of the western side of the Okavango Delta is tarred to Mohembo and so getting to Tsau, the turning-off point for Drotsky's, is much faster than before (Map 18).

At 1,5 km past the turning (north-east) to the village of Tsau, and the microwave tower, you will see a turnoff to the left (Map 19). It used to be marked with a signpost bearing the zebra logo of Botswana's museum and the legend 'Drotsky's Cave'. Don't rely on seeing it, however, and instead keep a sharp lookout! From the turning, the track is sand for 147 km to the caves. A four-wheel-drive vehicle is essential. Fold your wing-mirrors back at this point!

The first two-thirds of the route passes through wooded, undulating sand country, without any distinct pattern in the low dunes. This area was once flooded and part of the Okavango. Later you will come upon more distinct and larger fossil dunes. They mark the furthest reaches of the once far more extensive delta (Map 19). From here the sand is very heavy and the going slow. The 147 km from Tsau will take you 5 or 6 hours. An important junction not to miss is the turning signposted 'Xhaba Borehole' at 93 km from the start of the track. This is a new shortcut to the caves which saves 35 km and an hour-and-a-half in time. Turn left here. This route will take you past the borehole, an equal distance beyond it to the Gcwihaba River and the caves beside it.

The longer route is more arduous but worth doing, even if one is not going to Caecae. At 152 km, after crossing a particularly sandy dune, look out for a magnificent view over to the west. About 30 km away to the north-west you will see the Aha Hills. On the downhill slope there is a (rather rusted) signpost, with the Botswana Museum's zebra emblem, pointing to the left, and a bush track which follows the river valley 27 km to Drotsky's Cave. Continue straight on for 9,6 km to Caecae.

ROUTE 20: Drotsky's Cave-Aha Hills

Total distance: 47 km. Time: 2 hours.

The Aha Hills can be reached from the main Maun-Shakawe road. The easiest route is to turn off at the Drotsky's Cave turning, just north of the village of Tsau. (For details of the first section, see Route 19: Maun-Drotsky's Cave, maps 18 and 19).

Continue on that track for 155 km to the signpost to Drotsky's Cave, beyond which the village of Caecae is approximately 9,6 km. At this village the road turns north to the hills 10 km away. You can also get into the hills from further west by driving 9,2 km west of Caecae and turning north along the border fence on a perfectly adequate and frequently used track. Regardless of which route you take into the hills, it is possible to return via Qangwa and Dobe in the north. To do this, on either road drive north for approximately 50 km (from the line of Caecae). At that point the border track turns due east for 20 km past Dobe to Qangwa. On the more easterly track, you will come to a T-junction. Turn west to Dobe or east and travel directly to Nokaneng. The 160-odd km to Nokaneng is said to be exceptionally difficult. The road is deep sand for which a four-wheel-drive vehicle is a necessity. This route is not signposted.

ROUTE 21: Maun-Tsodilo (Map 18, page 224)

Total distances: via Sepopa 365 km   Time: 5-6 hours
via Ncamaseri 385 km
Shakawe-Tsodilo 68 km

There are now three tracks to Tsodilo: two from the south and one from the north. All lead from the fully tarred Maun-Shakawe road on the west of the Okavango Delta (see Map 18, and Republic of Botswana: Okavango 1:350 000). A four-wheel-drive vehicle is essential to get to Tsodilo from this road, however.

From Maun to the nearest turnoff at Sepopa is 320 km. Last petrol is at Etsha-6, although there is talk of a station opening at Gomare. The turnoff is signposted with the Botswana Museum's zebra logo and is 0,6 km before Sepopa. It is about 49 km to the hills. The first part of the journey is on a firm bush track. It is advisable to remove, or fold in, wing-mirrors. Just after half way you will encounter dune country. The valley floors are hard and driving is easy, but the route lies diagonally across the trend of dunes and a number of them must be crossed. The sand on the dunes can be very thick and loose. Total time from Sepopa turnoff to the hills can be anything from two to three hours.

A hitherto unpublicised route is to be found 25,5 km north of Sepopa. It is exactly 2,2 km before the Ncamaseri turnoff and some 300 m before a sign on the left-hand side of the road indicating 'Shakawe 32 km'. For a GPS reference of this important junction, see Map 18. If you turn and face the track you will notice a lone tree to its left, the palisade of a village to the right, a rough track behind you and no sign. It is 39 km to the hills from here. This route is slightly longer than the alternative route but the additional distance is on tar. This is now the recommended route but only for light trucks up to 1,5 tons, as it is not wide enough to take anything bigger.

For those approaching from the north the old Shakawe route (turnoff some 8 km south of the village) is no more and has been replaced by an appalling alternative. Although longer, the Ncamaseri track is faster.

If you want to try the Shakawe alternative as you are coming from the north, do not take the track opposite Shakawe Fishing Camp. Instead drive 5,5 km south on the tar until you hit the Samochima fence.

This is a new veterinary fence erected as an emergency measure to stop the spread of lung disease to Botswana's national cattle herd. Infection broke out in the area north of the fence and efforts are being made to contain it at this hastily erected front line. (This disease is almost always fatal to cattle but is not contagious for humans and the meat is perfectly safe to eat.) The Thamacha fence, between Etsha-13 and Sepopa marks the perimeter of a still larger 'containment' area. It is vital to Botswana's economy that this outbreak be controlled so please co-operate with the men at the gates.

Pass through the Samochima fence, turn west and follow it until you pick up the old road again on your left. The route is not recommended however. Not only is it longer (about 54 km of sand) but it is also extremely tough driving. You will have a foretaste of what lies in wait if you look at the sand facing you as you turn off the tar onto the south side of Samochima.

Note that Shakawe village has a clinic, a store and radio contact with Maun. Fuel is sold at the beautiful fishing camp at Shakawe, which caters for casual visitors. Electricity has reached the area from Namibia and telephones are soon to follow. Customs and immigration facilities are now available at Mohembo on the border.

ROUTE 22: Maun-Moremi-Savute (Maps 16 and 23, pages 222 and 229)

Total distances:	Time:
Bypassing Moremi: 183 km	3-5 hours

Direct via Moremi: 229 km   5-8 hours
including grand tour of Moremi: ± 350 km

Maps 16 (Nata-Maun) and 23 (Maun-Moremi-Savute-Kasane) in this book
at pages 222 and 229; Republic of Botswana: Chobe 1:350 000 and Okavango
Delta 1:350 000 Shell Maps of Moremi and Chobe by Veronica Roodt

Some people manage this route in an ordinary vehicle but this is not
recommended. There are no facilities for the general public along this
route, although water is obtainable. There is no fuel. For directions to
Maun see Route 13, Francistown to Maun, and maps 13 and 16,
Francistown to Maun. It is not within the scope of this book to provide
detailed maps of national parks, since these are usually available from
the Botswana Department of Wildlife. For this reason, only a large-scale
map of this section is included here. For more detail I highly recommend the excellent Shell maps of Moremi and Chobe by Veronica Roodt,
which are widely available in Botswana and in South Africa. I am grateful to these maps and Ms Roodt for verifying certain information used
here. There is little I can add to them except the GPS references included
on Map 23.

Remember: no campsites are available in Moremi or Chobe unless booked
and paid for in advance.

All the roads in this section are sand except for a tarred stretch between
Maun and Shorobe. After this point the surface is mostly sand or clay
which can be very slippery when wet. It is extremely difficult to cross
Mababe Depression when its 'black cotton' soil is wet.

The most direct route to Savute is to head north-east out of Maun on
the tar road to Shorobe (28 km — distances are from the last traffic circle
in Maun, near Crocodile Camp). At Shorobe you can buy locally woven
baskets, some of which are of a very high standard. Beyond Shorobe,
and 9 km from it, is a fork to the left. This leads past San-ta-wani to the
south gate of Moremi, but the road is exceptionally sandy and the going
slow, so it is not recommended. Continue beyond Shorobe to where the
tar ends 2 km further on (30 km from Maun) and you will arrive at the
Buffalo fence after an additional 19,4 km, a total of 49,4 km from Maun.
There is a critical junction 1,8 km beyond the fence. Left follows the
main route to Moremi South Gate (34 km) and the Moremi Reserve. For
Savute, however, continue north to Zankuyo village (24 km), 1 km beyond which the road splits. Either choice will get you to Mababe Gate
and Savute, but the right-hand fork is recommended as this will lead to

Mababe village (30 km) and will avoid the difficulties of Magwikhwe Sand Ridge. You will have to turn west out of the village and, after crossing the cut-line of Chobe National Park, will turn north again. From Mababe village to Savute is 77 km. At 10 km north of Mababe Gate in the Chobe National Park the road splits. Both roads go to Savute, but the right-hand fork is about 8 km longer and passes the margin of what used to be Savute Marsh.

It is likely that, during 1996 and perhaps for even longer, the public campsite at Savute will be undergoing reconstruction. It is advisable to check with the Department of Wildlife in Maun (Tel [267] 66 1265 or Fax 66 1264) before making plans to stay there.

If you choose to pass through Moremi you will arrive at the manned south gate with its public campsite. If not already paid at Maun, an entrance fee is expected for vehicles and passengers. The gate opens at dawn and closes at dusk.

From South Gate, there are two routes. The first (and more leisurely) is a drive around the Moremi peninsula to the North Gate. Mboma (± 50 km) is the western extremity. Continuing the circular drive you will come to Third Bridge and Cakanaca before arriving at North Gate (Khwai), having covered a total distance of about 120 km. The shorter and more direct alternative route is to travel from South Gate directly to North Gate (30 km), crossing a wooden bridge over the River Khwai just before the exit.

From North Gate the road turns east for 40 km and joins up with the main road from Maun to Savute. Approximately 34 km from North Gate you will come to the Magwikhwe Sand Ridge. This fascinating feature (which can best be seen in the vicinity of Savute) is a relic barrier beach from the days of Botswana's super-lake. Its summit stands at the highest level ever reached by the lake: 945 m above sea level. However, the immediate problem is to cross it. Four-wheel-drive is definitely needed. The sand is especially deep and soft as one crosses the ridge. Beyond it the road descends to the hard surface of Mababe Depression and no further problems should be encountered. It is approximately 12 km from the eastern foot of the ridge to the park boundary.

The south gate of Chobe National Park (also manned from dawn to dusk) is 58 km from Savute. An entrance fee must be paid, as for Moremi. The only official camping place is at the public campsite on the banks of the Savute Channel.

ROUTE 23 Savute-Kasane (Maps 20 and 23, pages 226 and 229)

Total distances: Time:
via Nogatsha 195 km   6-8 hours
via Kachebabwe 164 km   6-8 hours

Maps Republic of Botswana: Chobe, 1:350 000; Map 20 (Nata-Kazungula) and Map 23 (Maun-Moremi-Savute-Kasane) in this book at pages 226 and 229; Shell Map of Chobe by Veronica Roodt.

It is not within the scope of this book to provide detailed maps of national parks since these are usually available from Botswana's Department of Wildlife. For this reason, only a large-scale map of this section is included here. For more detail I highly recommend the excellent Shell map of Chobe by Veronica Roodt, which is widely available in Botswana and in South Africa. I am grateful to that map and Ms Roodt for verifying certain information used here.

There are two routes from Savute and the Mababe Depression northwards towards Kasane. Most people take the more westerly one which, although shorter, is far more difficult because of long stretches of deep sand. It does not appear to save much time.

A longer but generally easier route from Savute is to go eastward via Ngwezumba Dam. Not only do you see more of the park and, at certain times of the year, very much more game, but the sand road is often good, particularly after rain, and invariably better than the deep loose sand of the western route. However, the roads in this part of the world are extremely variable, so always expect the worst.

To follow this route start at the crossing of the Savute Channel itself and take the main road north, past the signposted turning to Linyanti. Before long, just after crossing an old and faintly discernible river channel, turn right to what is known as Harvey's or Khearoga Pan. (Going north here is the 'direct' route and passes through Kachekabwe and Ngoma Bridge en route to Kasane.) Continue east, passing Quarry Hill, which you can see clearly from the pan, on your left. At the 35 km point from where you turned off to Harvey's Pan, another track joins yours from the right and your direction now begins to swing increasingly northeast. Within 20 km you will start to follow the dry bed of the Ngwezumba River. After 114 km from the start you will reach a signposted junction. If you turn right here you enter the complex of roads around Ngwezumba Dam and have access to campsites at Tchinga and Nogatsha.

To get to Kasane by the most direct route, do not turn right but continue straight on. After 22 km you will come to a second intersection

where a right turn would also give access to Nogatsha and Tchinga
Continue straight for 36 km until you arrive at Nantanga Pans, 1 km
beyond which is the main road from Kasane to Ngoma Bridge. Turn
right for Kasane (22 km) or carry on straight to reach the Chobe River
(10 km).

ROUTE 24: Hunter's Road

Part 24A: Nata to Mpandamatenga (Map 21, page 227)

Part 24B: Mpandamatenga to Kazungula (Map 22, page 228)

These two routes are reported separately below: four-wheel-drive is essential although it may not always be used.

Warning: under no circumstances attempt this road at the height of the
rainy season. If there is standing water on flat ground, the route will be
impassable.

Timing your visit is critical to success. If it's too wet you can't get through
if it's too late in the year the pans will be dry and there will be no game
April/May through to July is probably the best time.

Maps: see maps 20, 21 and 22 at pages 226, 227 and 228. In addition, for
Route 24A refer to Republic of Botswana 1:250 000 series: *Nata Sheet 12*
Basutos Sheet 8, Kasane Sheet 4. Not absolutely necessary but good to have
are the 1:50 000 series: 1926 C1, 1926 A3, 1925 B2, 1825 D4 and 1825 D1
For 24B, refer to Republic of Botswana 1:250 000 *Kasane Sheet* 4.

Part 24A: Nata to Mpandamatenga

Total distance 239,2 km. Minimum time 1 day, recommended time 2-3
days.

Begin at the high-level bridge in Nata and take the tarmac road to
Kazungula. A remarkable grassed pan is crossed at 30 km and at 60,2 km
a veterinary fence is reached. Four kilometres after this a sign indicates
'Ngwasha Veterinary Camp' to the right (names and spellings are always a problem; Ngwasha is the Ngwahla I have been talking about).
Turn right and at about 14,5 km take the right fork which, with a little
common sense and good luck, will lead you to a T-junction which is the
border track at about 23 km from the tar. At this point the border is
fenced. The fence is just over a metre high and includes two steel cable
strands. Its function is a mystery, because it only extends for about a
kilometre to the north.

Turning north, the first part of this route is sand but the last third is 'black cotton' soil. If it's wet your vehicle will sink into this soil like a stone in quicksand. The soil needs five or six days of hot sun to dry out. Average speed on the sandy track (which was damp on both my visits) was about 10 km/h for the first 40 km. At 41 km from Ngwahla a strong track from the south-east joins the border road. I have not investigated this. From here on the track improved greatly and speeds of 20-25 km/h were possible all the way to Mpandamatenga. Four-wheel-drive was engaged only twice and then only for a few minutes. The vegetation is incredibly varied but watch out particularly for the *Baikiaea* woodlands, notably those at 5 km and 12 km from Ngwahla.

There are beautiful pans all the way. Tamafupa is reached after 27 km. At just over 34 km from the start is the group known collectively as Domtshetshu Pan. A little more than 200 m north of the 41 km junction with the road from the south-west, on the east side, is a feature rather unromantically called 'Cement Pan'. I do not know how it won this unfitting name for, when it has water in it, it is indeed a beautiful sight. Next follow: Kidney Pan, Stoffel's Pan (200 m inside Zimbabwe; not visited), Leadwood Pan (5 leadwood trees, 4 to north, 1 east), Hendrick's Vlei (3 leadwoods to north, 1 to south), Tibukai Pan (small, circular mudhole), Jolley's Pan (pair of tall mopane to south-west).

North of Jolley's Pan the sandveld country is left behind. Dune crests are replaced by a rocky substrate (decomposing basalt) that offers firm, fast and easy driving. The valleys that now start to appear are filled with 'black cotton' soil — lethal when wet! As you rise north out of Jolley's Pan a large tree on the left is a nice spot to have lunch and regroup before tackling the first vlei. After this comes Cream of Tartar Pan (6 mopane trees west side). At a point 6 km north of Cream of Tartar Pan is an important junction to note. If you turn south-west here you can reach the main tar road at a point 161 km from Nata (and 137 km from Kazungula) after a drive of 23,2 km. (From the main road, the microwave tower is a good indicator of the turnoff.)

From this junction on the Hunter's Road onwards the route is alternating hard basalt and soft black soil for the remaining 40-odd km to Mpandamatenga. Watch out for Border Beacon BB620 and the magnificent view from its ridge crest as you reach the watershed of the Deka River. Dawdle along the rest of this route for it is most beautiful scenery. Look out for the magnificent stand of acacia before reaching Mpandamatenga. Notice the track to the west just before you get to the border post, and turn there onto the road.

Part 24B, Mpandamatenga to Kazungula

Total distance 102 km. Minimum time 2,5 hrs, recommended time 1 day

This is a much easier and much more forgiving trip. It is shorter and the roads are better although, in the wet, you can only cross Kazuma Pan by using a kilometre or two of the Zimbabwe side (the two tracks are only 20 m or so apart).

Ask the customs officials at Mpandamatenga to show you how to get on to the border road, although you ought to be able to see where it curves off to the left a metre or two before the boom on the Botswana side. You don't need to clear customs or immigration.

After 25,8 km you will reach the edge of Kazuma Pan. There is a waterhole on the Botswana side where there is usually game. Notice the pan which stretches 15 km before you. The rest of the journey is straight forward. Map 22 should help you get through without difficulty. North of Kazuma the track is excellent hard sand. Notice the Leshoma River coming in the east about 88 km from Mpandamatenga and enjoy the open acacia woodland which its wide valley gives rise to. These last 15 km are a wonderful game drive.

The track north divides just before the respective Botswana and Zimbabwe border posts. Turn to the left (west) to join the tarmac road that leads 2,6 km to the Kazungula junction.

Distance table in km

The distance of the most direct route is shown on the chart. Measurements have been taken from the best available sources and all are subject to 5 % error.

The chart is a triangular road‑distance matrix (distances in km). Columns (origin) and rows (destination) are the same list of towns; many cells carry an alternative "via" routing. Best reading of the chart:

Destination \ Origin	Boxspits	Francistown	Gaborone	Ghanzi	Jwaneng	Kang	Kanye	Kasane	Kazungula	Lobatse	Mahalapye	Maun	Nata	Orapa	Palapye	Ramatlabama (South)	Ramokgwebane (North)	Selebi-Phikwe	Serowe	Seruli	Tsabong
Francistown	1229 (via Werda 792)																				
Gaborone	600 (via Sekoma 629)	437 (via Maun 777)																			
Ghanzi	847 (via Sekoma 704)	676 (via Kang)	513																		
Jwaneng	528	589	163	266																	
Kang	705	689	410	247	126																
Kanye	490	512	88	323	76	323															
Kasane	1419	490	1002	1351 (via Fwn)	1104 (via Fwn)	1037	1032 (via Fwn)														
Kazungula	1433	504	1016	1337 (via Fwn)	1090 (via Fwn)		1018 (via Fwn)	14													
Lobatse	512		72		126	373	50	1002	1016												
Mahalapye	992 (via Ghanzi/Sekoma 1250)	300	200	876	363	610	291	727 (via Nata 607)	741 (via Nata 621)	275											
Maun	1318	495	934	280	793 (via Ghanzi)	546 (via Ghanzi)		741		727 (via Fwn 1009)	734 (via Fwn 737)										
Nata	1064 (via Lobatse 793)	190	627	587	689		617	314 (via Fwn 744)	300 (via Fwn 730)	702 (via Fwn)	427	307 (via Fwn 737)									
Orapa	1311	240	526	1017	435	682	363	669	655	655	477	737	256 (via Fwn 430)								
Palapye		165	272	948	435		363	586		347	72	657	355	256							
Ramatlabama (South)		560	123	677	164	411	88	572		48	323	579	750	649	395						
Ramokgwebane (North)		82	519	859	682	929	610	657	594	594	319	645	272	322	247	642					
Selebi-Phikwe	1108	153	404	930	567	814	495	713	479	479	204	701	343	388	132	527	235				
Serowe	1136	209	316	981	479	726	407	597	419	419	116	585	399	212	44	439	291	176			
Seruli		93	344	870	507	754	435	583	391	391	144	585 (via Ghanzi 900)	283	328	72	467	175	60	116		
Tsabong	93 (in Bots 246)	984	547	618	507 (via Sekoma 384)	352 (via Tshane)	460	1488	1474	505	746	900 (via Ghanzi)	1174	1073	818	558 (tar)	1066	951	863	891	
Werda	390	839	402	580	239	314	315	1343	1329	360	601	860 (via Sekoma)	1029	928	673	403 (tar)	921	806	718	746	145

4. FACTORS AFFECTING YOUR CHOICE

SEASONS AND CLIMATE

Botswana is a huge country, roughly the size of France, and extends through nine degrees of latitude. This fact alone suggests considerable variation in climate. It is also landlocked and very nearly in the centre of the southern African subcontinent, on an elevated plateau approximately 1 000 m high. These factors contribute towards the low annual rainfall.

The seasons in Botswana are indistinct. Rains generally start in October or November and persist until March and April. Within that period, however, there may be long dry spells. With the cessation of rain in April, temperatures begin to fall and May is generally regarded as the first month of the dry, cool winter, characterised by clear sunny days and cold nights. Frosts are over by August and temperatures rise rapidly during the hot, dry period of September, October and November until the rains break again.

Although the rainy season is generally from October to April, there is great variation in the time of its arrival and departure, in the amount of rain that falls and in its distribution. The rainfall decreases from the north-east of the country to the south-west, and as it does so its variability increases. Thus the wet north-east might expect 600 mm of rain with a variability of about 30 per cent, whilst the drier south-west will receive, on average, only 200 mm, with a variability of about 80 per cent!

Generally the rain tends to fall in short, sometimes violent thunder-showers. Although rain may first fall in September, it is generally true to say that most of it falls in the months of December, January and February.

Temperatures can be quite extreme in Botswana, with the greatest range occurring in the south. The following table shows the mean maximum and minimum temperatures, in degrees Celsius, in four months of the year at five locations in Botswana.

	April	July	Nov	Jan
Kasane	30/15	25/8	33/19	30/19
Maun	30/15	26/6	34/20	30/19
Francistown	28/14	24/5	32/18	31/18
Gaborone	28/12	22/2	32/16	32/18
Tsabong	28/11	22/1	33/16	35/19

It is important to realise that these figures are only averages and that actual maximums and minimums can be very different. For example, there have been several reports of snow in the Kalahari and it is not uncommon for small amounts of water to freeze solid overnight in winter. On the other hand, maximum temperatures, especially in the hot months of October and November, can sometimes reach 40 °C or more.

BEST TIMES TO VISIT THE PARKS AND RESERVES

Botswana's national parks and game reserves have their own particular attractions at any time of the year. However, if your specific objective is to see game and to witness the great migratory herds, the following guide indicates the best times to visit.

Chobe National Park

The river front at Kasane and Linyanti. Good all year round but best from May to October.

Inland and the Savute area. From November to May, although if the Savute Channel is flooded or water remains throughout the year in the Mababe Depression, May to October also offers excellent viewing.

Moremi Game Reserve

Viewing here can be good all year round but the dry season months from May to November are usually best.

Okavango Delta

The Okavango is a vast wetland which varies in size throughout the year, as it is controlled largely by the rains that fall in Angola and flow into it via the Okavango River. The floods arrive at Mohembo, at the north-western end of the delta, as early as December, building up to a peak between January and March, but occasionally as late as May. These floods slowly work their way through the vastness of the delta in the succeeding months so that the highest levels in Maun, at the opposite end of the delta, are not recorded until July or August, or even in September. The delta is at its largest during June and July and at its minimum extent in December and January. Although fishing can be good throughout the year, the best months seem to be from August to February, whilst the best game-viewing months are from July to October.

Nxai Pan National Park

Successful game-viewing in this national park depends very much on whether or not rain has fallen. If the rains have been good, December to early April are excellent months. If they have failed, a visit to the park can be very disappointing from the point of view of seeing game.

Makgadikgadi Game Reserve

From the first rain, usually November, onwards until April, May and sometimes early June, the grasslands are occupied by herds of migrating antelope and their attendant predators.

Central Kalahari Game Reserve

The drought has severely reduced many of Botswana's game species and it would be unwise to expect too much of this reserve. As with Kutse, several good years of rain must elapse before we can hope for the return of game in substantial numbers. However, six watering points have been established in the northern half of the CKGR from Deception to Piper's Pan, and game of some kind will always be encountered. In the wet season animals will be more dispersed.

Kutse Game Reserve

It is unusual to see significant numbers of game in this reserve, particularly in recent years owing to the prolonged drought. Several good years of rain will be required before the game is likely to return in large numbers. Kutse is renowned for its excellent birdlife. Game is likely to be found near the pans at any time of year but October to April is usually best.

Mannyelanong Game Reserve

At this nesting colony of Cape vultures the birds are best seen in the winter months, from May to August or September.

Mabuasehube Game Reserve

The largest concentrations of game will be seen in the vicinity of these pans during the rainy season from October through to April.

Kalahari Gemsbok National Park

The park is divided by two major rivers, the Auob and the Nossob. Game-viewing is always good, one reason for the park being open all year round. However, it is particularly good along the Auob from June to October. The same is true for the Nossob from January until April. It is well worth paying a visit to the great dune-fields that stretch between the two rivers during the rainy months. Covered with lush vegetation, they make a most striking sight.

CHILDREN IN THE BUSH

Parents should think very carefully before taking younger children on holiday to the wildlife areas of Botswana. Apart from the long and often uncomfortable distances to be travelled, there is an element of danger.

Public campsites in the national parks are usually unfenced (although an electric fence has been used at Savute and may be put into use again) and there are no facilities where small children can play unattended, so constant watchfulness on the part of adults is required.

Operators refuse children under 12 and reluctantly accept children over 12, but there are no reduced rates for children. This is not so with Botswana's national parks and game reserves. In this case children of 8 years and below are allowed entry free and there is a reduced rate for those between 8 and 16 years of age. (See 'Park entry fees and regulations' on page 129.)

The following cautionary tale should illustrate quite vividly the dangers that a wilderness holiday can hold for children.

Savute campsite is situated next to the Savute Channel, which has been quite dry for the past few years. Some 50 m across the channel from one of the camping places is the skeleton of a crashed aircraft.

The ruin was an instant drawcard to the four children who had just arrived. With parents engrossed in setting up camp, the four bounded straight to the plane, exploring it and playing around it.

The underground water and the trees of Savute Channel are a constant attraction for thirsty elephants who are regular visitors to the area.

The inevitable happened and the children and a young bull elephant were in the same place at the same time. By the time the parents and children emerged from their busy oblivion, the elephant's looming bulk separated the two groups. The romance of the wild was suddenly a very frightening and threatening reality for the inexperienced city dwellers.

Fortunately, sheer fright froze all movement but the emotions and adrenalin were almost tangible. Perhaps that was what made the elephant quietly move on and away, averting a potentially very nasty situation.

BIRDLIFE: WHERE AND WHEN

At all times of the year there is an abundance of birds to be seen in Botswana, although in the colder months, between April and September, there are fewer birds around. During that time mostly resident birds will be seen, with only a few winter visitors and no European migrants. The warmer months, therefore, are best for birdwatching.

Another factor that strongly influences the number and species of birds is the availability of water. In a dry area there will be fewer birds; the same applies to a poor rainy season.

There are seasonal concentrations of birds in Botswana but they are difficult to predict. For example, at Lake Ngami very little will be seen if the lake is dry. If it has water in it, however, it is one of the most prolific bird localities in Africa. The same can be said of the salt pans in Botswana. The birdlife is very rich if there is water, but if there is none, a visit can be disappointing. This is particularly so of Makgadikgadi Pans, especially north-eastern Sowa Pan. Here, if there is water towards the end of the rainy season, millions of birds congregate, notably flamingos, pelicans and ducks. Yet if there is no flooding, relatively few birds will be seen.

Good areas for the keen birdwatcher are Chobe, the Okavango and the Limpopo valley. An experienced birdwatcher may expect to see up to 200 species in a week at Chobe or in the Okavango, including slaty egrets, shoebills and wattled cranes. Special sightings will include half-collared kingfishers, Pel's fishing owl and the African finfoot. In the

Limpopo valley it is not unusual to see 150 species in quick succession. In a dry part of the Kalahari, Mabuasehube for example, one might expect to see only 30 to 50 species of birds.

Botswana does boast one or two birds of particular interest to the specialist. The south-east is one of only two localities in southern Africa where the short-clawed lark occurs. In Ngamiland the black-faced babbler has been sighted. The only other place where this bird is found is Namibia.

There is a bird club in Gaborone which leads regular walks from the museum on the first Sunday of every month, starting at 6.30 am in summer and 7.15 am in winter. The secretary and committee are always delighted to assist visiting bird enthusiasts in any way they can. They can be contacted at P O Box 71, Gaborone, Tel (267) 35 1500.

FISHING: WHERE AND WHEN

There are three primary fishing areas in Botswana — along the Chobe River, in the Okavango Delta, and the Limpopo valley in the east. Much of the better fishing in the Limpopo is on private land and so not easily accessible to the visitor.

In the two other areas tiger fishing can take place throughout the year but is generally at its best from August to February when the water is low, although the annual flood can sometimes produce excellent sport. The best time to fish for bream and tilapia is also in these months. Barbel can be caught at all times of the year but low water levels give the best chance of success.

It is difficult to give more precise information about the best months for fishing, especially in the Okavango. Much depends upon which part of the delta one is visiting. The size and time of the flood has a major effect upon the quality of fishing and, as it varies greatly in volume and in time of arrival and can take five to six months to work its way through the entire system, there are a number of variables which will affect your choice. Having decided on a fishing holiday, the best course of action is to contact some of the fishing camps mentioned in this book and ask their advice.

In the Chobe/Zambezi area there are more than 91 species of fish, of which 24 are commonly sought after. Most visiting fishermen are interested in just two species: tiger fish and bream. Chobe's present tiger record is 9,8 kg and 5-6 kg catches are common. Chobe tiger, being lighter and leaner, are claimed by many to be a better fighter. Apart from tiger, bream and barbel, other popular species include pike, squeaker, western bottlenose, many dwarf species and yellowfish. This last, found both in the rapids and in the upper Zambezi, offers a particularly exciting challenge to the expert.

Still in its infancy, but immensely popular in South Africa, the new sport of fly fishing is spreading quickly into the more secluded preserves of the subcontinent. Chobe is no exception.

No licences are required for fishing in waters outside the national park but at designated places within its boundaries a fishing licence is necessary. This costs P5 for residents and P10 for non-residents. In addition, park entry fees for the boat and individuals must be paid. A bag limit of ten fish per person per day is imposed.

Arrangements can be made with local fishing companies to fish in Caprivi and Zambian waters. They will also take care of licensing, rod levy and immigration matters.

Trees and other snags on the bottom of the rivers and channels will take a heavy toll on your line, spoons and hooks. It is advisable, therefore, to have a large supply on hand. Steel trace and swivels are essential if you're after tiger fish. Do remember that crocodile and hippo still abound, particularly in the Okavango and in the Chobe. It is foolish to take unnecessary risks.

Because of aquatic weed control measures in force in Botswana, visitors may bring boats into the country only through certain designated points. There the boats will be sprayed and a permit issued. Such a permit is needed by all boats, regardless of whether they come from inside or outside the country, when they move between zones within Botswana. Import permits can be obtained from the Water Registrar, Department of Water Affairs, Private Bag 0029, Gaborone (Tel 360 7340/1 Fax 30 3508). Boats can be hired at Kasane.

5. PREPARING FOR THE TRIP

Although there is no real substitute for experience, it should not be necessary for people making their first safari into the wilds, especially the wilds of Botswana, to have to 'reinvent the wheel'. This section aims to provide some useful information so that you will be suitably prepared and equipped for a safari. There is nothing more frustrating, when you have arrived at a point 200 km from nowhere, than finding that the salt, toilet paper, tin-opener or film for the camera have been forgotten!

Ultimately, what you carry on safari is your personal choice and the suggestions given here should be regarded simply as guidelines. The experienced traveller may find little of use here but those who have not safaried extensively may well find this section helpful.

There are a few basic 'golden rules' worth keeping in mind:

1. Keep everything simple — you have come to see and enjoy, to get a break from home, not to take it with you. There is many an abandoned vehicle on the sides of Botswana's roads that collapsed and died from overweight!
2. Never leave a water point without filling all your water containers. You can allow roughly 5 litres of water per person per day as a guide for provisioning. This does not include an allowance for washing.
3. Never leave a filling station without replenishing your petrol or diesel — you may meet somebody else who needs it in an emergency.

WHAT TO TAKE

Accessories

If you're interested in wildlife, birds, the stars or just the endless vistas, binoculars are an absolute must. So, too, is a camera. For larger game a 200 mm lens is recommended and for birds a lens of a minimum 400 mm is necessary. A wide-angle lens of 35 mm or less is helpful in doing justice to the magnificent views. *A word of warning about optical equipment.* Botswana in general and the Kalahari in particular are known for their prodigious quantities of sand and dust. Take the greatest care, therefore, to protect delicate equipment. You will need considerable ingenuity and effort to do this. Merely carrying your equipment in its container or a cloth bag is not enough. The dust will get in. Some people carry cameras and binoculars in sealed plastic bags — and they also carry a spare supply of plastic bags. Professional photographers never wipe dust from a lens. Instead, dust should be blown off with compressed air, small canisters of which can be obtained from photographic shops.

Hats, sun blockout creams and sunglasses are essential, particularly if you are not used to the heat and the glare — both of which can be formidable. Insects can be a nuisance and repellents are recommended. Don't forget Lariam or chloroquine anti-malaria tablets (recommended for Botswana).

Some people regard a compass as a panacea to all problems of navigation. In Botswana this is certainly not the case unless (a) you know where you are to start with, (b) you have maps of the area you are in, (c) you know how to use a map and compass and (d) you can work by dead-reckoning (because there are very few landmarks to help you).

Clothing

During the day, throughout the year, a shirt or blouse and shorts or a light skirt are perfectly adequate. A pair of jeans or slacks, a long-sleeved cotton shirt and swimming costumes are all useful items of clothing on safari. A jersey or jacket is handy for the winter mornings. A useful combination is a warm hat or balaclava and a sleeveless waistcoat or jersey. If your head and chest are warm, the rest of your body feels warm. Dun colours are generally more suitable as they attract less attention and do not seem to draw tsetse fly to them as readily as do brighter colours. White is not really a practical colour, as it might not be possible to wash clothes as frequently as you might wish. Clothes should be of a hardy and durable material — thorns are a constant menace to delicate fabrics.

For night time during the summer months, day wear is quite sufficient. In winter, however, especially from May to August, it can get very cold at night. A change of warm clothing is therefore highly recommended. For the same reason, campers should have warm sleeping bags. Tracksuits are useful as they help to build up layers of insulation as the temperature drops, and they are comfortable for sleeping in. In winter also pack warm socks, gloves and a hat, cap or balaclava, especially if you're a little thin on top!

Shoes

There are as many opinions as to the correct footwear for the Kalahari as there are makes and types of shoe. The choice is yours, but these guidelines may help you. It is not recommended that visitors go barefoot. The sand can get too hot to walk on and your feet can actually blister. Thorns, insects and scorpions are other hazards. Heavy boots are a matter of choice but something lighter is really more practical. Choose a shoe that can be easily removed (so that the sand can be emptied out!) and is made of a porous material, something that is easy to wash and allows the foot to breathe. Open sandals, canvas shoes or running shoes are all suitable. A pair of 'flip-flops' is handy for use around the camp.

HEALTH PRECAUTIONS

Diseases

Malaria, a disease transmitted by infected mosquitoes, is encountered in all parts of Botswana and visitors are urged to take anti-malaria tablets. The type of malaria most commonly encountered is *Falciparum*, one of the complications of which is cerebral malaria, which can be a very serious condition indeed. Generally the malarial threat is worst in the northern part of the country. In this area you are advised to take anti-malaria tablets throughout the year.

There are two major schools of thought concerning the problem of malaria. One option is take nothing and treat it when you get it. Many of the locals use this approach, ignoring the prophylactics because they are not 100 per cent guaranteed against malaria and could mask the symptoms — a more dangerous situation because infection might not be correctly diagnosed. The alternative is to try and protect yourself against it in some way. This is the wisest course for visitors to Botswana. Those who come from a non-malarial region should not expose themselves to unnecessary risks and should take a prophylactic. Botswana pharmacists recommend the following:

Two days before arrival in the country, one Lariam (active ingredient mefloquine), followed by one a week during the visit and for four weeks after the visit. There have been reports of side-effects with this new drug but these can be reduced if the tablet is taken with a meal. Lariam is not recommended for those with high blood pressure. If Lariam is not preferred an alternative is two tablets of any chloroquine prophylactic two days before starting, followed by two a week thereafter and for four weeks after the visit. This tablet regime should be accompanied by two Paludrine (active ingredient proguanil) a day. This is because malaria resistant to chloroquine has been reported in Botswana, and if Paludrine is taken with it it provides stronger protection. Doses should be reduced for children.

Cerebral malaria is not a different variety of malaria. It is an infection so severe that the parasite has passed through the blood/brain barrier and is multiplying in the brain cells where many drugs cannot follow. If it is caught early enough, it can be treated. Severe difficulties will occur when there are long delays in diagnosis.

The best advice for avoiding malaria is, of course, not to get bitten in the first place. Sleeping under a net reduces the chances of being bitten by about 80 per cent. Wearing long socks, long pants and long-sleeved shirts in the evening is another smart move. These steps, backed up with the use of repellents, will be most effective in avoiding bites. Repellents include Mylol, Tabard and a long-lasting product called Bayticol.

AIDS is present in Botswana and routine precautions against contracting the HIV virus are no less important here than anywhere else. One in four men in the workplace is HIV-positive, as are one in four women reporting to ante-natal clinics in Francistown. There is no need to go to the extent of bringing your own needles in case of accident or emergency, although some people certainly do. Doctors, hospitals and clinics are well versed in standard anti-AIDS procedures. I have witnessed the use of new needles and watched the destruction of used equipment in a hospital.

Bilharzia is an ever-present threat in Africa, and Botswana, despite its dryness, is no exception. As a general rule, it is probably safe to assume that all rivers, streams and dams are infected, although not heavily. This is also true of the Okavango, especially around populated areas. The only way to avoid contracting the disease is to avoid bathing or wading in water. Curiously, bilharzia cannot be caught by drinking untreated, infected water. Saliva is sufficient to prevent contamination. The disease is easily cured today. Symptoms take at least six weeks to develop.

Trypanosomiasis, or sleeping sickness, a disease transmitted by the bite of an infected tsetse fly, is a very much reduced threat in modern Botswana. At its widest extent it occurs only in Ngamiland, in the area of Ngami, Okavango, Mababe and Chobe. Today it has been virtually eliminated and only small populations of tsetse fly exist. The fly can inflict a painful bite and, if you should contract the disease, its symptoms develop only after about two weeks. They include headaches and a fever. A blood test can quickly confirm if a patient is suffering from sleeping sickness. The condition is easily cured.

Rabies is endemic among many animals in Botswana. It is often marked by cases of unusual behaviour, which includes attacking humans or unusual friendliness towards humans. Recently a child in Maun came across a friendly mopane squirrel. He picked it up, took it to school and showed it to all his friends. The squirrel was rabid. All who handled it had to be treated for rabies.

In the case of a bite from a suspected rabid creature, it is important to get the patient to a hospital as soon as possible. A treatment is available which requires only five injections and is extremely effective, if administered quickly enough after the bite. If not, **death will result** (you have about 24 hours). Strange as it may seem, the most effective first aid is to wash the wound with soap and water; soap kills the virus. Any soap will do, including dishwashing liquid. There is now a vaccination which can be given for protection but it must still be followed by treatment in the event of a rabid bite.

Tick-bite fever commonly affects many people, especially newcomers to the country and, therefore, visitors. It is prevalent in the wet season, particularly in March and April and is passed on to humans from the bite of a tiny, pin-head size tick. The disease incubates for seven days and then manifests itself with severe aching of the bones, headaches, backaches and a fever. Although it can be serious and exceedingly unpleasant, it is a self-limiting disease and will run its course in three to four days. Typically, the symptoms include swollen and painful glands. Almost always an infected bite will be found — it will have a yellow head with a small black central spot. There is much controversy as to whether immunity can be acquired by stoically enduring the pain until the body's system defeats the infection. Medical experts in Botswana believe there is no merit in following this course and suggest instead that the sufferer report to a hospital where the disease is easily controlled through a course of tetracycline.

Finding ticks on your body is an experience you might have to get used to. They are easily dislodged, but care should be taken to remove the head as well as the body, or infection might result. Removing very small ticks can be a problem. A useful way is to smear them with Vaseline, grease or a commercial sealant. A drop on the tick causes it to release its hold and it can be pulled away when the sealant is removed.

Venoms

Scorpions are numerous in the sandveld of the Kalahari but care can be taken to avoid them. Simple precautions include shaking out clothes and emptying out shoes before putting them on. The unwary are often bitten while picking up firewood, and it is best to kick or knock the wood before handling it. Many scorpions live in trees, especially under loose bark. A sting can be extremely painful but it is not generally dangerous. The effects will wear off within an hour or so. The best treatment is to cool the site of the sting and to administer mild painkillers, if available. The San insist that the best cure is to catch and kill the creature, squeeze its innards onto the palm of your hand, mix it up and rub into the excoriated wound site!

Dealing with **snakebite** is not a simple matter. Broad spectrum anti-snakebite serums are available and you should consider taking one with you. Generally they have a short shelf-life and need to be kept constantly cool, if not refrigerated. This is not always easy to achieve. Sometimes, it has been claimed, an anti-venom injection has caused more problems than it has cured. You need to know your snakes and how to use the serum if you are going to carry it.

An alternative to a snakebite kit is a new method of treating snakebite which, to me, seems a far more attractive choice. Known as the Sutherland Method (after its Australian originator) or the Pressure Immobilisation System, it requires only a few crepe bandages.

It is not the intention here to explain the system in full but, essentially, it requires that the victim be rested, soothed and relaxed. The injured limb is completely bound — from one end to the other — with crepe bandages using firm but gentle pressure. The idea is to restrict the movement of the lymph system in which the poison is transported. *No tourniquet is applied.*

An advantage of the system is that, in contrast to the tourniquet method which can dangerously stop or hinder blood flow, the affected limb is not at risk on that account. You can learn more about this method from Johan Marais's book *Snake versus Man* and from most snake parks.

My recommendation is to study this method as it seems a sensible and hopeful compromise between risking the dangers of incorrectly administered serum and doing nothing at all.

Other

Visitors who wish to take sensible precautions should consider having a hepatitis A and B vaccination before entering the country. An alternative is an injection of immune globulin which will prevent you from contracting this common disease for about three months. It is also advisable to have a tetanus and a typhoid booster.

Venereal infections are quite common, especially gonorrhoea.

Water in the towns and villages is perfectly safe to drink.

The **sun** in the Kalahari is fierce and those whose skins are not used to it should wear hats and should apply total ultra-violet blockout creams. The **dust** in the dry season will irritate eyes which are not accustomed to it so take eye-wash solution with you. Mild attacks of **diarrhoea** are not uncommon. Lomotil, a non-prescription medicine, is an effective cure.

There are general **hospitals** at the following locations: Maun, Ghanzi, Gaborone, Francistown, Lobatse, Mahalapye, Serowe, Selebi-Phikwe, Molepolole, Kanye, Mmadinare, Mochudi, Ramotswa, Jwaneng and Orapa.

Many of the villages throughout the country have **medical clinics** staffed by trained personnel. These clinics should not be overlooked, especially when assistance is needed for less serious complaints. Many are in radio contact with hospitals.

First aid

If you intend to travel independently, and to the remoter areas, take a first aid handbook with you. Many lives have been lost unnecessarily through failure to take the simple precautions clearly outlined in such a book. In addition, you should carry a first aid kit — the Automobile Association, the Red Cross or any chemist will help you select suitable items for it.

Heatstroke may prove to be a problem and your first aid equipment should include salt tablets. Some people may find that the intensely dry air of the Kalahari causes congestion in the sinuses and, for this reason, a decongestant of some kind should also be included.

Infection can spread very rapidly so keeping clean on safari is important. It is possible, with practice, to complete a respectable bath with only three mugs of water! Sweat rashes often result from a combination of dirt and heat. Talcum powder will control this condition but cleanliness will help avoid it. Another aid to controlling infection is a styptic pencil. Rubbed on those annoying bites, it reduces the irritation — and hence the scratching — thus lessening the chance of infection from dirty fingernails.

VEHICLE SPARES

Always carry at least one spare wheel, a jack and wheel brace. A puncture repair outfit is of no use without tyre levers and both are a good idea to carry. Essential spares include fuses, tyre pump, tyre pressure gauge, lightbulbs, points, condensers, sparkplugs, a regulator, radiator hoses (top and bottom), fan belt, warning triangles, engine oil, a small coil of soft baling wire, jump leads, brake and clutch fluid and a full set of tools. Carry a spare set of keys and, ideally, find a place on the outside of the vehicle where they can be secured, hidden yet relatively easy to get at. Never leave the spare set in the vehicle! A tow rope and shovel are useful, and so is a hand-held spotlight.

It is only possible to give general guidelines on the availability of vehicle spares since what is required depends very much upon the make of vehicle and the particular problem. All the main centres — Gaborone, Francistown, Maun, Mahalapye, Lobatse — will stock the commonest spares for the most popular vehicles. Smaller towns, especially along the railway line, will be able to get them very quickly.

In the more remote areas garages are few and far between and proper spares almost nonexistent. This is sometimes offset, however, by the increasing levels of ingenuity and self-reliance that people in these areas have developed. In an emergency you will have to place your trust in these people and, while you may not get a very professional job, the chances of your being able to drive on are very good.

MAPS

The main source of official maps of the country is the Department of Surveys and Mapping, Private Bag 0037, Gaborone, Tel 35 3251. An excellent map catalogue can be obtained on request and it gives detailed information on what is available. Maps can also be purchased from the department's offices in Selebi-Phikwe, Maun and Francistown, but stocks are limited. They carry only the large, general maps of the country and the 1:50 000 maps of their immediate areas. The offices in Maun do sell maps, although the range is very limited. Special arrangements can be made to order and have them collected there.

A number of commercial enterprises such as curio and book shops sell a limited range of the more popular maps.

Residents of South Africa can obtain Botswana maps from the Map Office (Pty), 5 Kollege House, 46 De Korte Street, Braamfontein, Johannesburg at Tel (011) 339 4941/49 and Fax 339 4951. The staff there are very helpful and efficient.

For those considering close and detailed work in a small area of Botswana, especially in the more remote and featureless places, aerial photographs are recommended. These 230 x 230 black-and-white prints are available only from the department in Gaborone and will take a week from receipt of order. Recent maps giving medium-scale cover of the entire country at 1:50 000 are available.

Conventional six-colour maps are available in scales from 1:1 500 000 to the very popular 1:350 000 editions for the Okavango and for the Chobe areas. A mixture of monochrome and full-colour maps are available in the scales 1:500 000 and 1:250 000 for the whole country, whilst a series of 1:100 000 and 1: 50 000 cover the northern half, the east and the south-east of Botswana.

Street maps showing plot numbers and street names exist for Gaborone, Francistown, Selebi-Phikwe and Lobatse. A folding pocket road map, produced on behalf of Shell Oil, can be obtained from their offices (P O Box 334, Gaborone, Tel 35 3025 Fax 30 5827) and from the Department of Tourism, Private Bag 0047, Gaborone, Tel 35 3024.

PACKING YOUR VEHICLE

Botswana's roads are rough and facilities limited. Presuming that you have planned a lengthy trip, you will have to carry a lot of equipment and space willl be at a premium.

It makes sense, therefore, to give careful thought to the way you pack your vehicle. Besides, cornflakes soaked in petrol don't go down very well!

There are three basic rules to follow when planning your packing:

1. Wrap hard objects with sharp edges in a cover (an old piece of underfelt or something equally substantial).
2. Pack heavy objects at the bottom of the pile.
3. Strap everything down or pack inside boxes which are strapped down. Remember that the constant bumping and shaking, together with a copious layer of dust, will create abrasion that can rub through paint or canvas during a long journey.

You are going to be dealing with five types of gear:
1.   Food and drink
2.   Camping and cooking equipment
3.   Clothing
4.   Photographic
5.   Vehicle spares and fuel
Divide each of these into two categories: those you need immediately to hand and your bulk supplies.

Food and drink

You can get most basic foodstuffs within Botswana. It does, however, pay to plan your menus well in advance so that you have some idea of what you need to buy at what point.

It is worth carrying a large cool-box and planning for fresh meat and vegetables for the day you arrive and for 24 hours after you leave main towns. Remember, though, that Botswana is very hot, ice is not easy to come by and food will go off quickly. In addition, your vehicle's bouncing around will rapidly pulp soft vegetables and fruit, so tomatoes and peaches, for instance, don't last long. Onions and carrots do, however, and can add flavour to canned meals. Oranges are always refreshing.

Avoid 'pop-top' plastic bottles, the type containing oil or vinegar. Pressure can pop them open at very much the wrong time. Choose screw-top containers instead.

Decant foods such as sugar and dried milk from paper packets into screw-top containers and plan to have a '48 hour' tin that is readily to hand and a bulk supply that gets buried.

The following foodstuffs may be carried as basics:
bannock mixture, i.e. flour and baking powder to make a pan bread
lemon juice
instant potato powder
stock cubes for stews, etc.
rusks
glucose sweets
chewing gum
dried fruit
milk powder
coffee
teabags
Oxo cubes

peanuts
raisins
rice
butter/margarine
muesli mix
bread (when available)
cheese portions
sugar
salt
pepper
oil
vinegar

Fresh vegetables and fruit which last well include:
Potatoes (plus tinfoil to cook them in), cabbage, onions, carrots, oranges, lemons. Celery and tomatoes are refreshing but don't plan to keep them too long.

The following range of tinned food is useful:
Corned beef (an excellent base for stew)
pilchards
potatoes
tomato puree (for adding flavour to cooked foods)
baked beans
peas
pickled fish
tomatoes
cream (for treats)
luncheon meat
sweetcorn

All of these are good basics which can be eaten hot or cold and mixed and matched to make tasty meals. Obviously the tinned food range is enormous and you must choose according to your personal taste.

Work out your general menus in advance. You will probably find it best to pull out the food for the next 24 hours whilst in camp and pack it in a small box so that it is easy to get at. Then, if you are delayed the next day and camp late, a meal can be prepared quickly. There is nothing guaranteed to raise blood pressure more than getting into camp after dark and not being able to get a meal going until the whole vehicle has been unpacked. Everybody will probably be tired and fed up, particularly if it's raining, but a hot meal, quickly prepared, works wonders in restoring morale.

Camping gear

No experienced camper will need to be told what to carry but, for those who are a little uncertain, some guidelines are offered, drawn from personal experience.

Camping equipment in Botswana needs to fulfil a number of functions. You must be able to provide shade during the day and protection from dust and thorns on the ground. A large canvas sheet is ideal for both functions. It can also be used to help vehicles out of sand, to lie under when it rains and to catch rainwater for drinking or bathing. It will also keep you warm when wrapped around your sleeping bag.

Where there are likely to be predators, your camping gear must provide a totally enclosed area in which to sleep. Several incidents are recorded of lion or hyena taking a bite out of a sleeping person. It really does not make sense to sleep in the open without some kind of all-round cover, such as a lightweight tent with a built-in groundsheet.

Camp-beds are not necessary; you can sleep on the ground or on a foam or inflatable mattress. A small pillow is a good idea; unless you are practised at it, sleeping without a pillow is very uncomfortable.

Nights can be very cold during the Botswana winter when the clear open skies cause rapid heat loss from the earth. Warm sleeping gear is recommended. During the summer months mosquitos and biting insects can be a nuisance and a tent with a flyscreen or some kind of mosquito net is essential.

Pack your camping gear where it comes readily to hand — preferably on a roof-rack — and strap it down well before moving. Make extra sure that tent poles are firmly held in place. It is very useful to be able to get a camp set up quickly, particularly after a long day when you may have to try to do things in the dark. It is not a bad idea to practise a few times at home. It may seem like a simple exercise, but it can be complex and nerve-racking when you try to do it in the bush after dark!

Cooking utensils and other basic equipment

Keep cooking equipment simple and sturdy. Glass tends to become a casualty on safari. A small gas cooker (3 kg) with a single ring is useful. Take a spare cylinder too. (Useful tip: jets get easily blocked so either carry cheap replacements and a spanner or use one of the aerosol sprays, such as Q20, to blow the wrong way through the jet to clear it.) This is ample for three people. You can usually build a fire if you want to, but remember to collect wood before you arrive at campsites as the surrounding areas have usually been well stripped already.

A *potjie* (cast-iron pot), flat-bottomed or three-legged, is a worthwhile investment for fire cooking. Use the following checklist for cooking equipment:

gas cylinder plus ring, kettle, wooden platters, small jug (for ladling water/soup), tin-opener, braai grid (with clip to hold it closed), plates (melamine), mugs, knives/forks/spoons, chopping knife, Thermos flask, small spade (for toilet use, amongst others), plastic basin (for washing dishes, clothes and self), washing powder (in screw-top container), flat-bottomed *potjie* bowls, chopping board, small pan which can double as frying pan or cooking pan, plastic glasses, matches and/or lighter (waterproofed), paper towels/toilet paper (in a waterproof plastic bag or container), two 10-litre containers of water (preferably black plastic to prevent growth of algae), short length of washing line and pegs, dishwashing liquid (in screw-top container)

Divide all these things between a 'day' box and a 'kitchen' box, except the cooker and *potjie*. The 'day' box contains those things likely to be used whilst travelling — e.g. mugs, knives, forks, spoons, wooden platters, tin-opener. This enables you to stop and have lunch, invariably cold, without involving a major unpacking of the vehicle.

It is very convenient to be able to lift the box out, collect the cooker and despatch the cook to one side to get on with the meal whilst everybody else prepares camp. This is not as easily done if the various components are scattered around all over the vehicle.

Clothing

Big suitcases tend to be a nuisance. Several canvas holdalls are better than one large container. Because they are soft they can be packed more tightly and don't rub against other things. You can also separate your clothing into different uses with smaller containers, e.g. warm, night-time gear in one bag, daytime clothes in another, etc.

Plan to carry as little as is compatible with personal hygiene and comfort. You will be surprised how little you really need and clothing can be very bulky. Remember also that it is going to get crumpled up in the bags, so if you have a set of 'nice togs' for when you go out for a drink in town, they must be fairly crease-resistant.

Photographic

Part of the enjoyment of the trip for many people is taking photographs. That means camera equipment — at least the camera in present use — must be handy. Because of the dust it also means that it will probably travel in the passenger cab with you, and not in an open back or anywhere else exposed to dust. Don't rely on getting your particular film; bring plenty with you. As I often reproduce some of my shots I use a tripod whenever I can. A 35 mm colour slide going on an A4 page is enlarged approximately 44 times and so every blurring caused by movement is exaggerated. A tripod steadies the camera. I use a low ASA, because light is one thing there's always plenty of in Botswana!

Packing fuel and spares

Assume that fuel fumes will leak and so will the liquid, so put it somewhere out of the way. The roof is an option, but if you store your fuel here watch the high centre of gravity. A 200 litre long-range tank is another storage option, and so is plastic drums.

One useful tip is to keep two different size screwdrivers, an adjusting spanner and a pair of good pliers wrapped up in a cloth under or near your seat. It is surprising how many little things can be attended to with just these tools without the necessity of having to take the whole toolbox out of the 'depths' somewhere in the back.

6. CUSTOMS

BORDER POSTS

Botswana/Republic of South Africa

Border Post	*Times of operation*
Pontdrift	7.30 to 16.30 daily
Platjan	7.30 to 16.30 daily
Zanzibar	7.30 to 16.30 daily
Martin's Drift	7.00 to 18.00 daily
Parr's Halt	8.00 to 18.00 daily
Sikwane	7.00 to 19.00 daily
Tlokweng Gate	7.00 to 22.00 daily
Ramotswa	7.00 to 19.00 daily
Pioneer Gate	7.00 to 19.00 daily
Ramatlabama	7.00 to 20.00 daily
Pitsane Molopo	7.30 to 16.30 daily
Bray	7.00 to 17.00 daily
Makopong	8.00 to 16.00 daily
Bokspits	enquire before using
McCarthy's Rust	enqure before using

Botswana/Namibia

Mamuno	8.00 to 17.00 daily
Mohembo	6.00 to 18.00 daily
Ngoma	8.00 to 16.00 daily

Botswana/Zimbabwe

Mpandamatenga	8.00 to 16.00 daily (for non-commercial purposes only since there are no forwarding agents at this post)
Ramokwebane	6.00 to 20.00 daily
Kazungula Road	6.00 to 20.00 daily

Botswana/Zambia

Kazungula Ferry	7.00 to 18.00 daily

There are a number of additional points at which Botswana can be entered where there are no border posts on the Botswana side. The visitor is required to report to the nearest police station immediately. These points of entry are: Tsabong, Middelpits, Baines Drift, Buffel's Drift and Pilane.

Visitors should also note that there are no bridges across the Molopo River in the south, and that there are no high-level bridges across the Limpopo. Both rivers are liable to flooding and access may not then be possible.

It is important to remember that during public and school holidays border posts will be especially crowded. Although the staff try to prevent long delays, they are usually unavoidable. Do not try to rush through at opening time at the border posts on the main transport routes as the freight companies will be queued up waiting to get through. Either alter your travel times or try one of the lesser used border posts. Longest delays can be expected at Ramokwebane, Ramatlabama and Tlokweng.

AIRPORTS

	Times of operation
Sir Seretse Khama, Gaborone	6.00 to 22.00 daily
Maun	6.30 to 18.30 daily September-November & March-May 6.00 to 19.00 daily December-February 7.00 to 18.00 daily June-August
Francistown	7.00 to 18.00 Monday/Wednesday/Friday 7.00 to 16.30 Tuesday/Thursday/Saturday/Sunday
Selebi-Phikwe	6.00 to 18.00 daily
Kasane	6.00 to 18.30 daily
Jwaneng	7.30 to 16.30 weekdays only
Orapa	7.30 to 16.30 weekdays only

CUSTOMS REQUIREMENTS FOR VISITORS

All goods acquired outside Botswana must be declared on entry into Botswana. Goods acquired from within the Southern African Common

Customs Area (SACCA), comprising Botswana, South Africa, Swaziland, Namibia and Lesotho are free from customs duties but may be liable to sales tax and additional duties. However visitors may bring into Botswana, free of duty and, where applicable, sales tax, the following:

Wine — 2 litres. Spirits and alcoholic beverages — 1 litre and 6 x 340 ml cans of beer. Cigarettes — 400. Cigars — 50. Tobacco — 250 g. Perfume — 50 ml. Toilet water — 250 ml. Other new or used goods of total value not exceeding 500 UA per person. A Unit of Account is equal to R1,00. Minors, i.e. children under the age of 18, may claim these concessions, except in respect of tobacco and alcohol.

Sales tax is payable on most consumable items and is usually 10 per cent of the item's value. However it does vary, especially in respect of various alcoholic beverages. Please note that sales tax is charged on spare fuel carried in containers.

Permits

There are some items which require special permits. Permits in these cases would be obtainable from the ministries concerned, such as Wildlife, Mines and Agriculture, among others. If you are not sure whether a permit is necessary for a particular item, you can enquire at the Department of Customs & Excise, Private Bag 0041, Gaborone (Tel 31 2455).

If your vehicle is equipped with a two-way radio, a citizen band radio or a mobile telephone set, it is necessary to acquire a permit from the Radio Licence Office, Botswana Telecommunications Corporation, P O Box 700, Gaborone (Tel 35 8246/35 8000, Fax 31 3355). It is advisable to allow one month for the processing of this permit.

Food

Food may only be imported if it is for immediate and personal consumption. The importation of dairy products (with the exception of 3 dozen eggs and 2 litres of milk per person) and uncooked meat is prohibited without an import certificate issued by the Veterinary Department, Private Bag 0032, Gaborone (Tel 35 0500).

Please note that it is necessary to have a health permit from the veterinary department in order to transport meat within Botswana. They do check at the vet fences and may confiscate the meat or make you cook it and eat it there if you do not have a permit.

Firearms

The control of firearms in Botswana is very strict. There is a total restric tion on the importation of side-arms, automatic weapons and small-bore rifles (e.g. of .22 calibre). An import permit is required for any permitted weapon and can be obtained by writing in advance to the Officer in Charge, Central Arms Registry, Private Bag 0012, Gaborone (Tel 35 116' ext 2466).

Boats

In order to control the spread of aquatic weeds, the Department of Wa ter Affairs requires that no boat be brought into the country without a permit. This must be applied for in advance from the Department of Water Affairs, Private Bag 0029, Gaborone (Tel 360 7100). Boats will not be allowed into the country without this permit.

Persons in the country moving a boat from one zone to another also require a permit, which can be obtained from the same department.

ROAD TAX

For all foreign vehicles entering the country a road tax of P5,00 is charged

CURRENCY

Only the following currencies are accepted by the customs authorities cash or traveller's cheques in rand, sterling and United States dollars traveller's cheques only in Zimbabwe dollars.

All visitors and residents are permitted to carry with them when ei ther leaving or entering the country Pula notes and coins and/or foreign currency notes and coins up to a combined total of P5 000 per person without authorisation.

HEALTH CERTIFICATES

Inoculation certificates are not required at the moment unless you come from an African country north of the Zambezi, or Angola or northern Namibia, where yellow fever is endemic, when it is necessary to have been inoculated against yellow fever. You should be inoculated at leas 10 days before entering Botswana. The inoculation is valid for 10 years

It is advisable, however, for all travellers going beyond Gaborone to be inoculated against the following diseases and to carry an International Certificate of Vaccination:

Hepatitis A (now available for children as well as adults), rabies, typhoid, tetanus, polio (adults require boosters), meningitis (children under 6).

This is a wise precaution to take as there have been recent cases of these diseases in the remoter areas of Botswana and in neighbouring countries.

VISA REQUIREMENTS

Visas are not required of passport holders from the following countries:

All Commonwealth countries, Austria, Belgium, Denmark, Federal Republic of Germany, Finland, France, Greece, Italy, Liechtenstein, Luxembourg, Namibia, Netherlands, Norway, Pakistan, Republic of Ireland, Samoa (Western), San Marino, Sweden, Switzerland, United States of America, Uruguay and Yugoslavia.

Nationals of all other countries are required to obtain a visa. They should do so at least three months in advance of their intended visit, by writing to the Chief Immigration Officer, P O Box 942, Gaborone. Passport-size photographs are required for visa applications.

PETS

It is possible to bring domestic pets, such as dogs and cats, into Botswana with very little difficulty. For both dogs and cats you will need a movement permit issued by a state veterinarian indicating that the cat or dog has been inoculated against rabies. The rabies vaccine must have been administered not more than one year before the end of the intended journey and not less than one month before it commences. A certificate from a state veterinarian, certifying that the animal is in good health, is also required.

Movement permits have been drawn up by the following countries: Botswana, Lesotho, Swaziland, South Africa, Namibia and Zimbabwe. With this form, which is valid for 60 days, dogs and cats can be carried freely between each of these countries. If you bring a dog or cat with you into the country and intend to travel around with it, it is essential that you carry a valid movement permit. You will have to produce it at the numerous veterinary cordon fences through which you will pass. If you do not have such a permit, you will not be allowed to proceed.

Visitors from Zambia, producing equivalent documents, will also be allowed to enter the country with their pets. (It should be noted, however, that dogs and cats are not allowed in national parks or game reserves. There are kennelling facilities for both cats and dogs in Gaborone and Selebi-Phikwe.)

To bring horses into Botswana, it is necessary to have temporary export and import permits which must be arranged through the veterinary and animal health departments both in the country of origin, e.g South Africa or Zimbabwe, and in Botswana well in advance of the intended visit. This may involve an examination of the horse by a veterinarian and will require a Dourine test on mares within 21 days of travelling.

LENGTH OF STAY

If a visitor wishes to remain in Botswana for more than one month, he must obtain an extension of his entry permit from the nearest immigration department once inside the country. For non-residents, a total of 90 days a year is allowed. This regulation is strictly enforced.

MOTOR VEHICLES: LICENCES AND INSURANCE

Motor vehicles, caravans and trailers that are legitimately licensed and registered in their country of origin can be brought into Botswana by visitors and used by them for a period of six months. As in many other countries, all vehicles are required to hold a minimum third party insurance. Third party insurance valid within the SACCA is also valid in Botswana. Vehicles from these countries are therefore only required to pay the road tax. Vehicles registered elsewhere are required to obtain third party insurance at the border post. Vehicles from outside the SACCA are also required to obtain a temporary import permit which is valid for six months and can be renewed at the customs department.

Foreign driver's licences are valid for 6 months. Licences not printed in English should be accompanied by a written translation.

7. DRIVING AND YOUR VEHICLE

Botswana has more than 4 200 km of first-class tarmac roads. It is now possible to drive from Johannesburg, via Gaborone and Francistown, to both Maun and Kasane and through Serowe to Orapa on tar. In addition, the western side of the Okavango is tarred from Maun to the border at Mohembo. Before long the tar will reach Ghanzi and Mamuno on the Namibian border. Increasingly excellent roads are opening up the country to the motorist.

Not all roads, of course, are of such a good standard. There are many thousands of kilometres that range from rough or sandy tracks to gravelled surfaces and vary in quality from season to season from fair to execrable. If a good road surface is a critical factor for you, then you are advised to seek the most up-to-date information.

RULES OF THE ROAD

Speed limits

There are three general speed limits in Botswana. All main roads have an upper limit of 120 km/h. In towns and villages the general limit is 60 km/h. On the main road, some of the through routes are 80 km/h. All speed limits are signposted. National parks and game reserves impose their own limits, and these are indicated in the individual reserves. The Botswana police regularly set speed traps and offenders are prosecuted. New radar equipment has been acquired and the police are prone to sudden bursts of activity. Sophisticated arguments will not help you at all and, unfortunately, the fact that you are in a foreign-registered vehicle is likely to work to your detriment. The trick is not to get caught! Traps are often set in unlikely places on main roads, mostly in 80 or 60 km/h zones.

Safety belts

If a vehicle is fitted with safety belts, it is compulsory to wear them. A fine of between P10 and P30 is usually imposed, although the maximum penalty is P200.

Riding on the roof

Although the roof is an ideal position for game spotting and general viewing, this practice is against the law in towns and villages. Especially in the latter the police can be rather vigilant and will impose fines.

HAZARDS

Motorists should take great care to watch for animals on the road. This is a particular hazard on roads in Botswana and many lives have been lost in accidents caused by collisions with animals. Whether a road is fenced or not, there is always the possibility of cattle, donkeys, goats and game animals straying onto it. Often they are deliberately herded there to take advantage of grazing that would otherwise go to waste. At night the hazard is even greater, particularly in the cooler months when animals seek the warmth of the tarmac. Even with spotlights, dark animals on a dark road are extremely difficult for tired eyes to see. *The danger that animals represent cannot be stressed too greatly.*

Driving on high-speed roads at night is particularly hazardous in Botswana. Many locals regard the idea of driving on the Gaborone-Francistown road during the hours of darkness as suicidal. The road to Maun is no doubt regarded in the same way. Despite fencing, cattle and stock will stray onto the road. Numerous people have died tragically in the last few years after colliding with animals. Please be careful. Try not to drive at night on the main roads and if you have to, drop your speed by 20 km/h, make sure your lights are in perfect working order and exercise the greatest caution.

Even on secondary or minor roads, it is unwise to drive after dark. If you have no choice, then drive slowly and carefully. Good spotlights will help, but they must be well set and are of limited use in dusty conditions. Even the best spotlight cannot penetrate dust and they may in fact reduce visibility through the 'bounce' of the glare on the dust.

Accidents

The laws in Botswana relating to the reporting of accidents are similar to those elsewhere in southern Africa. If, as a result of a vehicle accident there is any injury to persons or damage to property, this must be reported to the nearest police station or police officer 'as soon as is reasonably practical and, in any event, within 48 hours'. Where there is minor damage only and no injury to persons, it is sufficient, with the agree ment of all the parties involved, to exchange names and addresses. Where an accident has taken place it is the duty of the driver to stop. Parties involved have a legal right to demand from each other names and addresses, details of vehicle registration numbers and ownership, insurance particulars and the names and addresses of any passengers who may be potential witnesses.

A difficulty often arises in cases where livestock has been killed or injured. Basically, there are two situations in which this can happen, i.e. where the road is fenced and where it is not. In the former case, that is on most but not all of the tarred main roads and few, if any, of the gravel and sand roads, theoretically the owner of the animal is responsible for any death, injury or damage caused by the presence of his animals. This is because it is an offence for a stock owner to allow his animals to stray onto the road. Thus it may seem that there is a good chance of a claim against him succeeding. In practice, however, such claims are usually dismissed because of the many defences which are open to the stock owner and the counter-claim of some contributory negligence on the part of the driver.

On an unfenced road it becomes even more difficult to determine responsibility for damages. In both cases therefore, the most practical solution is to try to avoid an accident in the first place. If you do have an accident, recognise that it is often easiest to pay compensation for the animal involved and accept the fact of damage to your vehicle. Litigation is going to be costly and lengthy and the outcome uncertain, quite apart from the fact that the owner of the animal may not have the resources to meet your damages.

VEHICLE BREAKDOWNS

Travelling in a four-wheel-drive vehicle in Botswana's remoter areas, you should be aware of the host of things that can go wrong. It is not possible to cover all the possible problems in one book, but one or two hints may help in a time of crisis.

Whatever else you remember to do, there is one golden rule of critical importance. *Keep calm.* No matter how much of a hurry you are in, if you've broken down, you are going to be late. Take a break while you gain control — make a cup of tea if necessary. Above all, think about your situation before you act. Many problems are caused by very small and sometimes unlikely things coming adrift. Electrics are the most common source of poor running or bad performance. Only as a last resort should you consider taking the carburettor apart!

Jacking up a vehicle

If you're stuck in mud, clay or deep sand, jack up the vehicle and put branches, planks or stones under the wheels. Sometimes, though, instead of the vehicle going up, the jack goes down, sinking into the ground. To prevent this, take the spare wheel off and use it as a base for the jack. Otherwise try a piece of plank, a board or a thick pad of folded canvas. Inflatable jacks are another option.

Flat battery and unable to push-start because of sand or mud

If there is no other battery and you have a generator fitted (as opposed to an alternator), try the following. Jack up one of the driving wheels and remove it. With the car jacked up, wind a long length of cord around the hub. Ask one or two of your companions to pull on the cord, rotating the wheel. With the ignition on and the vehicle in gear, start as in a normal 'push-start' situation (foot on the clutch as the hub builds up speed, foot off the clutch when maximum speed is reached). Make sure, if you are in a forward gear, that the hub is being rotated in the right direction. If you have an alternator, this won't work.

If there is a battery handy, then use jump leads. It is usual to connect them red to red and black to black, but this only works if the 'dead' battery still has some life in it. It is much better to connect red to red and the sound battery's black to the earth (engine block or body-work) of the stricken vehicle, especially if it is fitted with an alternator.

If you only have one piece of lead or wire, you can make an adequate earth connection by putting the two vehicles together, metal to metal (usually bumper).

A tip received from P Holmes of Cape Town sounds like a useful way of starting a petrol engine vehicle if you have a weak battery. He says 'remove every other sparkplug (in the firing order) from the engine. The load on the starter is greatly reduced and the higher cranking speed can be enough to get the engine going. Thereafter, the sparkplugs can be replaced and the HT leads fitted with the engine running. The noise is awful so plug the ears!'

Clutch and brake fluid

You should never travel without a supply of this fluid. However, if you are caught without it, there are emergency alternatives. Almost any liquid will do — water, urine, vegetable oil for cooking. *Never use minera oils* as they will rot the rubbers. Whatever is used must be flushed out as soon as possible.

Slave or master cylinder goes

Once you are moving, you can change gears without the clutch. With a bit of practice and experience this can be done smoothly and does not harm the gearbox. The problem is getting moving in the first place. Warm the engine and then switch it off. Engage first gear, depress the accelerator and turn the starter. This is not good treatment for the starter, but it will get you going, unless you are stuck in very deep sand — in which case you have a long wait or a long walk ahead!

BUSH BEHAVIOUR

Good behaviour in the bush is like good behaviour in any circumstances. It takes the form of courtesy and consideration, an awareness of the needs of others. The major difference is that bad behaviour in the bush can be extremely dangerous or even fatal. When you see headlines that tell you of another death somewhere in the wilderness, you might feel that the wisest way to behave in the bush is not to go there in the first place! But you needn't suffer any mishaps if you are disciplined enough to follow the simple guidelines below.

There are travellers' tales aplenty about close shaves with wild animals. After all, a holiday to the wilds of Botswana is all about getting back to unspoilt Africa with its dangerous wild animals and challenges to the traveller. It may be very tempting to get so close to the elephant that its eye fills the viewfinder of your telephoto lens. Resist the temptation. It is extremely unsafe for you, and besides, the more unfortunate incidents there are, the more likely it is that the authorities will draw up stringent regulations to control visitors to the wild areas. This will only end up curbing *your* freedom, which is one of the special features of a visit to the wildlife areas of Botswana.

When driving

Keep a respectful distance from wild animals. We humans do not relish invasion of our personal space. Wild animals feel particularly uncomfortable about close contact with humans and vehicles.

If you do find yourself close to animals, do some anticipatory planning and work out an escape route in case of need.

Be extremely wary of animals with young.

Do not move any distance from your vehicle unless you are accompanied by a guide who knows the area.

When camping

Never feed wild animals, although you may be tempted to do so. Resist the temptation by remembering that when you feed a wild animal you are probably signing its death warrant. One of Savute's inhabitants was a young elephant bull. He was an affable elephant who early on discovered that one of the delights of being around tourists was receiving handouts of food. Oranges, particularly, were an ecstatic and addictive new experience.

With his very fine sense of smell he found that he could track down oranges in tents and vehicles and he started helping himself. Sometimes helping himself required flattening a tent or breaking into a vehicle and the fact that humans were around was no deterrent.

Needless to say this behaviour brought a flood of complaints to the parks department and the elephant was eventually shot as a nuisance animal. Many would say that the wrong animal got the bullet.

Where there are game animals, *sleep in a tent or vehicle* but never in the open. Use a tent with a built-in flysheet that closes firmly so that no part of your body sticks out.

Carry all your rubbish out of the parks. After all, you managed to carry it all in with you. I know this can be difficult and that bags break. Double-bag it and leave it where there is an obviously working removal system in a town or at some park gates. But don't bury it. Unless you dig a monumental pit, it will be dug up and scattered. Many campers make a great effort to ensure that no rubbish is left lying around, sometimes burying it, leaving an immaculate campsite behind. They no doubt feel very self-righteous in leaving the place in a far better condition than their predecessors. However, it doesn't take too long before the monkeys, baboons and hyenas systematically go through the burial heap and unearth all the rubbish.

Don't camp in a hippo track. Watch out for game tracks and respect other creatures' right of way. This also applies to places like bridges. One party decided to sleep on the wooden bridge at Third Bridge because they had heard that the lion used it to cross the river and they were keen to see lion. They did! They also found out how difficult it was to move in a sleeping bag and to try to get six people through two Land Rover doors in a hurry. They were lucky — the lions were not hungry and did not panic and strike out.

Beware of crocodiles. When you are hot and dusty and arrive at great pools of water there is a temptation to plunge in. The Okavango has a very healthy crocodile population that includes some very large beasts. Many stretches of water will have a resident crocodile. They move very quietly and incredibly swiftly.

One unfortunate incident is recorded where a girl bathing at the edge of a pool was taken by a crocodile. The rest of the party heard a scream, ran to the water and found a cake of soap and a swirl of muddy water. The girl's body was never found.

Bathe only after you have had a thorough look around the area. Look for eyes and nostrils protruding just above the water and check along the nearby banks. Bathe with somebody keeping watch. Again the basic principle is, don't be afraid but do be aware that you are in wild Africa.

BUSH DRIVING

Driving in the bush is one of those things that is 'easy when you know how'. People's responses to driving in the bush for the first time seem to be one of two extremes: either it is seen as a 'piece of cake', no different from any other driving, or they become over-anxious, as if they are about to plunge into the maw of the unknown. This over-anxiousness seems inevitably to set up a self-fulfilling prophecy and something usually does go awry.

Gears

The first rule is to anticipate the hazards ahead. You will soon learn to recognise those dry sandy patches. Slow down and change into the gear in which you can negotiate the sticky patch *before* you reach it. Once you are in it, keep up your revs. If you have a rev-counter, you should not allow the engine to drop below 1 000 rpm. If this does happen, change down as quickly and smoothly as you can. Beware of 'snatching', i.e. accelerating too quickly, because this can shear a half-shaft or cause a wheel to spin and dig in. You need to find the balance between swiftness and smoothness.

Sand and mud

As most of Botswana is rather like a vast beach hundreds of metres deep, your biggest challenge is likely to be sand driving. However, the tips on sand driving apply equally to mud driving. Beware the 'black cotton' muds that occur in some areas. If it has rained and you see an area of very black surface ahead of you, take special care. The mud that forms in the black soils is sticky and tenacious and will thoroughly bog you down. Travel with a high-lift jack; they save a lot of time and effort if you do get stuck.

A general rule is to have hard tyres in wet mud — the idea being that they will 'cut down' through the soft material to a harder surface beneath — and over soft sand or a surface like a beach or Makgadikgadi, have soft tyres that will spread the load. Despite this advice, many people have very hard tyres in sandy country, hoping to reduce the number of punctures they get. My experience is that the sensible compromise works: soft tyres on deep sandy roads, hard tyres when there is no road and you're blazing a path through the bush.

Once stuck in sand, as in mud, lift the wheel(s) clear, place sticks and branches under it (watching for sharp pieces that might go straight through the tyre, adding to your problems!). Clear sand or mud away from the sides (in and out) of each wheel. It all adds to the burden if you leave it there.

When stuck down to the chassis, a good trick is to lift the whole of the back of the vehicle (a big advantage of a high-lift jack) and push sideways so that it slips off the jack and falls into a new set of tracks. Doing this alternatively front and back allows you to 'crab walk' in a chosen direction. Be very careful, though, because high-lifts are extremely dangerous. Make sure everybody is clear of the vehicle, especially children and dogs.

Sometimes you miss a gear change in really soft sand and have to do a standing start. This usually happens in low-ratio country so things will already be pretty bad. The trick when starting is to reverse a metre or two. This gives you enough run to keep moving. If you start out forward straight away you can dig yourself in and make matters worse.

Much of Botswana is blessed (or cursed) with challenges called sand ridges, part of the old lake shoreline, or relicts of an ancient desert. The sand is particularly tenacious and more than one party has turned back because of the ridges. Understanding the characteristics of sand will help you cope with this problem. As the temperature rises the tiny pockets of air between the particles of sand expand. When a heavy wheel drives over it there is a large volume of air to displace and the vehicle sinks in deep. In contrast, when it is cooler there is a smaller volume of air to displace, the sand is more compact and will support a greater weight. If you can do your sand ridge driving, therefore, in the cool of the morning, you will have fewer problems than in the heat of the day. The sand is also much more compact when wet, i.e. after rain.

Before you set off on your journey do make sure that you know your vehicle, especially if you are hiring or borrowing one. Do you know that free-wheeling hubs have to be engaged by hand before your four-by-four works? Have you made sure that a high-lift jack can be used on your vehicle? The lifting shaft must be clear, so it's usually placed under the bush-bars front or back. If you have no bars or equivalent, then you can't use the jack!

Makgadikgadi

Having been stuck here more times than I want to remember I consider myself an expert on getting out of the pans. Here's what I do.

Be very cautious if you drive across the surface of the pans in the Makgadikgadi. It generally looks like a caked grey, cold gravy, which may seem ideal for high-speed driving. Unfortunately, under the surface it is not all the same and without any warning you can find yourself axle-deep in cloying mud.

Never drive on Makgadikgadi without the 'hubs in'. Be ready to engage four-wheel drive at the slightest provocation. Be very wary of driving off into the blue across the open pan where there are no tracks. Stay on existing tracks or, if you do move away, stay close to shorelines. Keep your speed up (80 km/h or more). If you feel the surface give, or mud starts flying up from the wheels, *do not brake*. If the condition continues curve gently away towards the nearest shore. *Do not swerve suddenly.*

If you do go in and you have lots of friends and vehicles with you but no winch then:

Step one. When you feel yourself going and you know you've had it, let the vehicle come to a stop on its own. *Do not brake* and do not try to drive out.

Step two. With a friend at each wheel pushing, but, more importantly watching to report on which wheel spins, try gently pushing and driving out. Instantly stop if a wheel spins; you will only dig yourself further in.

Step three. Reduce tyre pressure to between 1,0 and 0,8 bars and repeat step two. Keep them this soft while you stay on the pan. Note: put the valve caps back. The valves will fill with mud if you don't and you'll have a major problem re-inflating the tyres. If this strategy does not work up to this point, you've now got to roll up your sleeves and do this thing seriously!

Step four. Remove all weight from the vehicle and repeat step three.

Step five. High-lift jack (if you haven't already used it).

Presuming that you have a winch, the problem here is that you probably have nothing to attach it to. Take the spare wheel off and dig a trench the exact width and depth of the wheel, at right angles to the front of your vehicle and within easy reach of the winch cable. Attach the cable to the wheel and sink the wheel deeply into the trench you have dug for it. This will give you something firm to pull against.

Wheel balance

Once, after completing the Hunter's Road in appalling conditions, I found my truck wobbling and shaking all over the tar. In fact, it was barely driveable at normal speeds. The problem? Mud sticking to the prop-shaft and wheel rims. When the mud is distributed unevenly and is hard and dry (as it had become after several hot and sunny days) it completely upsets the balance on wheels and rotating shafts. This causes a most uncomfortable drive and, more particularly, unnecessary wear on bearings. Stop and carefully dig off all the dried mud from both the outside and inside of the wheels, etc.

Steering

There is a tendency to 'fight' your steering wheel, trying to make it go where you think it should. If you are in an existing track the vehicle will more or less steer itself so all you need to do is keep your hands lightly on the wheel. One of the hardest lessons to learn is that in sand a vehicle's wheels behave quite differently from the way they do on tar roads. When it feels as though you have hauled and twisted the steering wheel so that the wheels must be pulled right round, stick your head out of the window and have a look. The chances are they are not even straight yet, never mind slewed around! It is worth the effort to find some 'tame' sand' in which to practise. (Sand is 'tame' when there is someone around to help you if you get stuck!)

Tyre pressure

If you find your vehicle getting stuck in sand you can try dropping your tyre pressure. It will depend on the load you are carrying and the nature of the vehicle, but you should aim for something in the region of 1,0 bar. This advice may also apply when you are in mud, depending on how deep it is. Within reason, the softer the tyre the better the traction as the tyre spreads, giving you a bigger 'footprint'. At low speeds this will not significantly shorten tyre life. Remember, however, that the likelihood of a puncture is increased and the clearance of the vehicle is lowered. This can be a problem if there is a high ridge down the middle of the track.

Radiators and grass seeds

If you are driving through grass, check your radiator and keep a close watch on your temperature gauge. If the needle starts to move up, stop and check the state of the radiator. Often in grass or on tracks with a grassed centre, the passage of the vehicle breaks off the seed heads. These penetrate the very fine air gaps that pass through your radiator. As they accumulate, the seeds insulate the radiator, preventing the air from flowing through and the heat from dispersing. You will have to remove as much of the seed material as possible and stop until the engine has cooled down somewhat. Whatever you do, do not open the radiator when it is very hot; always let it cool down first. Modern radiators are pressurised and the sudden drop in pressure means a rapid rise in engine temperature which can damage the engine! You also run the risk of a spurt of scalding steam which can injure you. If the radiator is seriously clogged, remove it (after draining and retaining the water) and clean each air space, one at a time, with stems of dry grass before replacing.

You can help reduce this problem by fitting a fine gauze screen of some sort in front of the radiator to prevent seeds from getting stuck.

A radiator is a surprisingly sophisticated piece of equipment and once every 100 000 km or so you should get an expert to check that it is in good order.

Exhausts

Over the years I have been collecting photographs of burnt-out vehicles in the Kalahari. Without putting too much effort into it, I think I have seen eight. In almost all cases the fire starts because of a thoughtless design fault; dry grass collects underneath the vehicle close to a hot exhaust. If you are driving long distances off-road or through thick grass you must stop and check thoroughly under the vehicle. Find out where grass collects, and remove it regularly.

Driving through water

Before proceeding through a patch of water, stop and examine it carefully. Walk through it to get some idea of its depth and the nature of the bottom. If it is even slightly risky, get into lowest-range low gear, even if you don't think it necessary. It's a bit late to try to change down when you're sinking, so rather go in slowly, steadily and over-powered, than fast and under-powered. Try to avoid submerging the exhaust. A slow passage creates less turbulence and less chance of getting electrics wet.

To avoid excessive wetting of the engine in the Okavango Delta many experts stop and remove the fan belt when faced with a long water crossing. This dramatically reduces the spray inside the engine compartment.

Gravel roads

Botswana has an active programme of upgrading main roads but there are still significant stretches of gravel along the main routes. If there is oncoming traffic you will find yourself enveloped in thick, blinding dust and this is very dangerous. There have been a number of horrific and fatal accidents on untarred main roads. These can be avoided with thought, anticipation and care. When you first see the oncoming vehicle, scan the rest of the road between you for other vehicles, pedestrians and the ubiquitous livestock. Switch on your lights so that you will be visible to any following oncoming vehicles, and slow down. Stop if you have any doubts about having a clear road ahead.

Despite the frustration of being behind a heavy truck and its billowing clouds of dust, be very cautious in trying to overtake. Rather pull over, have a cup of tea and let the vehicle ahead pull away. After all, you are on holiday and you can afford to relax rather than risk an accident.

8. NATIONAL PARKS, RESERVES AND WHERE TO STAY IN BOTSWANA

With the growth of the tourist industry and the general development of the country there is an increasing range of places to stay in Botswana. There are still some notable gaps, however. For example, no youth hostel facilities exist anywhere.

This section is divided into five categories — National parks and reserves, Small reserves, Private camping grounds, Hotels, and Lodges. Hotels in the main centres of Gaborone, Francistown, Lobatse and Selebi-Phikwe are used mainly by business people and government officials. Tourism is at present largely focused on the wildlife areas to the north, where tourist accommodation is mostly in lodges and at campsites.

These lodges are all very different in terms of ambience and personality, and are one of the delights of touring Botswana. In the descriptions of the individual establishments an attempt has been made to give some indication of the unique character of each.

NATIONAL PARKS AND RESERVES

Botswana is doing much to upgrade its national parks and reserves and to manage these protected areas in an ecologically sound manner. In an attempt to prevent overcrowding in the parks a booking system was introduced in 1995, and new facilities are being added constantly.

Reservations, park entry fees and regulations

National parks and game reserves in Botswana are open throughout the year. Altogether some 17 per cent of Botswana is devoted exclusively to wildlife reserves, apportioned as follows:

Four national parks: Chobe National Park, Nxai Pan National Park, Makgadikgadi National Park and the Kalahari Gemsbok National Park (which now incorporates Mabuasehube Game Reserve).

One wildlife reserve: Moremi Wildlife Reserve.

Five game reserves: Central Kalahari Game Reserve, Kutse Game Reserve, Mannyelanong Game Reserve, Gaborone Game Reserve and Maun Game Reserve.

At present bookings are required for the camping sites in Chobe National Park, Moremi Wildlife Reserve, Makgadikgadi National Park and Nxai Pan National Park. It is intended to include the central and southern parks and reserves in the booking system, but at the time of writing no advance reservations were required for these areas.

Public camping grounds in the parks are divided into individual campsites, each of which is designed to accommodate a maximum of six people. Groups of more than six people are required to book additional sites.

Most public camping grounds are serviced by ablution blocks with flush toilets, showers and handbasins, whilst many individual camping sites have concrete table/bench units and braai/barbecue stands. Water standpipes and litter bins are provided within the camping ground.

Although shower and toilet facilities are provided in many parks, water is frequently a problem. Supplies may be temporarily suspended for one of many reasons, including drought and the activities of game, especially elephant.

It is essential that advance reservations be made for campsites because if the camping grounds are full, any camper arriving without a prior reservation will only be allowed access into the park for the day.

Booking applications and enquiries should be made to:
Parks and Reserves Reservation Office
P O Box 20364
Boseja
Maun
(Tel 66 1265, Fax 66 1264)

The reservation office is located near the police station in Maun and is clearly signposted. It is open every day of the week throughout the year, including public holidays, from 7.30 am to 4.30 pm.

Reservations may be made up to 12 months in advance personally or by telephone, fax, telegram or letter. The information required when making a booking is:

Name of the park or reserve
Name of the public camping ground
Date of arrival and departure
Total number of persons and whether they are Botswana citizens, residents or non-residents.

After you have made a reservation a provisional booking form will be sent to you by the reservations office. Full camping fees are payable in advance, and the amount and date due will appear on the form. The payment date will usually be between two to four weeks from making the reservation, depending on where you live and how soon the reservation is. Entry fees are payable at the gate of the park or reserve.

All payments must be in Botswana Pula. Payments made to the reservations office may be submitted in one of the following ways:

Bank certified personal cheques

Postal orders or money orders, crossed a/c payee only

Bank drafts

Cash — only when the payment is made personally at the reservations office

Payments made at park or reserve entrance gates must be in cash.

When pre-payment for a reservation is received, an official receipt and confirmation form will be issued. It is essential to safeguard this as visitors will not be allowed to occupy the campsite without presenting the confirmation form at the park or reserve entrance gate. A second copy of the confirmation form, marked 'station copy', will also be issued. This must be presented at the entrance gate and will be retained by the gate attendant. Campsite reservations not taken up by 5.30 pm will be subject to re-letting and pre-payments will be forfeited.

Gate times at parks and reserves:

06.00-18.00 from March to September

05.30-19.30 from October to February

The reference number that appears in the top right-hand corner of the provisional booking/confirmation form must be quoted in any further business connected with that reservation.

Requests for alterations to your original booking should be made in writing or by visiting the reservations office personally. The alteration must be initialled to avoid any dispute at a later stage. Should there be an increase in the number of persons or length of stay, the difference can be paid on arrival at the park or reserve.

Refunds of pre-payments will only be made if notice of the cancellation is received in writing more than 30 days before the date of the reservation. Any applications for refund should be accompanied by the original receipt. If you wish to transfer your booking, then you must cancel your original booking and re-book, and the pre-payment can then be transferred to the new booking. This transfer of pre-payment may only be done once.

The schedule of fees that follows applied in 1995, but fees are subject to alteration without notice.

Entry fees in Pula/day:

Private parties	Citizens	Residents	Non-residents
Over 16 years	2,00	10,00	50,00
8-15 years	1,00	5,00	25,00
7 years and below	Free	Free	Free

Licensed, Botswana-based tour operators, established hotels and lodges			
Over 16 years	2,00	10,00	30,00
8-15 years	1,00	2,00	5,00
7 years and below	Free	Free	Free

Camping fees in Pula/night:

Private parties	Citizens	Residents	Non-residents
Over 16 years	5,00	10,00	20,00
8-15 years	1,00	2,00	10,00
7 years and below	Free	Free	Free

Licensed, Botswana-based tour operators, established hotels and lodges			
Over 16 years	1,00	5,00	10,00
8-15 years	0,50	2,00	5,00
7 years and below	Free	Free	Free

Vehicle entrance fee in Pula/day:

Botswana-registered	2,00
Foreign-registered	10,00
Registered operator's vehicle (per annum)	500,00
Excess weight fee for each 450 kg over 3 500 kg unladen	250,00

Fishing permit in Pula/day:

Citizens	Residents	Non-residents
1,00	5,00	10,00

Boat entrance fee in Pula/day:

All boats	5,00
Operators' boats (per annum)	150,00
Canoe/dugout	Free

Aircraft entrance fee in Pula/day:

Botswana-registered	2,00
Foreign-registered	10,00

CAMPSITES IN NATIONAL PARKS

Note: In all national parks and reserves collect and carry in your own firewood from outside the area. Wood will either be non-existent or exceedingly scarce, and very expensive when available.

Chobe National Park

Chobe has five designated camping areas.

Savute

The public camping ground at Savute is presently closed for refurbishment. The ablution blocks were in serious need of repair as they had been virtually destroyed by elephant desperately trying to get water. In the 1970s Savute Channel was a place of hippos and water. Since the 1980s, however, it has been totally dry.

A temporary campground has been created close to the original site. The only facilities it offers is water standpipes covered by rock and cement structures in an attempt to keep them elephant-proof, and 'long-drop' toilets enclosed by reed walls. It is hoped that the camping ground will be re-opened towards the end of 1996. Permanent water points have been established away from the campsite for the elephants.

Savute is still a fine place to see game of all kinds, which is part of the reason for its popularity.

Take care not to keep fruit, especially oranges, in your tent or vehicle as this can focus the unwanted attention of elephant on you.

Linyanti

Linyanti camping ground is on the banks of the Linyanti River and overlooks the Caprivi Strip. Although it does have shower and toilet facilities, the same provisos apply here as for all the other camps — don't count on them being operational.

Linyanti is a little off the beaten track and consequently appeals to those who prefer their wilderness to be more private.

Nogatsha and Tjinga

At present there are no ablution facilities at either Nogatsha or Tjinga, but temporary camping grounds established at both sites in 1996 will be upgraded to standard permanent camping grounds. There is usually water available at both these sites.

Serondela

Serondela is on the itinerary of every four-wheel-drive vehicle and every two-wheel-drive vehicle that passes through the area. So you will have to accept that if you are there in high season you will have many neighbours.

There are toilets and showers here which usually work. Watch out for the monkeys and the baboons, which have become increasingly bold and destructive.

Note that this camp will be closed shortly. It is being moved to Ihaha, on the Chobe River about 15 km further west. This move should significantly reduce the present overcrowding at the east end of the park.

Moremi Wildlife Reserve

There are four camping grounds in this reserve.

South Gate

This campsite, set among mopane trees, is just outside the reserve and is generally only used by people who arrive after the gate closes. Although there are toilets, there is no guarantee that the pump will be working. Showers are available.

Third Bridge

This is probably the most popular campsite in Moremi. Water, showers and toilets are available.

Xakanaxa

Showers, toilets and water are available. A number of safari operators have camps here and you may be able to hire a boat from the operators.

North Gate

This campsite lies just within the reserve and has shower and toilet facilities, as well as an ample supply of water under normal conditions.

Nxai Pan National Park

A good time to visit this park is during June and July, which is the springbok mating season, or during the wet season when there are a lot of zebra and gemsbok. Kori bustard are plentiful all year round.

The water at Nxai Pan is potable, but it is still a good idea to travel with extra water. It is necessary to have four-wheel-drive to get to Nxai Pan and to get around the park in the wet season.

This park has three camping grounds.

North Camp

This camp is situated on the northern edge of the pan and has ablution facilities, as well as water standpipes. It is set amongst mopane trees but there is little shade so it can become very hot.

South Camp

This camp is situated on the southern edge of the pan. The camp has four sites set among purple-pod *Terminalia*, which provide plenty of shade. There are ablution facilities, water standpipes and picnic tables.

Baines' Baobabs

An informal camping ground exists at Baines' Baobabs. There is no water here.

Makgadikgadi Game Reserve

This reserve is set in beautiful countryside and should be enjoyed for that. The animals are very skittish and hard to find as there has been a lot of poaching on the outskirts of the park. The poaching is difficult to control as the park is surrounded by cattle posts. It is also difficult, with the limited number of game guards stationed here, to keep out the donkeys and goats which wander into the park.

In the wet season large herds of zebra can be found in the eastern part of the reserve. It is also a good place to see raptors.

It is advisable to take drinking water as the water here is very salty and quite sulphurous.

There are two camping grounds in the reserve.

Xhumaga

This camp is set on the Boteti River in a large sandy area beneath beautiful, mature *Acacia erioloba* trees. There are four sites here with toilets, showers and water. The river does not always have water in it, so check first if you are set on a water camp.

Njuca Hills

Views from this immense fossil dune are stunning. This camp has no water. There are two campsites with pit latrines.

Kutse Game Reserve

Some 25 numbered campsites have been established at Kutse. These have been located around various pans. Some of them have pit latrines but others have no facilities at all, so it is essential to carry all your own water. Camping is not allowed outside designated camping areas. A visitors' map is available at the gate which indicates the various campsites.

Central Kalahari Game Reserve

Although visitors are permitted in this reserve there are, as yet, no facilities available. There is, however, plenty of space!

Kalahari Gemsbok National Park

The South African National Parks Board provides the facilities in this park. There are three lodges, each with camping facilities of the highest standards. Entry to this park is through South Africa or Botswana.

Although Mabuasehube Game Reserve has been incorporated into this park, access to it is still through Botswana. No facilities exist in Mabuasehube and it is advisable to take your own water.

Mannyelanong Game Reserve

This reserve, created solely to protect a vulture nesting colony, has no facilities. It is a few kilometres outside the village of Otse, some 50 km south of Gaborone.

Entrance is free but you are requested to stop at the game scout camp and register when entering. Access to this park is allowed only during September and October and from the end of February to mid-April so as not to disturb the breeding birds.

The game reserve includes much of the mountain on which the colony is situated as well as a fenced area which demarcates the actual nesting site. The fenced area is strictly out of bounds. Even approaching it noisily or in haste can disturb the nesting birds and this is detrimental to their proper conservation. A handy rule of thumb: if the birds take flight as you approach, you've upset them. Be more cautious.

Gaborone Game Reserve

This reserve opened in 1988 on the initiative of the Kalahari Conservation Society and the Department of Wildlife and National Parks. Created mainly for educational purposes, it consists of 5 km² of varied habitat on the edge of the Ngotwane River in Gaborone. Fees of P1,00 per person and P2,00 per car, plus 50 thebe per person for picnics, make it an inexpensive outing.

Despite its tiny size, this remarkable reserve is one of the most visited protected areas in Botswana.

Within the reserve will be found a wide range of mammals including white rhino, kudu, eland, wildebeest, impala, gemsbok and zebra. The rhino are kept in a separate area with strengthened fencing, although much of the other game is able to move freely between this area and the rest of the park.

There is a good network of roads, two picnic sites with toilets, water and braai sites, a visitors' information centre with a mini museum, and a game-viewing hide overlooking a permanent artificial waterhole. A bird hide should be completed in 1996 in the marsh area of the park. Viewing is best in the early morning and is also quite good in the evenings. The reserve is open from 6.30 am to 6.30 pm every day.

Maun Game Reserve

This small reserve, 3 km² in extent, is situated on the banks of the Thamalakane River opposite Riley's Hotel. The aim of the park is to provide wildlife education facilities. Entrance is free and visitors may walk around the park, where it is possible to see a variety of antelope. A visitors' centre is being erected.

Francistown Game Reserve

Land has been allocated on the Shashe River to develop an educational park which will be developed in the near future.

SMALL AND/OR PRIVATE RESERVES
Khama Rhino Sanctuary
The Khama Rhino Sanctuary Trust, P O Box 10, Serowe.
Tel 43 0713/43 0420/43 0520.

The Khama Rhino Sanctuary lies 30 km north of Serowe on the Orapa road in the central district of Botswana. A community trust established in 1992, the sanctuary is dedicated to the safeguarding and breeding of Botswana's last rhinos, which were in danger of being poached out. It is situated on 4 400 ha of Kalahari sandveld with the Serowe Pan, a large calcrete depression, in the centre of the reserve.

At the time of writing the entry fee was P10 per vehicle plus an additional P2,50 per person. Children under 18 are free. There is a charge of P20 per vehicle for camping.

This reserve not only has the largest breeding herd of rhino in Botswana, it is also home to a diverse range of antelope and smaller mammals such as bat-eared foxes. Leopard tracks have been seen. There is abundant birdlife with a large variety of raptors.

The sanctuary is still being developed but is open to visitors. Campsites with ablution facilities are available and self-catering chalets are being built. The campsites and the chalets are situated in stands of mongongo trees (*Phytodendron rautanenii*), which provide each site with privacy.

As some of the areas in the park have deep sand it is advisable to use four-wheel-drive vehicles when driving around the sanctuary. If you do not have such a vehicle, it is possible to go on organised game drives.

Mokolodi Nature Reserve
P O Box 170, Gaborone. Tel 35 3959. Fax 31 3973.
Restaurant bookings: Tel 32 8692. Fax 32 8568.

Accommodation	Facilities	Activities
Chalets	Restaurant	Game drives
Dormitory	Licensed	Game walks
Booking essential	Education centre	Elephant walks
	Conference facilities	Rhino walks
	Curio shop	

The reserve opened its gates in 1994. It was established by the Mokolodi Wildlife Foundation, which aims to further environmental education and to conserve the flora and fauna of south-eastern Botswana.

Mokolodi is 15 km south of Gaborone on the Lobatse road. Animals you may see there include white rhino, giraffe, warthogs and zebra. There are also four young African elephants that have been trained by mahouts from Sri Lanka. You may, at quite a price, arrange to go on an elephant walk in the park with these elephants or with the rhino.

Accommodation is available in five thatched en-suite chalets set among rocky outcrops overlooking a waterhole. Each chalet has a small fridge, a gas stove and an outside braai area. Dormitory accommodation is also available for backpackers, at a very good rate.

An entry fee is charged per person and for the vehicle, unless you are only going to the restaurant. The gate opens at 7.00 am and closes at 6.00 pm. Only those going to the restaurant may enter after 6.00 pm. The restaurant closes at 6.00 pm on Sundays and does not open on Mondays.

Nata Sanctuary

See Route 12: Sowa Pan on page 69.

PRIVATE CAMPING GROUNDS

Francistown

The Marang (see Lodges, p. 146)

Gaborone

St Clair Lion Park
Tariff: Budget
P O Box 238, Gaborone. Tel & Fax: 37 2711.

The Lion Park lies about 20 km south of Gaborone on the road to Lobatse in a large tract of private land. It provides facilities for camping and caravans with communal ablution blocks, braai stands and electricity points. Kennelling facilities are also available. There is a restaurant and bar which opens at 5.00 pm on weekdays but operates all day during the weekend. It is not usually necessary to book. There is a gate fee.

The Lion Park has other attractions too. As the name suggests there are lions, albeit in enclosures. The 4x4 Club holds four-wheel-drive challenges on specially laid out courses. Picnic spots are available. The Lion Park Equestrian Club will also provide horses and lead game rides through the adjacent Mokolodi Nature Reserve or, if you prefer, you can organise a game drive within the confines of the extensive Lion Park itself.

Gweta

Gweta Rest Camp (see Lodges, p. 146)

Kasane

Chobe Safari Lodge (see Lodges, p. 149)
Kubu Lodge (see Lodges, p. 150)
Buffalo Ridge Campsites
Tariff: Budget
P O Box 55, Kasane. Tel 65 0430. Fax 65 0223.

This new camping ground at Ngoma is set up on the ridge overlooking the Chobe River. This camping ground is ideal for those who arrive after the gate to the Chobe National Park has closed for the night, or who are waiting to cross over into the Caprivi.

There are ablution facilities and each campsite has a tap. It is possible to purchase bags of very good firewood at the gate.

Maun

Audi Camp (see Lodges, p. 153)
Crocodile Camp Safaris (see Lodges, p. 154)
Island Safari Lodge (see Lodges, p. 154)
Sedia Hotel (see Lodges, p. 155)
Sitatunga Safaris (see p. 156)

Moremi & Central Delta

Gunn's Camp (see Lodges, p. 160)
Oddballs (see Lodges, p. 163)

Nata

Nata Lodge (see Lodges, p. 170)
Nata Sanctuary (see Places to visit — Sowa Pan, p. 36)

Western Delta

Fish Eagle Lodge/Drotsky's Cabins (see Lodges, p. 180)
Guma Lagoon Camp (see Lodges, p. 181)
Shakawe Fishing Camp (see Lodges, p. 183)

HOTELS

Botswana has no grading system for hotels. Price can be used as an indicator of the quality of the hotel. Many of the hotels are owned by the Botswana-based Cresta group and are all of a good standard. Some of the Cresta hotels have recently become affiliated to the Best Western international hotel franchise. The following is a list of hotels and their addresses.

Cresta Central Reservations:
Botswana: Tel 31 2431. Fax 37 5376. Telex 2434 BD
Zimbabwe: Tel 70 3131. Fax 79 4655. Telex 26679 ZW
South Africa: Tel (27) (012) 341 4440. Fax 341 4449.

Francistown

Best Western Thapama Hotel & Casino
Private Bag 31, Francistown. Tel 21 3872. Fax 21 3766.

The Marang Hotel (see Lodges, p. 146)

Tati Hotel
P O Box 15, Francistown. Tel 21 2255. Fax 21 5079.

Grand Hotel
P O Box 30, Francistown. Tel 21 2300. Fax 21 2309.

Gaborone

Best Western President Hotel
P O Box 200, Gaborone. Tel 35 3631. Fax 35 1840.

Cresta Lodge
Private Bag 00126, Gaborone. Tel 37 5375. Fax 37 5376.

Gaborone Travel Inn
Private Bag 00127, Gaborone. Tel 32 2777. Fax 32 2727.

Gaborone Sun
Private Bag 0016, Gaborone. Tel & Fax 35 1111.

Oasis Motel
P O Box 30331, Gaborone. Tel 35 6396. Fax 31 2968.

Morning Star Motel
Box 177, Gaborone. Tel 32 8301.

Grand Palm Hotel & Casino
P O Box 2025, Gaborone. Tel 31 2999. Fax 31 2989.

Ghanzi

Kalahari Arms
P O Box 29, Ghanzi. Tel 59 6311.

Lobatse

Cumberland Hotel
P O Box 135, Lobatse. Tel 33 0281. Fax 33 2106.

Mahalapye

Mahalapye Hotel
P O Box 526, Mahalapye. Tel 41 0200.

Maun (see Lodges, pp. 153-156)

Palapye

Botsalo Travel Inn
Tel 42 0245. Fax 42 0587.

Selebi-Phikwe

Best Western Bosele Hotel
P O Box 177, Selebi-Phikwe. Tel 81 0675. Fax 81 1083.
Syringa Lodge
P O Box 254, Selebi-Phikwe. Tel 81 0444/019. Fax 81 0450.

Serowe

Serowe Hotel
P O Box 150, Serowe. Tel 43 0234.

LODGES

The tourist industry in Botswana is in a state of flux with much development and many changes being made. New lodges are always opening, while old ones sometimes close down. The lodges that have been included in this guide may, however, be relied on for their consistent hospitality and service.

Staying in a lodge is not the same as staying in a five-star establishment; a lodge will not offer the predictable sameness of hotel chains that

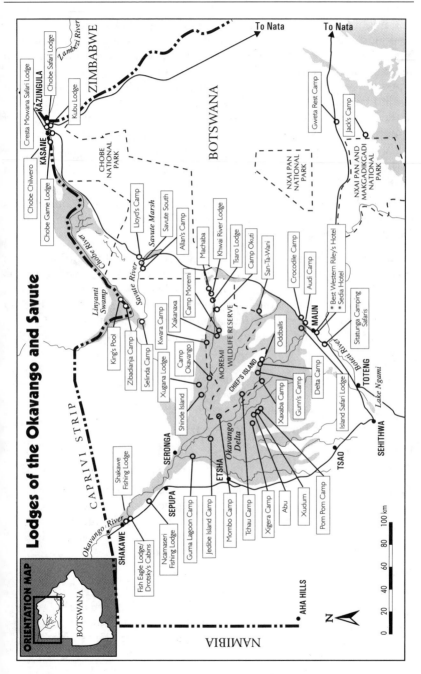

Lodges of the Okavango and Savute

you might find anywhere else in the world. Each lodge has its own character and this is especially true of those which are individually owned. You may well enjoy five-star service, but it will be very different from that laid down in the list of requirements for a grading system.

As you read through the descriptions of the lodges in this section you should be able to develop a feel for what to expect. This section is intended to help you choose where to stay and how to construct the kind of holiday that will suit both your interests and your pocket.

The lodges are grouped by area and the areas are arranged in alphabetical order. At the beginning of each section there is a brief description of the area.

Heading each lodge description is a summary; this is for quick reference to determine the type of accommodation offered, the tariff level, facilities and activities.

Parking: A perpetual — and so far unresolved — problem for motorists driving to Maun and flying on to one of the many camps and lodges is where to park safely. If you are lucky the booking agency may let you park 'in the yard round the back'. But such yards are usually of limited size. There is the airport, but that is probably not the safest place to leave your car. Hotels and the larger safari camps in Maun are the solution most resort to.

List of lodges in Botswana (by area)

Francistown	The Marang
Gweta	Gweta Rest Camp
Kasane	Chobe Chilwero
	Chobe Game Lodge
	Chobe Safari Lodge
	Cresta Mowana Safari Lodge
	Kubu Lodge
Makgadikgadi	Jack's Camp
Maun	Audi Camp
	Crocodile Camp Safaris
	Island Safari Lodge
	Best Western Riley's Hotel

	Sedia Hotel
	Sitatunga Camping Safaris
Moremi & Central Delta	Abu Camp
	Camp Moremi
	Camp Okavango
	Camp Okuti
	Delta Camp
	Gunn's Camp
	Khwai River Lodge
	Kwara Camp
	Machaba
	Mombo Camp
	Oddballs
	Pom Pom Camp
	San-ta-wani
	Shinde Island
	Tchau Camp
	Tsaro Lodge
	Xakanaxa
	Xaxaba Camp
	Xudum
	Xigera Camp
	Xugana Lodge
Nata	Nata Lodge
Savute	Allan's Camp
	Lloyd's Camp
	Savute South
	King's Pool
	Selinda Camp
	Zibadianja Camp
Tuli	Jwala Game Lodge
	Mashatu Game Reserve
	Stevensford Game Reserve
	Tuli Lodge
Western Delta	Fish Eagle Lodge/Drotsky's Cabins
	Guma Lagoon Camp
	Jedibe Island Camp
	Ncamaseri Lodge
	Shakawe Fishing Lodge

Francistown area

This is not usually a major port of call for tourists. It is one of the olde
towns in the country and is the hub of economic activity in the area. It
has good road and rail links to major sources of supply so, from the
visitor's point of view, it is a good place to pick up motor spares and
basic necessities.

THE MARANG Tariff: Budget (camping) Medium (hotel)
P O Box 807, Francistown. Tel 21 3991/2/3. Fax 1 2130. Telex 2264 BD

Accommodation	*Facilities*	*Activities/attractions*
Hotel with rooms	Licensed	Birdlife
Chalets	Restaurant	Walks
Camping	Swimming pool	
Booking advisable	Telephone	
	Telex	
	Conference facilities	
	Packed lunches	
	Tourist advice and maps	
	Satellite TV	
	Shop	

The Marang, whose name means 'the place of sunbeams', is situated
just outside Francistown on the banks of the Tati River. Huge acacia trees
lush green lawns, thatched roofs and genuine comfort all make the
Marang an outstanding hotel.

Choose from wood and thatch chalets by the river bank, or air-condi
tioned rooms. Whichever you decide on, you will enjoy the beauty and
tranquillity this hotel offers.

The atmosphere is relaxed and friendly and, like many guests before
you, you will leave intending to return again.

The Marang also has a beautiful, shady campsite with hot water and
clean ablution blocks. There is a terrace and an à la carte restaurant, a
swimming pool, conference room and a most attractive bar constructed
out of kiaat wood from Nata.

The Marang has become 'the place' to stop over on the long road to
the Okavango and Chobe.

Gweta area

Gweta is a small village, just off the main tourist route.

GWETA REST CAMP Tariff: Medium
P O Box 124, Gweta. Tel 61 2220. Fax 66 0493. Telex 2487 BD

Accommodation	Facilities	Activities/attractions
Rondavels	Licensed	Pan excursions
Camping	Restaurant	
	Bottlestore	
	Curios	
	Swimming pool	

Gweta lies just off the main road from Francistown to Maun, some 99 km west of Nata. The rest camp is well signposted. Gweta, an appealing village, is set among tall palm trees and is the gateway to the Makgadikgadi Pans and game reserve.

The rest camp offers accommodation in thatched rondavels or provides camping facilities. There is an open-air restaurant and bar under hatch.

Game drives into the Makgadikgadi Pans and game reserve can be organised, as well as trips on four-wheeler motorbikes.

Kasane area

Kasane is currently experiencing considerable growth and development. Tourism is certainly one of the driving forces, and the tar road from Nata has made the area much more accessible.

There is an ever-growing range of food and liquor available here. You can buy diesel and petrol and some repairs can be undertaken at Chobe Engineering, which is a few kilometres out of town on the Kazungula road.

CHOBE CHILWERO Tariff: High

Linyanti Explorations, P O Box 22, Kasane. Tel Kasane 65 0505. Fax 65 0352. Telex 2901 BD or Okavango Explorations, Private Bag 48, Maun. Tel & fax 66 0528. Telex 2962 BD. Also Hartley's Safaris, P O Box 69859, Bryanston, 2021, South Africa. Tel (011) 789 6214. Fax (011) 886 1815/789 9218. Telex 42 9795 SA

Accommodation	Facilities	Activities/attractions
Chalets	Licensed	Birding
Booking essential	Gift shop	Game-viewing
	Radio	Cruises
		Game drives
		Game flights
		Boating

Chobe Chilwero is perched on top of the small escarpment between Kasane and the main entrance to the Chobe National Park. Take the road out of Kasane to the national park. Just past Chobe Safari Lodge, look for a road to the left that crosses a small culvert bridge and heads up the hill. Follow this road for 5 km. Kasane is also accessible by air and guests can arrange to be collected from the airstrip.

Chilwero is a beautiful example of imaginative building using local materials. Poles and thatch have been used boldly in the double-storey main building, which nestles under a magnificent sweep of thatched roof. The dining room is dominated by a vast refectory table made locally of kiaat, an indigenous tree famed for the splendour of its wood.

Around the striking central building are eight A-frame chalets with en suite shower, basin and toilet. Sited 100 m above the plain below, Chilwero offers some of the best views in Botswana.

All meals, accommodation, game-viewing activities, national park fees, laundry and transfers between Chilwero/Kasane/airport are included in the tariff.

The lodge closes from December until the end of February.

CHOBE GAME LODGE Tariff: High
P O Box 32, Kasane. Tel 65 0340. Fax 65 0280/65 0223. Telex 2765 BD
Also P O Box 2602, Halfway House, 1685, South Africa.

Accommodation	Facilities	Activities/attractions
Hotel	First aid	Birding
Booking essential	Licensed	Game-viewing
	Restaurant	River cruises
	Swimming pool	Game drives
	Shop	Boating
	Telephone	
	Radio	

Chobe Game Lodge is 12 km west of Kasane. Drive through the town towards the Chobe National Park. The road changes to a firm but frequently corrugated dirt road. Four kilometres outside Kasane is the entrance to the national park. You will have to stop at the gate, fill in the appropriate forms and pay the park entrance fees. Visitors arriving at the gate and producing proof of their reservations will be charged the lower 'Operators' park fees. There is a main road that leads directly to the game lodge, or you can choose various scenic options.

Chobe is a tranquil enclave of luxury in the midst of the African bush. Green lawns and lush gardens contrast with dry, dusty, wintry landscapes.

From the spacious entrance hall, a gallery of striking African art, the main building steps down to a river vista. It is a place of romance and has worked its magic on many people, perhaps the best known being Liz Taylor and Richard Burton, who celebrated their second marriage here in 1976.

Accommodation is in pleasingly appointed rooms with bathrooms en suite. For those who desire privacy, for a few pula more there are four luxury suites each with its own private swimming pool. Other guests have access to the large lodge pool set in lawns on the riverbank. The hotel is currently planning a discount system in its accommodation rates for all bona fide citizens and residents of Botswana. The lodge does have a self-drive rate for accommodation for people using their own four-wheel-drive vehicles and members of the Kalahari Conservation Society will receive, on production of a valid membership card, a 25 per cent discount on the Botswana bed and breakfast rate.

Amidst this luxury, it is all too easy to forget that you are a guest in the domain of the animals. Be prepared for reminders such as bushbuck and warthog grazing on the lawns, the colourful birdlife, troops of baboons and even elephants and hippos, which come to feed on the trees and green lawns.

If the lure of big game has brought you to Chobe, you can go game-viewing by boat or by open motor vehicle, if you do not have your own. Early morning and late afternoon are the best times for this. The hotel has a Cessna 207 at Kasane airstrip and can provide flights to Moremi, Savute, Okavango or Victoria Falls. For the rest, there is the appeal of relaxing beside the pool, or taking a 'sundowner' cruise which combines game-viewing by boat, watching the sunset and enjoying light snacks and ice-cold refreshments after the heat of the day.

CHOBE SAFARI LODGE Tariff: Medium
P O Box 10, Kasane, Tel 65 0336. Fax 65 0437. Telex 2762 BD

Accommodation	*Facilities*	*Activities/attractions*
Hotel	First aid	Birding
Chalets	Licensed	Game-viewing
Camping	Restaurant	River cruises
Booking essential	Swimming pool	Fishing
	Curio shop	Game drives
	Bottlestore	Game flights
	Telephone	Boating
	Fuel	
	Conference room	
	'Local' pub	

Chobe Safari Lodge is on the western outskirts of Kasane, overlooking the Chobe River. Once you have reached Kasane, take the main road towards the national park and you will see the hotel on the right-hand side of the road, just before you leave town.

Apart from the hotel itself, there are 22 thatched rondavels and a grassed campsite. It is not unusual for elephants to stroll through the campsite at night browsing on the trees. They are unlikely to harm campers if they are not disturbed but they are quite awesome close up. This is a popular spot for fishermen and you can hire boats to take you further afield than just the riverbanks. Game drives can be arranged and, when you are neither game-viewing nor fishing, you can cool off in the residents' pool. A daily sunset cruise, on a 25-seater double-decker boat, is arranged by the hotel. The vessel has bar facilities and is excellent for birdwatching and game-viewing.

Transfers can also be arranged to luxury tented camps in Photo Africa private wildlife concession areas. (See the list of safari operators for more information on Photo Africa Safaris.)

The hotel is conveniently located close to a bank, garage and general store.

KUBU LODGE Tariff: Medium
P O Box 43, Kasane. Tel 65 0312. Fax 65 0412. Telex 2768 BD

Accommodation	*Facilities*	*Activities/attractions*
Hotel	Licensed	Birding
Chalets	Restaurant	Game-viewing
Rondavels	Swimming pool	Walks
Camping	Shop	Game drives
Booking essential		Fishing
		Boating
		River cruises
		Mobile safaris

Take the tar road from Kasane to Kazungula. Some 10 km from Kasane you will see signs to Kubu Lodge that will direct you down towards the river. The lodge is about 1 km from the main road.

Kubu Lodge used to be the site of the Employment Bureau of Africa (TEBA) recruitment office for the Kasane area. It bears many signs of the old colonial era, with exotic trees such as jacarandas and flamboyants planted round the settlement. The old houses have wide verandas which are closed in with mosquito gauze.

Among large and ancient trees are 11 wooden chalets with thatched roofs and three thatched rondavels overlooking the lower Chobe River and offering comfortable accommodation. There is a two-storey restaurant of wood and thatch with a small cocktail bar, a lounge and an extensive balcony with a superb and refreshing view. This is the perfect place for a sundowner! The kitchen produces excellent home-cooked meals.

The swimming pool is a delight in the heat of a Kasane summer and is a welcome facility even in the middle of winter. Scenic boat trips on a skimmer, a flat-bottomed boat, down to the confluence of the Zambezi and the Chobe rivers can be arranged and are particularly beautiful at sunset and sunrise. A trail has been laid out amongst the trees allowing for a close-up view of the birds and the many bushbuck resident at Kubu Lodge. In addition, there are daily game drives with professional guides in open Land Rovers to Chobe National Park.

Campsites are laid out along the river and there are brick and thatch ablution facilities of a high standard. As part of maintaining the 'quality' of camping life, numbers are restricted and so it is advisable to book during the busy seasons of Easter, June and July.

It is from Kubu Lodge that Steve Griezel of African Odyssey organises safaris into the Chobe area.

CRESTA MOWANA SAFARI LODGE Tariff: High
P O Box 266, Kasane. Tel 65 0300. Fax 65 0301. Central reservations: South Africa Tel (012) 341 4440. Fax (012) 341 4449. Botswana Tel 31 2431. Fax 37 5376

Accommodation	Facilities	Activities/attractions
Hotel	Licensed	River cruises
	Restaurant	Game drives
	Shops	Fishing
	Conference facilities	Game-viewing by
	Poolside coffeeshop	helicopter
	Poolside bar	Horseback trails
	Cocktail lounge	Day trips to
	Swimming pool	Victoria Falls

Mowana Safari Lodge will be found on the eastern outskirts of Kasane, overlooking the Chobe River. The gate to the lodge is easily identified by the large baobab which grows next to it — Mowana means baobab in Setswana. The hotel is a statuesque, double-storey building opening out onto the banks of the Chobe River. The thatch and wood which has been used so abundantly in the building enable the lodge to blend in with the environment. Try to time your first entrance into the reception area at sunset so that the baobab growing in the main amphitheatre of the hotel is backlit by the setting sun — a truly breathtaking sight.

Accommodation is in luxurious air-conditioned rooms, each with en suite bath and shower. Each room also has its own mini bar and tea/coffee facilities. Mosquito nets and electric mosquito protectors are provided to prevent guests being bitten by mosquitos.

The cocktail lounge is situated high above the Chobe and affords sweeping vistas of the river and of the opposite bank.

Game drives in open-air safari vehicles can be taken into the Chobe National Park and game-viewing boat trips or helicopter trips may also be arranged. For those who would rather lounge by the pool there are poolside coffeeshop and bar facilities.

Makgadikgadi

JACK'S CAMP & SAN CAMP Tariff: High
P O Box 173, Francistown. Tel 21 2277. Fax 21 3458

Accommodation	*Facilities*	*Activities/attractions*
Luxury tents	Game-viewing	Birding
Booking essential	4x4 quad bikes	Guided walks

Uncharted Africa operates the only permanent camps in the Makgadikgadi. The camps adjoin the Makgadikgadi National Park and so have access to the vast salt pans and to Baines' Baobabs.

These camps pride themselves on their traditional atmosphere and pay attention to the little details which make your stay so memorable Persian carpets in the luxury en suite tents, damask tablecloths and bone handled silver cutlery.

Riding on the pans on the 4x4 motorbikes you are able to explore this unique area and enjoy the sight of the grass plains teeming with zebra and wildebeest or the waterbirds during the wet season. You may even make some archeological and anthropological discoveries on this remnant of Africa's great super-lake. A San tracker is also available to lead you on game walks.

Guests may fly in to the airstrip near the camp or drive to Gweta where they will be met and taken to camp.

Maun area

Maun has developed into a major centre boasting M-Net, good eateries, franchise take-away joints, supermarkets and gift, craft and curio shops. Many of the older residents still find it difficult to accept the motor cars that now drive around Maun, since the tar road has provided access to ordinary vehicles.

Maun is the main administrative town for the north-western districts and many government offices are situated here. Extensive banking facilities are also available. In Maun you can buy just about anything you might need for yourself or your vehicle.

Maun has a large population of Hereros, refugees from Namibia at the turn of the century. The strickingly dressed women in their long, colourful Victorian dresses will tempt the photographer to reach for his camera. Be warned, though: unless you have previously negotiated both the photograph and the payment, you will not be popular.

AUDI CAMP Tariff: Budget
Private Bag 28, Maun. Tel 66 0599. Fax 66 0581

Accommodation	*Facilities*	*Activities/attractions*
Erected tents	Bar	Mekoro
Camping	Restaurant	Boats
	Swimming pool	4x4 hire
		Game flights
		Game drives
		Budget safaris

Audi Camp is situated on the bank of the Thamalakane River. To get there leave Maun on the Nata road and turn left (north) after crossing the bridge over the Thamalakane. Audi Camp is 13 km away on the road to Moremi.

For those who are too weary to erect their own tents there are erected tents with fold-up mattresses which sleep two people, but there is also plenty of space to put up your own tents. There are four showers with lots of hot water.

A restaurant provides both a regular menu and light snacks and you can choose between a Continental breakfast or the full traditional English fare. This is a good place to stop over on your way to Moremi.

CROCODILE CAMP SAFARIS Tariff: Medium
P O Box 46, Maun. Tel 66 0265/66 0796. Fax 66 0793. Telex 2487 TWILD
BD

Accommodation	Facilities	Activities/attractions
Chalets	Licensed	Birding
Camping	Restaurant	Mekoro
Booking essential	Telephone	Game drives
	Radio	Fishing, Boating
		Canoes

'Croc Camp' must be one of the best-known camps in Botswana. Started by the famous crocodile hunter Bobby Wilmot, it is one of the oldest tourist camps in the Maun area. It is situated on the bank of the Thamalakane River, the water level of which varies according to the time of year and the nature of the annual floods.

Access to this camp has improved since the road to Shorobe has been tarred. Leave Maun on the Nata road and turn left (north) after crossing the bridge over the Thamalakane. Crocodile Camp is 15 km away on the road to Moremi.

Close to the river are newly constructed brick and thatch chalets with en suite facilities and electricity. Also set amongst the riverside trees is the focal point of the camp — the bar. Bar dinners are available at a very reasonable price and are great! There is a good restaurant.

The camping area is set back from the river. There is an ablution block with hot and cold showers and flush toilets.

Crocodile Camp Safaris, as their name suggests, also organise a wide range of mobile safaris, both by boat and vehicle, into the Okavango and throughout Botswana. Each safari is accompanied by a licensed professional guide. For more details the owner Jane Elliot should be contacted.

ISLAND SAFARI LODGE Tariff: Medium
P O Box 116, Maun. Tel & Fax 66 0300. Telex 2482 BD

Accommodation	Facilities	Activities/attractions
Lodge	Licensed	Safaris
Chalets	Restaurant	Boating
Camping	Bar	Mokoro trails
Booking advisable	Swimming pool	Birding, Walks
	Shop	Helicopter game flights

Starting from Maun, take the tar road north-west from the junction near the airport. Carry on when the tar stops. After a total of some 10 km, just before the Matlapaneng bridge, you will see, on your left-hand side, signposts directing you towards Island Safari Lodge.

The lodge is situated under a canopy of fine old trees and one is aware of constant birdsong and the chatter of squirrels. The two-, three- or four-bedded brick cottages are thatched and all have hot and cold showers. There is a restaurant and bar.

The campsite is also set among the trees lining the river and there are good ablution facilities. The birdlife is a constant delight, even if you are not a keen birdwatcher.

BEST WESTERN RILEY'S HOTEL Tariff: Medium plus
P O Box 1, Maun. Tel 66 0204, 66 0320. Fax 66 0580. Telex 2418 BD. Central reservations: Tel 31 2431. Fax 37 5376. Telex 2434 BD

Accommodation	*Facilities*	*Activities/attractions*
Hotel	Licensed	See below
Booking essential	Restaurant	
	Hair salon	
	Shop	
	Telephone	
	Radio	
	Bottlestore	

Riley's Hotel is in the centre of Maun. The original hotel, with its unique frontier atmosphere, has been substantially renovated. Ever expanding to meet the energetic growth of Maun, Riley's now has 16 double air-conditioned rooms, three air-conditioned executive suites and 32 twin rooms, 12 of which have air-conditioning. All these rooms have en suite facilities. The large and immaculate swimming pool is extremely popular, as are Harry's Bar and the Motswiri Pool Bar. Deep, shady verandas surround two sides of the hotel and overlook the river.

Riley's is within easy walking distance of banks, curio shops, a garage, supermarket and liquor stores.

SEDIA HOTEL Tariff: Medium
Private Bag 058, Maun. Tel & Fax 66 0177

Accommodation	*Facilities*
Hotel	Licensed
Chalets	Restaurant

Accommodation	*Facilities*
Camping	Swimming pool
	Volleyball court

The Sedia Hotel is located 5 km out of Maun on the road to Matlapaneng and is on the south-west side of the Thamalakane. Take the road out of town north-west from the airport junction.

The hotel has 24 double rooms and a restaurant. There are also six cottages, each with a double bed and two single beds, for those who wish to self-cater. All are relatively near the river. There is a swimming pool and a volleyball court. Camping facilities are also available.

SITATUNGA CAMPING SAFARIS Tariff: Budget
Private Bag 47, Maun. Tel & Fax 66 0570/66 0258

Accommodation	*Facilities*	*Activities/attractions*
Camping	First aid	Birding
Booking advisable	Licensed	Walks
Chalets	Shop	Fishing
Tents	Bottlestore	Crocodile farm
	Radio	

Approaching Maun from the direction of Nata, take the 'Maun South' turnoff, cross the Thamalakane River and turn left, on the tar road, at the junction opposite Ngami Toyota. The camp is 12 km further on, to the left, and is well marked with signs to the crocodile farm.

The general camping area is situated at the main entrance to Sitatunga Camp and is attractively laid out in a well wooded area. Taps bring water to the campsites and firewood is provided. There are hot showers and flush toilets. A unique attraction of this camp site is John Seaman's Crocodile Farm, which you are invited to tour by arrangement with the staff. A shop sells general provisions and liquor at the entrance to the campsite.

Moremi area and Central Delta

Moremi is something of a mecca for wildlife enthusiasts. There are no places to buy food or fuel in this area so once you leave Kasane or Maun to enter Moremi you must be fully self-contained. A four-wheel-drive vehicle is essential. The country is flat and well vegetated, with extensive areas under water after the annual flooding. There are four camping areas in Moremi — at North and South gates, Third Bridge and Xakanaxa.

ABU CAMP (Elephant back safaris) Tariff: High
Private Bag 332, Maun. Tel 66 1260. Fax 66 1005

Accommodation	*Facilities*	*Activities/attractions*
Luxury tents	Radio	Elephant back safaris
Booking essential	Air transfers	Game drives
		Night drives
		Guided walks
		Mekoro

Abu Camp is located on the banks of the Nxabega River in the south-western part of the Okavango Delta. This camp is named after Randall Moore's legendary film-star elephant, Abu. Abu has starred in films such as *Circles in the Forest* and *Power of One*, and here in the delta leads a herd of 13 adult and young elephants.

Travelling with this elephant family allows visitors a unique opportunity to approach and interact with a wide variety of game as they blend in with nature. Guests are transported on the backs of the four adult elephants in custom made two-seater saddles. The younger elephants accompany the adults and provide a constant source of interest and amusement as they play and swim.

Abu Camp nestles under African ebony trees overlooking a lagoon. Accommodation is in five luxurious en suite safari tents. Sundowners and meals are eaten out in the shade of a giant fig tree.

Access to Abu Camp is by air only — a 20-minute flight — followed by a short drive. Tariffs include air transfers, acommodation, all activities, all meals and drinks and a daily laundry service.

CAMP MOREMI Tariff: High
Private Bag 198, Maun. Tel 66 1243. Fax 66 0037 or Desert & Delta Safaris, P O Box 1200, Paulshof 2056, South Africa. Tel (011) 807 3720. Fax (011) 807 3480

Accommodation	*Facilities*	*Activities/attractions*
Tented camp	Licensed	Birding
Booking essential	Restaurant	Game-viewing
	Radio	Walks
	Swimming pool	Boating
	Curio shop	Canoeing
	Observation	River cruises
	platform	Fishing

Camp Moremi is situated on the beautiful Xakanaxa Lagoon in the Moremi Reserve. Only 22 guests can be accommodated in walk-through safari tents with open-air private hot showers and flush toilets (they can be covered in the rainy season!). Each tent is furnished with Rhodesian teak furniture, colourful woven rugs, designer linen and matching interior blinds.

Shaded by giant ebony trees, the magnificent Moremi Tree Lodge is an elegant thatch and timber structure comprising a main lounge, wildlife reference library, dining room and cocktail bar cooled by overhead punkah-punkah fans. The large sundeck affords an excellent view of the lagoon.

The daily rates include all accommodation, all meals, all drinks, all scheduled game-viewing activities, park entrance fee and a laundry service. Honeymooners are catered for.

Camp Moremi provides a complete lodge experience with its game drives through Moremi Reserve, its opportunities for fishing and its boat visits to the heronries on Gadikwe and Xakanaxa Lagoon.

CAMP OKAVANGO Tariff: High
Private Bag 198, Maun. Tel 66 1243. Fax 66 0037 or Desert & Delta Safaris, P O Box 1200, Paulshof 2056, South Africa. Tel (011) 807 3720. Fax (011) 807 3480

Accommodation	*Facilities*	*Activities/attractions*
Tented camp	Licensed	Birding
Deluxe suite	Restaurant	Game-viewing
Booking essential	Radio	Walks
	Swimming pool	River cruises
		Fishing
		Boating
		Canoeing

Camp Okavango is situated on remote Nxaragha Island in the heart of the Okavango Delta. Unashamed luxury blends with the Africa of yesteryear in the elegant thatch and lethaka (reed) main building which houses a cocktail bar, lounge and dining room, while the expansive open-air patio caters for al fresco meals and evenings around a blazing fire. Camp Okavango's silver service dinner served by candlelight is renowned among seasoned travellers.

Shaded hammocks, reading benches and a delightful sundeck and plunge pool provide relief during the hot midday hours.

Camp Okavango accommodates only 22 guests in walk-through safari tents with open-air private hot showers and flush toilets (they can be covered in the rainy season!). Each tent is furnished with Rhodesian teak furniture, colourful woven rugs, designer linen and matching interior blinds.

The daily rates include all accommodation, all meals, all drinks, all scheduled game-viewing activities, park entrance fee and a laundry service.

Honeymooners are catered for and, for those who demand the ultimate in exclusivity, Camp Okavango boasts 'Jessie's Suite', where your stay includes private game-viewing activities.

Camp Okavango is the ideal base from which to discover the delta's wetland ecosystem. All game-viewing activities are conducted by experienced resident naturalist guides and include canoe and boat trips. Guided nature walks on the neighbouring islands can be arranged and the fishing is excellent.

CAMP OKUTI Tariff: Medium
Private Bag 47, Maun. Tel & Fax 66 0570/66 0258

Accommodation	Facilities	Activities/attractions
Chalets	First aid	Birding
Booking essential	Licensed	Game-viewing
	Restaurant	Boating
	Radio	Fishing
	Curio shop	

Camp Okuti is situated in the Moremi Reserve on the banks of the Xakanaxa Lagoon. It is accessible by road or by air from Maun.

The camp is privately owned by John and Ursula Seaman and has a delightfully informal atmosphere. To help preserve this asset the number of guests is limited to a maximum of 20 persons.

The accommodation is enchanting, with comfortable brick and thatched chalets and en suite bathrooms sheltering beneath tall trees and overlooking the beautiful lagoon. The daily rate includes all activities, all meals and all drinks.

A visit to Camp Okuti is a special experience for those who like to combine in one safari the attractions of the Okavango Delta and the rich and exciting game-viewing opportunities of the Moremi Game Reserve.

DELTA CAMP Tariff: High
P O Box 39, Maun. Tel 66 0220. Fax 66 0589. Telex 2484 BD Also Box 52900, Saxonwold 2132, South Africa. Tel (011) 788 5549. Fax (011) 788 6575. Telex 42 2302 SA

Accommodation	Facilities	Activities/attractions
Chalets	Licensed	Birding
Booking essential	Radio	Game-viewing
		Mekoro
		Walks
		Fishing

There is no access to this camp by road, so it is not a place for a casual visit. Arrangements must be made to fly in. There are daily flights to the camp from Maun.

Delta is one of the oldest camps in the Okavango. It nestles unobtrusively under tall trees, the reed, wood and grass of which it is built blending harmoniously with the setting. The camp sleeps no more than 16 guests at a time. Activities at Delta focus on birdwatching, game-viewing and fishing. It is a good place from which to explore the waters of the Okavango by mokoro, under the guidance of a professional game guide — there are a maximum of two guests per guide.

All meals, drinks and excursions are included in the daily tariff.

GUNN'S CAMP Tariff: Medium
Private Bag 33, Maun. Tel 66 0023. Fax 66 0040. Telex 2612 BD

Accommodation	Facilities	Activities/attractions
Luxury tents	Licensed bar	Mekoro
Campsite	Meals	Boat safaris
	Shop	Game-viewing
	Radio	Game walks
		Birding
		Fishing

Gunn's Camp is situated on the Boro River, opposite Chief's Island in the Moremi Reserve. The camp is set on two small neighbouring islands, each densely wooded and graced with tall palms. There is no way into this camp except by water or aircraft. They try to schedule flights as close as possible to your requested time.

On one island is the camping site with its toilets and showers, barbecue area, bar and supply store. Camping and cooking equipment is available for hire, and you can buy basic non-perishable provisions. The second island offers seven large twin-bedded tents, each with its own en suite facilities.

Mokoro safaris can be arranged while in the camp. People may go out for two or three days or just for a few hours if they prefer. It is also possible to take a powerboat excursion along the many channels and lagoons or walk on the islands in the surrounding delta.

KHWAI RIVER LODGE Tariff: Medium
Gametrackers, P O Box 100, Maun. Tel 66 0302. Fax 66 0153. Telex 2648
BD

Accommodation	*Facilities*	*Activities/attractions*
Chalets	First aid	Birding
Booking essential	Swimming pool	Game-viewing
	Shop	Walks
	Radio	Game drives

Khwai is not a casual, drop-in destination — so make prior arrangements if you intend to spend a night there. From the north gate of Moremi
Reserve, head in an easterly direction for 8 km. There are a number of
roads to choose from, so direction-finding is something of an act of faith.
If you need help enquire at the north gate before you leave. The lodge
overlooks the river.

Khwai is one of the largest lodges in the delta. The thatched main
complex of dining room, bar and lounge is open to the elements. After
your evening meal, coffee, liqueurs and tales of the day are served up
around the fire outside. Accommodation is in individual chalets scattered among the trees. Each has its own shower, basin and toilet.

Game drives take clients into surrounding reserves to see wildlife.
The rest of the time can be spent around the pool, or viewing the birds
and game from the grounds of the lodge. Keep an eye out for elephants,
which love the lodge's young fig trees. The elephants are no respecters
of humans who might be in their way.

Khwai's resident hippo are a source of great interest. It is hard to believe that these creatures, which look so somnolent in the water, kill more
humans than any other animal in Africa.

Rates are fully inclusive.

KWARA CAMP Tariff: High
P O Box 119, Maun. Tel 66 0086. Fax 66 0632. Central reservations: P O
Box 651171, Benmore, 2010, South Africa. Tel (011) 884 1458/9. Fax (011)
883 6255. Telex 42 8642 SA

Accommodation	*Facilities*	*Activities/attractions*
Luxury tents	First aid	Game drives
Booking essential	Radio	Walking
		Mokoro trips
		Fishing

Kwara Camp is situated on the northern reaches of the delta, bordering
onto the Moremi Game Reserve. The camp has a lovely view of a hippo

lagoon and the permanent waterways of the delta beyond, and is flanked on either side by grassy floodplains of the mainland.

Each of the four furnished en suite tents is raised on a metre-high teak deck overlooking the lagoon. Guests have no need to leave their balconies to see the abundant animal and birdlife in front of the camp. The dining room and the bar area, under canvas, are also positioned on a raised platform providing good views of both the floodplains and the lagoon.

Guests usually fly in, landing at the private airstrip where they are met by camp staff and transferred to the camp.

The camp is within easy access of a waterway that leads into the main rivers, making it possible to take half-day mokoro trips and to walk on the nearby islands. Game-viewing is good in this area, and drives with an experienced guide are available.

MACHABA Tariff: Medium
Ker & Downey, P O Box 40, Maun. Tel 66 0211-3. Fax 66 0379. Telex 2485 BD

Accommodation	Facilities	Activities/attractions
Luxury tents	Licensed	Game drives
Booking essential	Restaurant	Night drives
	Radio	Birding
	First aid	

Machaba lies in the heart of big-game country on the banks of the Khwai River, right opposite Moremi Game Reserve.

You can drive in but most people fly and there is a short transfer from the airstrip to the camp.

Accommodation is in luxury tents with every convenience and really good showers and ablutions. You can look forward to long evenings of conversation and convivial company round a blazing campfire in the middle of a tented camp.

For the photographer, there is an enormous range of game animals to choose from, both in the reserve and outside it. Leopard, elephant, buffalo, lion and giraffe can all be expected. The rich birdlife also offers good photographic opportunities. The night game drives are a fascinating experience and open another dimension of the wilderness experience.

MOMBO CAMP Tariff: High
P O Box 119, Maun. Tel 66 0086. Fax 66 0632. Central reservations: P O

Box 651171, Benmore 2010, South Africa. Tel (011) 884 1458/9. Fax (011) 883 6255. Telex 42 8642 SA

Accommodation	*Facilities*	*Activities/attractions*
Luxury tents	First aid	Game-viewing
Booking essential	Radio	Game drives
	Plunge pool	Walking
		Birding

Mombo Camp lies within Moremi and is situated on Mombo Island, which adjoins the northern tip of Chief's Island. This camp overlooks the wide open plains where the savanna meets the delta and is best known for its excellent game-viewing.

Guests are accommodated in the ten furnished en suite tents which are lit at night by solar-powered electricity. The separate dining and living/bar area overlook the open plain in front of the camp. Morning and afternoon game drives on the plains enable you to get good sightings of the abundant big game and spot, if you are lucky, some of the more unusual bird species found in this area. In the heat of the day guests may cool off in the plunge pool.

Guests usually fly in, landing at the private airstrip where they are met by camp staff and transferred to the camp.

ODDBALLS Tariff: Budget-Medium
P O Box 39, Maun. Tel 66 0220/339. Fax 66 0589. Telex 2484 BD Also Box 52900, Saxonwold 2132, South Africa. Tel (011) 788 5549. Fax (011) 788 6575. Telex 42 2302 SA

Accommodation	*Facilities*	*Activities/attractions*
Camping	Licensed	Birding
Booking essential	Restaurant	Game-viewing
	Shop	Mokoro trips
	Radio	Walks
	Camping	Fishing
	equipment	

To get to this camp you have to be flown, usually from Maun, which is quite an experience. The aerial views of the delta are fascinating and, particularly in winter, offer a complete contrast from the barren dryness of the area around Maun.

Oddballs is situated on the edge of Chief's Island, where you can camp and then explore the delta by mokoro. The decor is quaint and original. The bar is built around a tall tree and leaky mekoro are given a new lease of life serving as ingenious cupboards. At the campsite you will find hot showers and flush toilets. Campers may come prepared with their own food and gear, although there is a shop where a limited range of tinned foods, clothing and curios can be bought. It is also possible to hire camping equipment. Self-catering chalets are available.

It is to the credit of the management of Oddballs that they are meticulous in seeing that every bit of rubbish from the sites they use in the delta is removed.

POM POM CAMP Tariff: Medium
Ker & Downey, P O Box 40, Maun. Tel 66 0211-3. Fax 66 0379. Telex 2485 BD

Accommodation	Facilities	Activities/attractions
Luxury tents	Licensed	Game walks
Booking essential	Restaurant	Game drives
	Radio	Fishing
	First aid	Birding
		Boating
		Mekoro

This is a fly-in island camp in the heart of the permanent delta. Part of the Ker & Downey group, it meets all their well-known standards for excellence and concern for clients' needs.

From the hippo which inhabit the lagoon fronting the camp to the game that you'll encounter either by vehicle or on game walks, this camp permits a closeness to the Okavango and its inhabitants that you'll find hard to match.

Certainly, it is a wonderful place for the enthusiastic photographer. As with the Okavango generally, the birdlife is enormously varied and plentiful and one does not have to be a fanatic to enjoy this startling variety.

Being able to venture forth in a mokoro brings the delta home to you in an intensely personal and unforgettable way.

SAN-TA-WANI Tariff: Medium
Gametrackers, P O Box 100, Maun. Tel 66 0302. Fax 66 0153. Telex 2648 BD

Accommodation	Facilities	Activities/attractions
Chalets	First aid	Birding
Booking essential	Radio	Game-viewing
		Walks
		Game drives

San-ta-wani, one of the earlier lodges built in the delta, is set among beautiful riverine trees. The buildings are of brick and thatch. Evening meals are served under the stars — weather permitting, which is most of the time — in a reed-fenced boma. The chalets are spacious and each has an en suite toilet and a basin. Showers are a short distance away. In the chalets you will find a printed checklist of the area's birds, mammals and trees so that, if you are so inclined, you can have the satisfaction of recording your sightings. Clients are taken on game drives on request.

Daily rates are fully inclusive. San-ta-wani will be closed during 1996 for refurbishment but will open again in 1997.

SHINDE ISLAND Tariff: Medium
Ker & Downey, P O Box 40, Maun. Tel 66 0211/2/3. Fax 66 0379. Telex 2485 BD

Accommodation	Facilities	Activities/attractions
Luxury tents	Licensed	Game-viewing
Booking essential	Restaurant	Fishing
	Radio	Birding
	First aid	Boating
		Mekoro

This is another luxury tented camp. Located in the region of the big river systems of the north-west, it is an island overlooking its own exclusive lagoon.

Typically, therefore, one will spend time in boats (both motor and mekoro), exploring the delta and experiencing its wonders at first hand. There are plenty of opportunities to get out and walk among the game on some of the bigger islands.

A special feature of the area is that it tends to be favoured by the sitatunga antelope, and there is a good chance that you may be lucky enough to see this elusive creature.

Boat trips to Gadikwe Lagoon can show you breeding colonies of herons, egrets, cormorants, pelicans and storks or, if you prefer, there is excellent fishing.

TCHAU CAMP Tariff: High
P O Box 119, Maun. Tel 66 0086. Fax 66 0632 Central reservations: P O Box 651171, Benmore 2010, South Africa. Tel (011) 884 1458/9. Fax (011) 883 6255. Telex 42 8642 SA

Accommodation	Facilities	Activities/attractions
Luxury tents	First aid	Game-viewing
Booking essential	Radio	Walking
		Motorboat excursions
		Mokoro trips
		Birding

To get to Tchau, guests land at Xaxaba airstrip and then travel for 45 minutes up the Boro channel to Chief's Island on which the camp is situated.

This is an exclusive camp which only accommodates ten people. The furnished en suite tents blend in unobtrusively with their surroundings and there is a separate reeded dining and bar area. The camp is lit at night by solar-powered electricity.

Most of the guests' time at this camp is spent walking on the island or exploring the waterways, either in mekoro or on motorboats.

TSARO SAFARI LODGE Tariff: Medium
c/o Okavango Explorations, Private Bag 48, Maun. Tel & Fax 66 0528. Telex 2962 BD. Also Hartley's Safaris, P O Box 69859, Bryanston 2021, South Africa. Tel (011) 708 6214. Fax (011) 886 1815/789 6218. Telex 42 9795 SA

Accommodation	*Facilities*	*Activities/attractions*
Chalets	First aid	Birding
Booking essential	Licensed	Game-viewing
	Swimming pool	Walks
	Shop	Game drives
	Art gallery	
	Radio	
	Covered hide	
	Conference facilities	

Tsaro is situated on the eastern side of Moremi on the banks of the Khwai River. Access is by plane only.

Tsaro is graciously luxurious and quite different from the majority of lodges in the delta. Here brick and mortar take the place of the more usual reeds and poles. The impression is of arriving at an elegant private home as a guest of the family — and that is very much the ambience of Tsaro. Walk through the front door and your eye is drawn from a sparkling pool in a white-walled courtyard to a suspended mokoro, now no longer plying the waters of the delta but serving as an attractive plant container. The U-shaped courtyard opens onto a vista through shady trees, over lush green lawns, to the wild beyond.

Tucked unobtrusively to the side are the guests' chalets. No simple round huts these, but intriguing split-level units where the bedroom looks down onto the sitting-room and the elegant bathroom has a sunken double bath. The camp accommodates a maximum of 16 clients at a time.

There is a shop with a small selection of clothes and curios, local artifacts, books and film.

Guests are taken out on early-morning game drives and it is well worth the effort to follow the rhythm of the bush and rise just before the sun. Tsaro's game drives have many surprises to delight the receptive guest. Game walks are also offered, accompanied by a licensed, armed, professional guide. Birdwatching and boat excursions are a speciality and take place from a second camp at Xugana Lagoon.

XAKANAXA Tariff: Medium
Private Bag 26, Maun or Moremi Safaris, P O Box 2757, Cramerview 2060, South Africa. Tel (011) 465 3842/3. Fax (011) 465 3779

Accommodation	Facilities	Activities/attractions
Luxury tents	First aid	Birding
Booking essential	Licensed	Game-viewing
	Radio	River cruises
	Curio shop	Game drives
		Fishing
		Flights
		Mekoro

One may fly in to Xakanaxa by arrangement from Maun, or one may drive there. The camp is 130 km from Maun. If you are driving, turn west inside Moremi Reserve, just a short distance from the north gate. The distance to Xakanaxa Lagoon is approximately 50 km. The route is signposted.

Xakanaxa is situated on the edge of the Xakanaxa Lagoon, one of the most beautiful in the delta. Under a canopy of giant trees there is luxurious accommodation for up to 20 guests in twin-bedded safari tents each with en suite facilities. A relaxed, rustic and friendly atmosphere prevails in this camp. Indigenous building materials have been used wherever possible — the dining room is open-fronted with reed walls and a thatched roof — and the tents and the reception and dining area have been carefully positioned to maintain privacy.

Bird and game-viewing trips by boat or vehicle can be organised to suit a client's taste. A speciality of this area is to be found between the months of July and October, when there are large nesting colonies of marabou storks, openbill and yellowbilled storks and herons. Fishing in the lagoon is exciting and rewarding — providing one's concentration does not suffer from the repeated intrusions of curious but inoffensive hippo!

XAXABA CAMP Tariff: Medium
Gametrackers, P O Box 100, Maun. Tel 66 0302. Fax 66 0153.
Telex 2648 BD

Accommodation	Facilities	Activities/attractions
Chalets	Swimming pool	Birding
Booking essential	Shop	Mekoro
	Radio	Walks
		River cruises
		Flights
		Boating

To get to this camp, deep in the Okavango Delta, you have to travel by air, usually from Maun. It is not a place for a casual drop-in as you pass. Booking is most important as Xaxaba is a very popular camp, especially during the busier months of the tourist season.

Xaxaba offers a range of facilities. These include boating, mokoro rides, fishing and walks through the incredibly beautiful floodplains of the delta. Aircraft flights can be arranged on request. A luxury camp of reed chalets is set in this 'place of tall trees', and as you wander through the camp you will see that the trees are discreetly identified, giving their common, scientific and Setswana names.

The daily tariff is fully inclusive.

XIGERA CAMP Tariff: High
P O Box 119, Maun. Tel 66 0086. Fax 66 0632. Central reservations: P O Box 651171, Benmore 2010, South Africa. Tel (011) 884 1458/9. Fax (011) 883 6255. Telex 42 8642 SA

Accommodation	Facilities	Activities/attractions
Luxury tents	First aid	Game drives
Booking essential	Radio	Game walks
		Mekoro
		Fishing
		Birding

Xigera is considered by many to be one of the loveliest camps in the Okavango. One of the most westerly, it is far from the large river systems yet is still in the permanent part of the delta facing on to its own delightful (and private) lagoon.

The camp is on a small island which is reached from the 'mainland' by means of a quaint wooden bridge. The eight furnished walk-in tents are set among towering evergreens that keep in the warmth in winter and provide shade during the hot summers. The separate bar, dining and lounge area is also under canvas.

Clients usually fly into Xigera, landing at the private airstrip where they are met and driven a short distance to the island.

Xigera is located on the western edge of the !Xo flats, and there are remarkable opportunities for walking among the game on innumerable islands. There's a good chance of seeing the elusive sitatunga. You can also travel by mokoro and slide silently through the reeded river channels to encounter the prolific birdlife at close quarters. This area is one of the best for Pel's fishing owl.

XUDUM Tariff: High
Ker & Downey, P O Box 40, Maun. Tel 66 0211-3. Fax 66 0379. Telex 2485 BD

Accommodation	*Facilities*	*Activities/attractions*
Luxury tents	Licensed	Game-viewing
Booking essential	Restaurant	Birding
	Radio	Night drives
	First aid	Mekoro
		Game walks
		Fishing
		All-terrain vehicles
		Game drives
		Elephant back safaris

Xudum is nestled on a sand tongue surrounded on three sides by a deep lagoon formed by the Xudum River. Mahogany and machaba hardwoods shade the seven luxury en suite tents. The lounge and dining area, also under canvas, overlooks the lagoon.

The wooden deck on the point of the peninsula is the perfect place to view life in the lagoon and on the floodplains. Over 300 species of birds have been identified in this area, making it a paradise for birdwatchers. The deck is also an ideal venue for a sundowner.

Xudum offers a variety of non-traditional safari activities, including exploratory drives in amphibious all-terrain vehicles and walking or riding through the bush with trained African elephants. To ensure that guests really enjoy this bush experience and feel the benefits of this camp, visits to Xudum are for a minimum of three nights.

XUGANA LODGE Tariff: Medium
Okavango Explorations, Private Bag 49, Maun. Tel & Fax 66 0528. Telex 2962 BD. Also Hartley's Safaris, P O Box 69859, Bryanston 2021, South Africa. Tel (011) 789 6214. Fax (011) 886 1815/789 6218. Telex 42 9795 SA

Accommodation	*Facilities*	*Activities/attractions*
Huts on stilts	First aid	Birding
Booking essential	Licensed	Game-viewing
	Shop	Walks
	Radio	Cruises
	Conference	Mokoro trails
	facilities	Fishing
	Swimming pool	Boating

Access to Xugana is by air only. Note that the weight restriction is 25 kg per person.

The lodge is on one of the largest lagoons in the delta and a record catch of tiger fish has been made within hailing distance of the lodge's bar! Bream and catfish are also plentiful. All types of tackle are available at the lodge shop.

The lodge provides accommodation for no more than 16 guests at a time in eight reed and thatch mesasa (huts) on stilts, set around indigenous trees overlooking the lagoon. Each mesasa is mosquito-proofed and has an en suite shower, toilet and basin.

Many rare birds are found here, with over 400 bird species having been identified. The sitatunga is also seen in this area.

The Okavango Delta has attracted some of the world's celebrities. Xugana's most notable guest was Prince Charles, who spent several days at the lodge in 1984.

Nata area

Nata village has really expanded and now boasts three filling stations: Shell, Engen and BP. The Shell garage is attached to Sua Pan Lodge, which also has a take-away shop and a bottle store. Sua Pan Lodge is owned by Thompson Masuku and provides the opportunity to overnight while on your journey further afield.

The chief attractions in Nata, however, are Nata Sanctuary and Nata Lodge. For more information on Nata Sanctuary see Places to Visit – Sowa Pan (p. 36).

NATA LODGE Tariff: Budget
Private Bag 10, Francistown. Tel 61 1260. Fax 61 1210

Accommodation	*Facilities*	*Activities/attractions*
4-Bed furnished	Airstrip at	Birding
safari tents	Nata	4x4 excursions to
Chalets	Licensed	Makgadikgadi Pans

Accommodation	Facilities	Activities/attractions
Camping	Restaurant	Ostrich breeding
Booking essential	Shop	farm
during the	Petrol	
holiday season	Diesel	
	Swimming pool	

Nata Lodge is some 10 km south of Nata on the main tar road from Francistown, and is well situated as a stop-over point for visitors to Maun, the Okavango Delta, Chobe National Park, Victoria Falls and Zambia. It is clearly signposted — so keep your eyes open for the distinctive logo of the helmeted guineafowl.

The attractive A-frame cottages, each with a private shower and toilet, stand among tall ilala palms, marula and monkey thorn trees. The site is near the north-eastern edge of the great Makgadikgadi Pans, an area of unique beauty.

In times of good rains, this portion of the pan floods and might retain an initial metre or more of water for several years. At such times, flamingo, pelican and other water birds appear in tens of thousands. The lodge will organise sunset pan trips into Nata Sanctuary at your request.

To deal with the thirst that builds up on a long journey, the lodge has a thatched bar next to the large swimming pool. There is also a restaurant with an à la carte and a 'snack' menu. The area generally is considered to be excellent for birdwatching — mainly because of the diversity of habitats close to the lodge.

Campers are particularly welcome here, and there are brick and thatched ablution blocks with lots of piping hot and cold water, all in a cool and shady campsite.

Savute area

A fuller description of Savute and its particular attractions is given on page 31. Here the landscape differs from that of Moremi and Chobe. After pervading flatness, it is a pleasing change to see the hills in this area and there are San paintings on some of the rocky outcrops.

Savute can be very dry and you should carry water. The Savute campsite suffers from the attention of elephants who have a habit of digging up the plumbing, leaving the campsite without water.

ALLAN'S CAMP Tariff: Medium
Gametrackers, P O Box 100, Maun. Tel 66 0302. Fax 66 0153. Telex 2648
BD

Accommodation	*Facilities*	*Activities/attractions*
Tented camp	First aid	Birding
Booking essential	Licensed	Game-viewing
	Radio	
	Laundry	

The chalets are A-frames built of local woods and have shower, basin
and toilet en suite. The heart of the camp is a large tent where the cooking, eating and drinking takes place.

Allan's Camp is aimed at those who are touring Botswana in their
own vehicles or who are part of a camping safari. The camp is mainly
used by these overland safari companies.

The frequent dryness of the surroundings does not make Savute the
kind of place that appeals to all, so it is not a place to stay for any length
of time unless you are one of the cognoscenti.

LLOYD'S CAMP Tariff: Medium
P O Box 37, Maun. Tel 66 0300. Fax 66 0205 or c/o Okavango Explorations, Maun. Tel & Fax 66 0528. Telex 2962 BD Also Hartley's Safaris, P O
Box 69859, Bryanston 2021, South Africa. Tel (011) 789 6214. Fax (011)
886 1815/789 6218. Telex 42 9795 SA

Accommodation	*Facilities*	*Activities/attractions*
Tented camp	First aid	Birding
Booking essential	Licensed	Game-viewing
	Radio	Game drives
	Game-viewing hide	

Once you have reached the public campsite at Savute, take any road that
heads approximately west along the southern bank of the Savute Channel. Lloyd's Camp is about 1 km from the public campsite. Lloyd Wilmot
will fly guests from Maun or Johannesburg to the camp.

If luxurious isolation from the wild is what you seek, this is not the
camp to visit. A *National Geographic* cover picture in 1983 showed Lloyd
digging a waterhole for a thirsty elephant standing within a trunk's touch.
The photograph was taken just in front of the camp. It epitomises Lloyd's
approach to wildlife — he believes in allowing his clients close encoun-
ters.

The camp, which provides double tented accommodation for only 12
people, is perched on the bank of the Savute Channel and looks down

onto what was the only source of surface water during the drought years of the early 1980s. There is an unobtrusive hide which offers a spectacular view of game visiting the waterhole. You can virtually count the vertebrae in an elephant's backbone. At night a spotlight is in constant use and many a guest has been held spellbound at a window, fascinated by the nightlife of the wild.

This camp is closed from December until February.

SAVUTE SOUTH Tariff: Medium
Gametrackers, P O Box 100, Maun. Tel 66 0302. Fax 66 0153. Telex 2648 BD

Accommodation	*Facilities*	*Activities/attractions*
Tented camp	First aid	Birding
Booking essential	Radio	Game-viewing
		Game drives

Savute South was set up at a time when no permanent structures were allowed in national parks, so both the communal area and the client accommodation are in tents. The blocks housing the showers, toilets and basins (built when the rule about no permanent structures was bent somewhat) are a short distance away from the tents — the significance of which will become clear. Savute is big-game country so staying inside your tent is a wise precaution, for the shadows abound with serious predators and thirsty elephants.

Nocturnal visits to toilets are out of the question. Once the staff have escorted you to your tent at night, that is where you stay. Each tent is provided with a chamber pot, an essential part of the furniture. Gametrackers are, however, upgrading their facilities and soon the tents will boast en suite bathrooms.

KING'S POOLS Tariff: High
Sable Safaris, Private Bag 209, Maun. Tel 66 0571. Fax 66 0571

Accommodation	*Facilities*	*Activities/attractions*
Luxury tents	Licensed	Game drives
Booking essential	Curio shop	Night drives
		Boat safaris
		Guided walks

King's Pool camp is situated in the Linyanti Swamp and is bordered by the Linyanti River and Chobe Game Reserve. It was named after King Gustav of Sweden, who honeymooned here in the 1970s with his bride Queen Silvia.

Sixteen guests can be accommodated in this exclusive camp in walk-in tents with en suite facilities.

This area is renowned for its large herds of elephants, and is situated on a major elephant migration route. The rare roan and sable antelope are also found here.

This camp operates from mid-April through to December. The rates include everything except air charter transfers in and out of the camp. Sable Safaris will organise these transfers on request.

SELINDA CAMP Tariff: High
Linyanti Explorations, P O Box 22, Kasane. Tel 65 0505. Fax 65 0352. Telex 2901 BD

Accommodation	Facilities	Activities/attractions
Luxury tents	Radio	Game-viewing by
Booking essential	Licensed	vehicle
	Curio shop	Game-viewing by
		boat
		Walking
		Night game drives
		Fishing

Selinda Camp is located on the banks of the eastern Selinda Spillway overlooking open floodplains, within a private wildlife area known as the Selinda Reserve. Less than a kilometre away is the exit point on the Linyanti (Chobe) River from which the famed Savute Channel leaves, in those years when it mysteriously chooses to flow. Equally enigmatic in its unpredictable flow patterns is the Selinda Spillway, which also enters the Linyanti near here.

This camp can accommodate no more than 12 people at a time in twin-bedded luxury safari tents. Each tent has its own private shower, toilet and hand basin.

This is big-game country and there are few animals occurring in Botswana that you will not spot as you drive or walk among the game in the care of your professional guide. Limited field sports are also available on request.

Selinda can be reached by air or by road, but this is definitely four-wheel-drive territory. The daily rate includes all meals, accommodation, game-viewing activities, national park fees, laundry and transfers between Chilwero/Kasane/airport. The camp is closed from December to the end of February.

ZIBADIANJA CAMP Tariff: High
Linyanti Explorations, P O Box 22, Kasane. Tel 65 0505. Fax 65 0352.
Telex 2901 BD

Accommodation	*Facilities*	*Activities/attractions*
Luxury tents	Radio	Game-viewing by
Booking essential	Licensed	vehicle
	Curio shop	Game-viewing by
		boat
		Walking
		Night game drives
		Fishing

Zibadianja is a small exclusive six-bed tented camp situated near the Zibadianja Lagoon in the private Selinda Reserve. Each tent is mounted on raised wooden platforms and has en suite facilities. The tents also have a flysheet and shade net cover. The bar area is outside, beside the campfire.

All game drives in this private wildlife area are conducted by professional guides and limited field sports are available on request.

At this camp, like all the other Linyanti Exploration camps, you can be assured of exceptional quality and service.

This camp can be reached by air or by four-wheel-drive vehicle and is closed from December to February. The daily rate includes all meals, accommodation, game-viewing activities, national park fees, laundry and transfers between Chilwero/Kasane/airport.

Tuli area

Tuli is an area of Botswana that deserves far more attention than it gets at present. It lies to the east of the Kalahari sands and the rocky landscape is full of interesting hills and valleys. This is also an area of great historical and archaeological interest. It is rich in game and the landscape is very favourable for game-viewing.

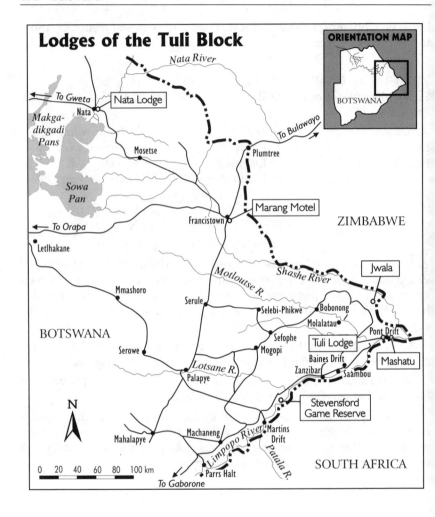

Lodges of the Tuli Block

JWALA GAME LODGE Tariff: Budget
P O Box 781900, Sandton, South Africa 2146. Tel 883 3711. Fax 884 3943

Accommodation	*Facilities*	*Activities/attractions*
Bush camps	Airstrip	Birding
Booking essential		Game-viewing
		Bush walks
		Game drives
		Night drives

Travelling from Johannesburg, take the road to Pontdrift where you will pass through customs and immigration. If you go via Pietersburg and Alldays, the journey takes about 5,5 hours. The border post closes at 4 pm. An alternative is to fly into Tuli Lodge, where customs and immigration formalities can be completed, and then to the Jwala Game Lodge airstrip.

The Jwala Game Reserve bush camp, Lenketa, offers the true bush experience: no electricity and no fences. Set in unspoiled riverine bush, the camp consists of five twin-bedded log cabins on stilts, with a well-equipped communal kitchen, gas fridges and stove, and a dining area. All bedding, cutlery and crockery is supplied. There are hot and cold showers and flush toilets.

Water near the bush camp means that there is often elephant, lion and other wildlife around.

The camp is available on a group basis and the price includes collection from the Pontdrift border post and game drives in an open Landcruiser.

MASHATU GAME RESERVE Tariff: High

P O Box 2575, Randburg 2125, South Africa. Tel (011) 789 2677. Fax (011) 886 4382. (Note: all bookings must be made through travel agents in Botswana or through the address given above.)

Accommodation	Facilities	Activities/attractions
Luxury chalets	Licensed	Game drives
Luxury tents	Private bar	Game walks
Booking essential	Fully catered	Night drives
	Swimming pools	Birding
	Conference room	

Located in the north-east Tuli Block, the Mashatu Game Reserve's closest border crossing into South Africa is at Pontdrift. Fly-in facilities are available and customs and immigration clearance at the airfield can be arranged when booking.

Air charter and fly-in packages can be booked either in Johannesburg or in Gaborone. Driving time from Johannesburg is 5-6 hours via Pietersburg and Alldays. The driving time from Gaborone is much the same. Self-drive guests are met at the border by game reserve staff and transported to the camps.

Mashatu is the largest privately owned conservation area in southern Africa. The area has a remarkable diversity of landscape and wildlife and its elephants are particularly well known. Other large animals to be found there include lion, leopard, cheetah, giraffe and many of the antelopes. There are two commercial camps at Mashatu.

Main Camp accommodates a maximum of 30 guests in luxuriously appointed air-conditioned rondavels and chalets. This camp makes an ideal venue for corporate clientele and senior management seminars as well as catering for the needs of foreign and local travellers who enjoy a certain amount of luxury during their bushveld holiday.

A feature of the camp is a thatched observation bar, the 'Gin Trap' overlooking a floodlit waterhole. There is also a filtered swimming pool. Day and night game drives are conducted in open four-wheel-drive vehicles and walking tours, led by experienced rangers, are also offered.

Tent Camp is a luxury tented camp accommodating a maximum of 14 guests. The character of the camp is entirely rustic, although every convenience is available to guests: the tents are insect-proofed and each has an en suite shower and toilet. Features of the camp are its very personalised atmosphere and the aura of wilderness which prevails. There is a swimming pool and game outings are conducted in the same manner as at Main Camp.

The tariff includes all meals, teas, coffees, snacks, accommodation, safaris in open Landcruisers, transfers to and from the Tuli airstrip and the Pontdrift border post.

STEVENSFORD GAME RESERVE Tariff: Budget
Manica Travel, P O Box 1188, Gaborone. Tel 35 2021. Fax 30 5552. Kudu Travel, Private Bag 00130, Gaborone. Tel 37 2224. Fax 37 4224. Travel Bags, P O Box 556, Selebi-Phikwe. Tel 81 4106. Fax 81 4107

Accommodation	*Facilities*	*Activities/attractions*
Chalets	First aid	Birding
Self-catering	Swimming pool	Game-viewing
Booking essential	Waterholes	Game drives
	Hides	Horse riding
		Walks

After crossing the border into Botswana at Groblersbrug/Martin's Drif and driving a further 8 km, turn right at Sherwood Ranch, onto the Sherwood Ranch/Selebi-Phikwe road. Immediately after the veterinary barrier on this road there is a well signposted entrance to the reserve.

The camp of this 3 500-ha reserve is built in beautiful riverine habitat, close to the banks of the Limpopo River. Accommodation is provided in thatched, rondavel-type chalets. Game Bird Lodge has three rooms each with two beds and en suite facilities and its own boma with dining, bar and kitchen facilities. The other chalet has two beds and two bunk beds, en suite facilities and its own private boma with a galley kitchen and dining facilities. Clients must bring all their own consumables; all other equipment, i.e. bedding, crockery, electric fridge and stove is provided. Firewood is also available.

Stevensford is open all year round with the swimming pool proving very popular in the summer months. There are six permanent waterholes and several hides from which to view and photograph game and birds, while horse riding through the bush is an unforgettable experience. When the Limpopo flows it is possible to go boating and fishing.

Each room has a list of the game and birds sighted at Stevensford and guests are invited to inform the camp manager of any new sightings.

TULI LODGE Tariff: Medium

Reservations: Tel (011) 482 2634. Fax (011) 482 2635 or Tel (011) 726 6894 or Fax (011) 726 4473 or a South African or Botswana travel agent.

Accommodation	*Facilities*	*Activities/attractions*
Chalets	Licensed	Birding
Booking essential	Swimming pool	Game-viewing
	Luxury conference	Foot safaris
	venue	Game drives
	Hides	Night drives

Clients can fly into Tuli Lodge from Lanseria near Johannesburg, or they can drive there. For the fly-in guests customs facilities are organised by the lodge.

If approaching from South Africa, drive to Pontdrift. The lodge is about 7 km from the border in a westerly direction. About 2 km beyond the border there is a road to the left signposted 'Tuli Lodge'.

Vehicles can safely be left at the border post and guests will be transferred by Tuli Lodge vehicles. One can drive through but it is not advisable due to the road surfaces and the possibility, at any time during the summer months, of the Limpopo coming down in flood. (If the river should flood, you can enjoy the thrill of being hauled across a raging flooded African river in a wire cage suspended on a steel hawser! It's great fun and perfectly safe.)

As the most popular time to visit the wildlife areas of Botswana is winter, when the bush is dry, dusty and brown, Tuli Lodge makes a most dramatic impression. Visitors think they have arrived at an oasis. At any time of year the garden is breathtaking. Its design is bold and the effect a beautiful, harmonious blend of indigenous trees and all manner of plants.

The buildings have also been sensitively designed to blend and complement the setting — the bar embraces a tree, and the dining room seems to be part of the garden with its etched glass panels protecting but not separating one from the world around.

Tuli Lodge can accommodate 38 people in its luxury en suite rooms and has sophisticated conference facilities for up to 40 people.

Apart from merely relaxing in the beauty of the surroundings, guests are also taken on game drives. The sparkling swimming pool is an attraction for the sun worshipper.

Western Delta area

The western part of the Okavango Delta is the place for fishing enthusiasts and several fishing camps have been established here. This is the home of Botswana's famous basket-makers. It is fascinating to visit villages such as Nokaneng, Gomare and Etsha, and to meet the basket-makers there. It requires time and patience, but the effort can be rewarded with some really special baskets.

Two other attractions of the Western Delta are the Tsodilo Hills and Drotsky's Cave. Full details about these places are given in Chapter 2. A quick way through the Caprivi Strip is also described in that chapter.

FISH EAGLE LODGE/DROTSKY'S CABINS Tariff: Medium
Private Bag 01, Shakawe. Tel & Fax 66 1206

Accommodation	Facilities	Activities/attractions
A-frame chalets	First aid	Fishing
Reed huts	Licensed	Birding
Houseboat	Radio	Boating
Camping	Boat hire	

Probably the most distant of the Okavango lodges from Maun, Drotsky's as Fish Eagle Lodge is sometimes called (in honour of its owners), can be reached by tarred road or by air.

If you are into fishing on the big rivers of the Okavango, this is the place for you, for the camp overlooks the main river as it flows down the 100 km of panhandle. This is also a birdwatcher's paradise; the birdlife is good all year but particularly spectacular from September to December.

There is a choice of very comfortable accommodation and the rates are moderate. Five-metre powerboats are available for daily or hourly hire so this is an ideal opportunity for independent travellers visiting the Western Delta by road to take a day or two off, camp and explore the waterways.

A unique aspect of this camp is the opportunity to hire a houseboat (minimum of six people) and spend time out in some of the remotest parts of the delta.

GUMA LAGOON CAMP Tariff: Budget (camping) Medium (luxury tents) P O Box 66, Maun. Tel 66 0351 / 66 0978. Fax 66 0571

Accommodation	Facilities	Activities/attractions
Luxury tents	First aid	Motorboats
Self-cater	Radio	Mekoro
tents	Licensed	Bird walks
Camping	Restaurant	Bird drives
Booking essential	Airstrip	Fishing

This camp, surrounded by palm trees, papyrus and reed beds, is situated on the banks of Guma Lagoon in the north-west delta. Guma Lagoon is one of the largest lagoons in this area.

Guma has a warm family atmosphere and most of the clients at this camp have been here before. There is a choice of facilities: camping, self-catering accommodation in furnished and serviced wilderness tents and full accommodation in nine luxury en suite tents.

For those camping or staying in self-catering accommodation it is possible to book meals. Special rates are available for large groups or families staying for six days or more in the fishing season.

There are two ways to get to Guma: by air or by road. The road is tarred to Etsha-13 but the last 11 km must be undertaken by four-wheel-drive. The camp provides parking under shade-cloth with a watchman for saloon cars and arranges a four-wheel transfer into camp.

Geoff Randall manufactures 'real' fibreglass mekoro here in an attempt to preserve the trees.

The main activity of this camp is fishing, which is excellent all year round.

JEDIBE ISLAND CAMP Tariff: High
Private Bag 14, Maun. Tel 66 0086. Fax 66 0632 Central reservations: P O
Box 651171, Benmore 2010, South Africa. Tel (011) 884 1458/9. Fax (011)
883 6255. Telex 42 8642

Accommodation	*Facilities*	*Activities/attractions*
Luxury tents	First aid	Birding
Booking essential	Radio	Game-viewing
	Swimming pool	Mokoro trails
		Boating
		Fishing
		Walking
		Sunset cruises

The island is located in the north-west of the Okavango Delta and has
deep water all year round. The annual variation in water level is little
more than 35 cm!

There are no roads here and no vehicles. Jedibe is strictly a water experience. The two main activities are mokoro trails and boating, allowing guests to experience the two very different habitats in the area.

To the north-east of the camp are the big rivers and large open expanses of water. Elsewhere, the floodplains are accessible only by mekoro.

Walks under the supervision of licensed professional guides are undertaken on the larger islands. Guests may also go on sunset cruises on
a double-decker boat.

Accommodation is in luxury tents with en suite facilities and there is
a large thatched lounge, dining room and bar area.

This region is one of the best in Botswana for Pel's fishing owl. You
can also expect to find pygmy geese, swamp boubou, western banded
snake eagle, Heuglin's robin and slaty egrets.

As far as game is concerned, you can expect to see buffalo, hippo,
crocodile, sitatunga and red lechwe.

NCAMASERI LODGE Tariff: Medium
Private Bag 23, Maun. In South Africa, Tel (011) 788 3923. Fax (011) 880
8401

Accommodation	*Facilities*	*Activities/attractions*
Thatched en suite	First aid	Birding
chalets	Licensed	Fishing/Boating
Booking essential	Restaurant	Walks

Accommodation	Facilities	Activities/attractions
	Radio	Aquatic game-
	Airfield	viewing
	Curio shop	Houseboat safaris
		Mokoro trails
		Tsodilo Hills/San

This island lodge, set amongst giant riverine trees on the north-west panhandle of the Okavango Delta, is accessible by air or vehicle followed by a short boat ride to the island. Ncamaseri Lodge is a small, intimate camp accommodating 12 guests in luxury en suite chalets, each with its own private wooden deck overlooking the floodplain. It is a mecca for the fisherman or birdwatcher and also offers river safaris for four guests in two luxury cabins on the *Kubu Queen* houseboat. Alternatively, this may be used for day safaris or sundowner cruises for Ncamaseri guests. The lodge is renowned for its excellent cuisine. It is also famed for the remarkable horse safaris organised by Barney Besterlink. A combination of horse safari, a stay at the lodge and a night or two on the houseboat is something you'll never forget!

SHAKAWE FISHING LODGE Tariff: Medium
P O Box 12, Shakawe. Tel 66 0822/823. Fax 66 0493

Accommodation	Facilities	Activities/attractions
Chalets	First aid	Birding
Camping	Licensed	Walks
Booking advisable	Swimming pool	Fishing
	Radio	Boating
	Meals	Tsodilo Hills

Shakawe Fishing Lodge, one of the first tourist camps to be established, has been in operation since 1969. It has recently been renovated and refurbished.

The lodge is situated 375 km from Maun and 30 km from Mohembo on the Botswana/Namibian border. Both of these roads are tarred so access to the lodge by road is no problem. There is also a good airstrip at Shakawe, but there are no customs/immigration facilities so clearance must be obtained in Maun. The lodge will organise transfers to and from the airstrip.

The lodge is perched on a high bank overlooking a bend in the Okavango River. Birdwatching is outstanding, owing to the wide range of habitats (riverine bush, savanna and semi-desert) found in a small area.

Accommodation is in five large brick and thatch chalets with en suite facilities and five two-room tents set under thatch with separate ablution facilities. These tents should be replaced by chalets in 1996.

The campsite, set under trees, also overlooks the river and there are ablution blocks with hot and cold showers and flush toilets. Firewood is available. Campers can either cater for themselves or eat in the dining room on request.

The best time for fishing is from April to November. The bream are good in June and July and the best time for taking on the fighting tiger fish is from August to October.

The lodge will arrange day visits to the Tsodilo Hills for guests, but only at the discretion of management, as the road is very poor.

Credit card facilities are not available at the lodge as there are no banking facilities in Shakawe at present.

MOBILE SAFARI OPERATORS

If you are unable to provide your own transport for exploring Botswana or if you prefer to take advantage of others' expertise to take you off the beaten track, there are a number of operators who run mobile safaris in Botswana.

A mobile safari is a commercial safari operation which moves from place to place by boat, vehicle or both, camping in the bush or using the facilities offered by some of the fixed camps or national park campsites

Starting points

There are basically two categories of starting point, those outside Botswana and those within. The closer you can get to your main area of interest under your own steam, the cheaper the safari will be.

The main starting points in Botswana are Gaborone, Kasane and Maun

There is a good quality tarred road to Gaborone and Kasane and any reasonable car can get there from South Africa, Zimbabwe or Zambia. Maun can only be reached from Nata, the track from Kasane via the Savute or from the borders with Namibia. The road from Nata to Maun is tarred; the road via Savute varies in condition depending upon the time of the year and how much traffic has been on it, but it should not be tackled unless in a four-wheel-drive vehicle.

Trying to keep abreast of all the mobile safari operators in Botswana is a daunting undertaking!

Below is a list, with addresses and contact numbers, of all the established and reputable mobile safari operators known to me. It includes those based in Botswana as well as in neighbouring countries.

If an operator or his company has been in operation for 10 years or more this appears in brackets after the name (e.g. +12).

It is now possible to go on a number of different and unusual types of safaris such as walking safaris, elephant back safaris and horseback safaris. So brief information about the specialist safaris has been included after the traditional safari operators.

After this appears a series of variables which you need to consider before making a final decision as to which operator you intend to choose. These variables have a strong influence on the cost of the safari you are planning.

I suggest that, after considering these, you contact your own travel agent, or one of those listed on pages 197-198 and let their recommendations guide you to the final choice. After all, the agents are right on the spot, especially those in Maun, and have first-hand knowledge of the mobile safari business.

List of known mobile safari operators

All of whose Botswana staff are understood to hold Professional Guides licences.)

Afroventures (+20)	P O Box 1200, Paulshof 2056, South Africa. Tel (011) 807 3720. Fax (011) 807 3480 P O Box 232, Kasane, Botswana. Tel 65 0456. Fax 65 0119
Capricorn Safari (+10)	P/Bag 21, Maun, Botswana. Tel 66 0351. Fax 66 0571. Telex 2612 BD
Crocodile Camp Safaris (+10)	Box 46, Maun, Botswana. Tel 66 0265. Fax 66 0493. Telex 2487 BD
Drifters (+10)	P O Box 48434, Roosevelt Park 2129, South Africa. Tel (011) 486 1224. Fax (011) 486 1237

Go Wild (+10)

P O Box 56, Kasane, Botswana. Tel 25 0237. Fax 25 0223. Telex 2763 BD

Island Safaris

P O Box 116, Maun, Botswana. Tel 66 0300. Fax 66 0205. Telex 2482 BD

Kalahari-Kavango Safaris (+10)

P/Bag 053, Maun, Botswana. Tel 66 0981

Karibu Safaris (+10)

P/Bag 39, Maun, Botswana. Tel 66 0493 or P O Box 35196, Northway, Durban 4065, South Africa. Tel (031) 83 9774. Fax (031) 83 1957

Kitso Safari (+10)

P O Box 236, Maun, Botswana. Tel & Fax 66 0493. Telex 2487 BD

Koro Safari (+20

P/Bag 22, Maun, Botswana. Tel 66 0205

Nata Lodge (+10)

P/Bag 10, Francistown, Botswana. Tel 61 1260. Fax 61 1210

Okavango Wilderness Safaris (+10)

P/Bag 14, Maun, Botswana. Tel 66 0086. Fax 66 0632. Central Reservations P O Box 651171, Benmore 2010, South Africa. Tel (011) 884 1458/9. Fax (011) 883 6255

Overland Safaris (+10)

P O Box 82, Warden 9890, South Africa. Tel (058) 643 0646. Fax (058) 643 0670

Papadi Safaris (+10)

P O Box 3684, Honeydew 2040, South Africa. Tel (011) 679 3525. Fax (011) 475 5369

Penduka Safaris (+20)

P O Box 55413, Northlands 2116 South Africa Tel & Fax (011) 883 4303

Penstone Safaris (+20)

P/Bag 13, Maun, Botswana. Tel 66 0351. Fax 66 0571. Telex 2612 BD

Peter Comley Safaris (+10)	P O Box 55, Kasane, Botswana. Tel 65 0234. Fax 65 0223
Sitatunga Camping Safaris (+10)	P/Bag 47, Maun, Botswana. Tel & Fax 66 0570/66 0258
Soren Lindstrom (+20)	P O Box 236, Maun, Botswana. Tel 66 0822. Fax 66 0493
Thandamanzi Safaris	P/Bag K24, Kasane, Botswana. Tel 65 0440. Fax 65 0314

Specialist safaris

(Many of the lodges also offer special excursions, such as mokoro trails, houseboat safaris and fishing safaris.)

Hunting safaris

Hunters Africa	P O Box 11, Kasane. Tel 65 0385. Fax 65 0383
Linyanti Explorations	P O Box 22, Kasane. Tel 65 0505. Fax 65 0352
Safari South	P O Box 40, Maun. Tel 66 0211/66 0212/66 0213. Fax 66 0379
Vira Safaris	P O Box 119, Maun. Tel 66 0284. Fax 66 0593 or P O Box 1602, Gaborone. Tel & Fax 37 2309

Horseback safaris

Okavango Horse Safaris	African Horse Safari Association, 36 12th Avenue, Parktown North 2193, South Africa. Tel (011) 788 3923. Fax (011) 880 8401

Elephant back safaris

Elephant Back Safaris	P/Bag 332, Maun. Tel 66 1260. Fax 66 1005

Walking trails

Linyanti Explorations	P O Box 22, Kasane. Tel 65 0505. Fax 65 0352

Canoeing trails

Linyanti Explorations	P O Box 22, Kasane. Tel 65 0505. Fax 65 0352

Factors affecting price

When you plan to travel with a mobile operator there are various aspects that you will need to consider. Use the list of factors below to help you make your choices. Discuss them with a travel agent who is experienced in this field. The nature of your choices will affect the price.

Do-it-yourself or full service: the degree to which you are prepared to physically participate in the day-to-day chores of safari life is a considerable factor influencing cost.

Level of service: some companies ask you to 'help here and there', others want you to do nothing, while some go to the extreme of pampering you as in the great and fabled East African safaris of the colonial era.

Ready made vs tailor-made packages: whether the safari is a standard package or whether it is tailored to your precise requirements.

Number of days

Number of people

Distance travelled

Places visited: you pay extra for visiting expensive places, such as Chobe National Park and Moremi Game Reserve. You also pay for exclusivity and for complete privacy.

Company's reputation: you can expect to pay a little more for the security of a good reputation based on many years of good service.

Guide's reputation: sometimes you will have to pay a premium for the leader or guide you would like to use.

Extras: such things as a flight above the Victoria Falls, or an extra trip by mokoro may not be part of the 'package'. Try to check these.

Speciality tours: often the price of the safari is influenced by specialised purposes. For instance, a horseback trail, birding, photography, etc.

9. MISCELLANEOUS INFORMATION

LANGUAGE AND CUSTOMS

Every language and culture has its own norms and customs of behaviour. Politeness in one society may be the height of rudeness in another. A good place to start is with simple courtesy and respect for the people you deal with. Using a few phrases of the local language can help to smooth the flow of communication.

A number of different languages are spoken in Botswana but as Setswana is the official language, greetings in this language will be understood throughout the country.

A basic lesson in Setswana will help you unravel the difference between the words Botswana, Batswana, Motswana and Setswana. The root 'tswana' takes on various meanings when different prefixes are added to it. So *Botswana* is the country; *Motswana* means one of the people of the country; *Batswana* is the plural, meaning more than one person of the country; *Setswana* is the language of the country.

The Batswana set great store by politeness and courteous greeting. You don't have to be a great linguist to take your first step. In fact it must be one of the easiest languages in which to be polite. Go back to what was probably the very first word you ever uttered — Ma. Lengthen the m sound as though you were about to start humming. Say 'Mma' and you have learnt the courteous form of addressing women in Botswana.

Adding 'Mma' onto a communication in English immediately makes it sound so much more polite — 'How much is this basket, Mma?'

The courteous form of addressing men is 'Rra'. The same principle applies, i.e. lengthen the r sound - 'Rra'.

The equivalent of 'Hello' in Setswana is 'Dumela', the stress being placed on the middle syllable. Marry your new word with the appropriate form of address and you have made a very useful investment in communicating with the people you will meet.

If you have no further linguistic ambitions the only other word to learn is 'Go siame', which is a general all purpose end to a conversation that means 'It's all right'.

PUBLIC HOLIDAYS

New Year's Day — 1st January, public holiday — 2nd January, Good Friday (variable), public holiday on the Saturday following Good Friday, Easter Sunday, Easter Monday, Ascension Day (variable), Sir Seretse Khama Day — 1st July, President's Day — 17th July, public holiday on the day following President's Day, Botswana Day — 30th September, public holiday on the day following Botswana Day (if Botswana Day falls on a Saturday or Sunday then it will be celebrated on the following Monday), Christmas Day — 25th December, Boxing Day — 26th December.

(During public holidays, all government offices, banks, businesses and shops are closed. Some of the larger shops may offer shortened trading hours. Public transport may alter normal schedules.)

BANKS

There are four commercial banks in Botswana: Barclays Bank of Botswana Ltd, Standard Chartered Bank of Botswana Ltd, First National Bank of Botswana Ltd and Stanbic Bank of Botswana Ltd.

The banks provide high branch coverage backed up by agencies and automatic teller machines (ATMs) in all the major towns of Botswana.

Barclays' opening times:
Main branches: Monday to Friday   8.30 to 14.30
Saturday   8.30 to 10.45

First National Bank's opening times:
Main branches:
Monday to Friday   9.00 to 12.45 2.15 to 15.30
Saturday   8.30 to 11.00

Standard Chartered's opening times:
Main branches: Monday to Friday   8.15 to 14.00
Saturday   8.15 to 10.45

Stanbic's opening times:
Main branches: Monday to Friday   9.00 to 15.30
Saturday   9.00 to 11.00

Banks are not open on public holidays. All these banks operate agencies around the country. The agencies do not always follow standard opening hours, opening for shorter periods and often not on Saturdays. Opening times can be ascertained on enquiry.

Such agencies all maintain current and savings accounts and should cash traveller's cheques. They will not deal in foreign currencies, except for the changing of rands and pula. Except by special arrangement, they will not be able to issue foreign exchange or traveller's cheques.

GOVERNMENT OFFICES AND HOURS

Government office hours are Monday to Friday: 7.30 to 12.30, 13.45 to 16.30.

The following is a useful list of postal addresses and telephone numbers of some government ministries and departments:

Ministry	Gaborone address	Telephone/s
Office of the President	P/Bag 001	35 0800
Agriculture	P/Bag 003	35 0500
Commerce & Industry	P/Bag 004	360 1200
Finance & Development	P/Bag 008	35 0100
Health	P/Bag 0038	35 2000
Labour & Home affairs	P/Bag 002	360 1000
Local Govt., Lands & Housing	P/Bag 006	35 4100
Director of vet. services	P/Bag 0032	35 0616
Dept Wildlife & National Parks	P O Box 131	37 1405
Registrar of Companies	P O Box 102	360 1290
Central Statistics Office	P/Bag 0024	35 2200
National Archives	P O Box 2994	360 1000
National Museum and Art Gallery	P/Bag 0014	37 4616
Dept of Immigration	P O Box 942	37 4545
Dept of Surveys & Lands	P/Bag 0037	35 3251
Police Headquarters	P/Bag 0012	35 1161
Dept of Civil Aviation	P O Box 250	37 1397
Dept Customs & Excise	P/Bag 0041	31 2455
Central arms registry	P/Bag 0012	35 1161 x 2466
Tourism department	P/Bag 0047	35 3024

ENTERTAINMENT

Many of the facilities indicated below are arranged by private clubs or hotels for their members or guests and are not usually available to the public. However, proprietors are most approachable and usually willing to allow visitors to use the facilities, sometimes on payment of a

small fee. Restaurants have not been listed in detail, mainly because of
the frequent changes in ownership, name and quality that are common
in this trade.

	Gaborone	Francistown	Lobatse	Maun
Cinema	*	*	*	
Theatre	*			
Cabaret	*			
Casino	*	*		
M-Net	*	*	*	*
Restaurant	*	*	*	*
Golf	*	*	*	
Squash	*	*	*	
Tennis	*	*	*	
Swimming	*	*	*	
Sailing	*	*		
Canoeing	*	*	*	

MEDICAL FACILITIES

Botswana has hospitals and health centres throughout the country. In
Gaborone the state hospital is Princess Marina Hospital (Tel 35 3221)
and in Francistown it is Jubilee Hospital (Tel 21 2333). In Gaborone there
is excellent medical and emergency service available at the Gaborone
Private Hospital, Private Bag BR 130, Gaborone. Tel 31 0999. Fax 30 1998.

Medical Rescue International has been operating in Botswana since
1991 and offers immediate and professional help in a medical emergency.
They have a network of qualified medical staff, ambulances and rapid
response vehicles equipped to advanced life support level and are able
to provide medical air evacuations with trained flight personnel and
appropriate equipment. They may be contacted at MRI Botswana, Private Bag BR256, Gaborone. Tel (Admin) 30 3066. Tel (Emergency) 30 1601.
Fax 30 2117.

VETERINARY SERVICES

There are limited veterinary services in Botswana. There are state vets
in many of the main centres but only private vet clinics in Francistown
and Gaborone. Tlokweng Veterinary Clinic in Gaborone offers a good
and reliable 24-hour veterinary service. They may be contacted at: Veterinary and Agricultural Consultants, P O Box 201028, Gaborone. Tel &
Fax (24 hrs) 32 8689. They are situated on the outskirts of Gaborone in
Tlokweng, on the main road to the South African border.

PETROL AND DIESEL

Petrol and diesel are available throughout the country from one of the following fuel companies: Caltex, Engen, Shell or Total. Prices frequently change and there is a variation in prices across the country. In general, the more remote the supply the more expensive it will be. The greatest range is about 15 per cent above the lowest (Gaborone) price. Petrol and diesel are approximately the same price.

Fuel is available on all the main routes through the country. It is sold at an increasing number of outlets, on a 24-hour basis in Gaborone, Francistown, Mahalapye and Serowe.

At all other centres fuel sales tend to be limited to approximately 6 am to 6 pm. However, it is generally true that the more remote the area the more amenable the owner will be to negotiation on this point.

The list that follows is of the more remote places, all of which generally sell fuel from 7 am to 6 pm. Some close for lunch and some close on Saturday afternoons and Sundays. The places are:

Artesia, Bokspits, Bray, Charles Hill, Dukwi, Etsha, Kang, Kanye, Lerala, Masunga, Metlobo, Metsemotlhaba, Mmadinare, Mmathethe, Mochudi, Mosopa (Moshupa), Nata, Parr's Halt, Phepeng, Pitsane, Phitshane-Molopo, Ramokgwebane, Sefophe, Sekoma, Sherwood Ranch, Shoshong, Sikwane, Takatokwane, Tonotha, Tsabong, Tshesebe, Tutume, Werda.

SHOPPING

Most day-to-day consumer items are readily available in the larger centres. There are an increasing number of shops in Gaborone such as one might find in a modern shopping complex elsewhere, which are not only concerned with supplying the basics but also stock luxury items.

There are good supermarkets in Lobatse, Gaborone, Mahalapye, Palapye, Selebi-Phikwe, Francistown and Maun. Kasane also has a small supermarket. In these towns you will also find good clothing stores, bottlestores, hardware shops, chemists, bookshops and curio shops. In the larger centres imported fresh vegetables can usually be purchased without difficulty. Mondays and days following public holidays may sometimes present the shopper with unexpected temporary shortages, particularly of fresh products such as milk and vegetables.

Hours of trading are generally from 8 am to 5 pm, although bottlestores open at 10 am and close at 7 pm, Monday to Saturday. Some shops close for an hour at lunchtime. Sunday trading takes place at some of the supermarkets in the larger centres. Again, in most of the larger centres at least one shop remains open until as late as 8 or 9 pm, selling the usual range of essential household requirements. This type of general dealer often remains open on public holidays as well. During such holidays, all government offices, businesses, banks and shops are closed, although many of the supermarkets in the larger centres have special shortened trading times.

Botswana does not have a sophisticated photographic market; if you are using specialist film, it is best to bring it with you. Colour slide film is only available in the main centres and in some of the safari camps. There is a small danger that it might be out of date or have been ill-protected against the heat and thus damaged. Some centres can process several types of colour prints on the 'one hour' processing machines which are becoming common, but all colour slides and prints that do not fit these machines are sent for processing outside the country.

In the small villages around the country, shopping is a very much more precarious activity. Almost every village has its store or stores and a bottlestore or 'liquor restaurant'. Some of these outlets stock an amazing range of goods, while all will have at least the basics — sugar, dried milk, tea, some kind of coffee, cigarettes, soap and soap powders, tinned fruit, corned beef, etc. The bottlestores usually restrict themselves to soft drinks, beer and the cheaper spirits — but they are occasionally capable of unearthing an unexpected bottle of wine or a good whisky! Most of the stores on the main routes have refrigerators but in the remoter areas you will get nothing cold and nothing fresh.

PUBLIC TRANSPORT

Air

Botswana has its own airline, Air Botswana, which provides connections between the following centres: Gaborone, Francistown, Kasane, Maun, Johannesburg, Lusaka, Harare, Victoria Falls and Windhoek. The following international airlines have scheduled service to Botswana: Comair from Johannesburg to Gaborone; British Airways from London to Gaborone; Air Zimbabwe, in collaboration with Air Botswana, from Harare to Gaborone; and Namib Air from Windhoek to Maun.

There are taxis available at all airports to convey the traveller to his hotel, if no other arrangement has been made. Some hotels collect their guests.

Buses

There are reliable, regular long-distance bus services between the main towns and villages of Botswana. Numerous buses work these routes in a somewhat unscheduled manner. To make use of this service it is necessary to get to one of the signposted bus-stops on the route you wish to take — and simply wait. These facilities are far more common on the tarred roads and to villages close to the main towns. In the rural areas, on dirt roads, they exist hardly at all.

If you are starting in one of the larger urban areas you can ask for directions to the bus terminus. Most centres now have them. It is from this point that almost all the buses start their journeys and it is much easier to find one going to your destination.

There is a daily bus service from Gaborone to Harare leaving from the bus terminus next to the station. It is also possible to take a Greyhound coach either to or from Johannesburg and Gaborone on Monday, Thursday, Friday or Sunday. These coaches leave from Kudu Service Station in the Mall and can be booked through travel agents or in South Africa through Greyhound offices.

Rail

The railway line from Mafikeng to Bulawayo in Zimbabwe enters the country at Ramatlabama in the south, passing through Lobatse, Gaborone and most major towns in the east, continuing to Francistown and Plumtree in the north. There are a number of passenger services.

There is a night train which leaves Mafikeng at 4.30 pm every day, stops at all stations and arrives in Bulawayo around midday the following day. There is also a reverse service down to Mafikeng. This train offers an economy class and a sleeper class.

Daily trains run to and from Gaborone and Francistown in the morning and the evening from Monday to Thursday. On Fridays there are also trains running to and from Gaborone and Francistown in the afternoon. These trains offer first class and economy class facilities.

Botswana Railways also offers special commuter services to and from Pilane and Gaborone, and Lobatse and Gaborone. The train fares are all very reasonable.

HITCH-HIKING

Conditions for the hitch-hiker in Botswana are little different from those elsewhere; there is an element of risk and this varies from time to time. On the main routes it is more difficult to get a lift, but this is compensated for by a higher volume of traffic. Often you will be asked to contribute towards petrol costs. In rural areas there is far less traffic but drivers seem more disposed to offer a lift.

TELEPHONE SYSTEM

Botswana has one of the most advanced telecommunications systems in Africa with automatic telephone exchanges in the larger towns and some smaller towns.

All of these exchanges are connected by an internal trunk-dialling system and there is international direct dialling.

In areas where there are no telephones, emergency messages can be passed by two means. The police will accept messages, including international telegrams. Most of the professional hunters and safari operators operate a radio network, through which messages can be passed.

Telex and facsimile services

There are public telex services at the post offices in the following centres: Francistown, Gaborone, Lobatse, Palapye and Selebi-Phikwe. Facsimile terminals are available at the Botswana Telecommunication Corporation offices in Gaborone and Francistown.

Many of the bigger hotels will also allow you to use their facsimile facilities if you are resident in the hotel.

OFFICE SERVICES

Gaborone
Gestetner Botswana
P O Box 838, Gaborone. Tel 32 5921. Fax 32 5922.
Photocopying and facsimile facilities.

Lobatse
Churchill Office Agencies
P O Box 55, Lobatse. Tel 33 0636. Fax 33 0109
Secretarial services: typing, photocopying, facsimile facilities; insurance; and photo developing — will send films to Gaborone.

Maun
Ensign Agencies
P O Box 66, Maun. Tel 66 0351. Fax 66 0571
General office services, telephone and facsimile facilities.

Kasane
Kasane Enterprises
P O Box 55, Kasane. Tel 65 0234. Fax 65 0223. Telex 2763 BD
Secretarial and office agency; travel agency; forwarding of messages and parcels; telephone, facsimile and telex facilities; and radio contact with most safari operators.

Selebi-Phikwe
M & M Secretarial
P O Box 379, Selebi-Phikwe. Tel 81 0626. Fax 81 0364. Telex 2244 BD
Secretarial services: typing, photocopying; facsimile and telephone facilities.

TRAVEL AGENCIES

Maun

Bathusi Travel & Safaris	P/Bag 44, Maun. Tel 66 0647. Fax 66 0664. Telex 2612 BD
Bonaventure Botswana	P O Box 201, Maun. Tel 66 0503. Fax 66 0502. Telex 2616 BD
Merlin Travel	P/Bag 13, Maun. Tel 66 0351/66 0635. Fax 66 0571/66 0036
Okavango Wilderness Safaris	P/Bag 14, Maun. Tel 66 0086. Fax 66 0632
Travel Wild	P O Box 236, Maun. Tel 66 0822/66 0823. Fax 66 0493

Francistown

VIP Travel	P/Bag 225, Francistown. Tel 21 6600. Fax 21 4526

Gaborone

Manica Travel	P O Box 1188, Gaborone. Tel 35 2021. Fax 30 5552. Telex 2523 BD
Kudu Travel	P/Bag 00130, Gaborone. Tel 37 2224. Fax 37 4224
Travel Centre	P O Box 1950, Gaborone. Tel 30 4360. Fax 30 5840
Travel Promotions	P/Bag 00130, Gaborone. Tel 30 5283. Fax 37 4224. Telex 2470 BD
Travel Wise	P O Box 2482, Gaborone. Tel 30 3244. Fax 30 3245

Kasane

Kasane Enterprises	P O Box 55, Kasane. Tel 65 0234. Fax 65 0223. Telex 2763 BD

Selebi-Phikwe

Travel Bags	P O Box 556, Selebi-Phikwe. Tel 81 4106. Fax 81 4107

AIRCRAFT CHARTER AND MAINTENANCE

Air charter

Gaborone

Executive Charter	P/Bag SK6, Gaborone. Tel 37 5257. Fax 37 5258
Kalahari Air Services & Charter	P O Box 41278, Gaborone. Tel 35 1804/35 3593. Fax 31 2015
Okavango Air	P O Box 10088, Gaborone. Tel 31 3308. Fax 35 6949

Maun

Aer-Kavango	P O Box 169, Maun. Tel 66 0393. Fax 66 0623
Air Xaxaba	P/Bag 13, Maun. Tel 66 0302. Fax 66 0571
Delta Air	P O Box 39, Maun. Tel 66 0044. Fax 66 0589
Elgon Air	P/Bag 198, Maun. Tel 66 0654. Fax 66 0037

Ngami Air	P O Box 119, Maun.
	Tel & Fax 66 0530
Northern Air	P O Box 27, Maun.Tel 66 0385.
	Fax 66 0379
Sefofane Air Charter	P/Bag 159, Maun.
	Tel & Fax 66 0778
Wildlife Helicopters	P/Bag 161, Maun.
	Tel & Fax 66 0664

Kasane

| Air Chobe | P O Box 280, Kasane. |
| | Tel 65 0532/65 0795. Fax 65 0223 |

Aircraft maintenance

There are two aircraft maintenance businesses in Botswana.

In Gaborone, Kalahari Air Services and Charter offer full servicing for all types of aircraft, including jets. Servicing ranges from routine maintenance to 50-, 100- and 2 000-hour servicing and re-builds.

In Maun, a general maintenance service is offered by Northern Air, including 50- and 100-hour servicing.

VEHICLE HIRE

Gaborone
Avis Rent A Car, Sir Seretse Khama Airport. P O Box 790, Gaborone. Tel 31 3039. Fax 31 2205. Telex 2723 BD. Also at Grand Palm Hotel, Tel 30 4282 and Gaborone Sun Hotel, Tel 30 3000. Van & Truck Hire, (vans, trucks and 4 x 4s). Plot 5649, Nakedi Road, Broadhurst. P O Box 916, Gaborone. Tel & Fax 31 2280. Holiday Car Rentals, Queens Road, The Mall, Gaborone. Tel 35 3970 (airport). Fax 31 4894.

Francistown
Avis, Francistown Airport. P O Box 222, Francistown. Tel 21 3901. Fax 21 2867. Holiday Car Rentals, Bluejacket Street, Francistown. P O Box 717, Francistown. Tel 21 4524. Fax 21 4526.

Maun
Avis Rent a Car, opposite Maun Airport. P O Box 130, Maun. Tel & Fax 66 0570. Holiday Car Rentals, Maun Airport. P/Bag 13, Maun. Tel 66 0820. Fax 660 3791.

Kasane
Avis Rent a Car, Cresta Mowana Safari Lodge, P O Box 339, Kasane. Tel 65 0144. Fax 65 0145. Holiday Car Rentals, Chobe Safari Lodge, P O Box 197, Kasane. Tel 65 0226. Fax 65 0129.

FOUNDATIONS AND DIPLOMATIC MISSIONS IN BOTSWANA

Diplomatic representatives

Embassy of the Republic of Angola
P/Bag BR 111
Gaborone
Tel: 30 0204 Fax: 37 5089

British High Commission
P/Bag 0023
Gaborone
Tel: 35 2841 Fax: 35 6105

Embassy of the People's Republic of China
P O Box 1031
Gaborone
Tel: 35 2209 Fax: 30 0156

Embassy of The Federal Republic of Germany
P O Box 315
Gaborone
Tel: 35 3143/35 3806 Fax: 35 3038

Embassy of France
P O Box 1424 Gaborone Tel: 35 3683/37 3863
Fax: 35 6114

High Commission of India
P/Bag 249
Gaborone
Tel: 37 2676 Fax: 37 4636

The People's Bureau of the Socialist People's Libyan Arab Jamahiriya
P O Box 180
Gaborone
Tel: 35 2481 Fax: 35 6928

High Commission of the Federal Republic of Nigeria
P O Box 274
Gaborone
Tel: 31 3561 Fax: 31 3738

Royal Norwegian Embassy
P O Box 879
Gaborone
Tel: 35 1501/2/3 Fax: 37 4685

Embassy of the Russian Federation
P O Box 81
Gaborone
Tel: 35 3389/35 3739 Fax: 35 2930

South African High Commission
P/Bag 00402
Gaborone
Tel: 30 4800/1/2/3/4 Fax: 30 5502

Embassy of Sweden
P/Bag 0017
Gaborone
Tel: 35 3912 Fax: 35 3942

Embassy of the United States of America
P O Box 90
Gaborone
Tel: 35 3982 Fax: 35 6947

High Commission of the Republic of Zambia
P O Box 362
Gaborone
Tel: 35 1951 Fax: 35 3952

High Commission of Zimbabwe
P O Box 1232
Gaborone
Tel: 31 4495 Fax: 30 5863

Consular offices and trade missions

Royal Danish Consulate
P O Box 367
Gaborone
Tel: 35 3505 Fax: 35 3473

Consulate Office of The Republic of Cuba
P O Box 40261
Gaborone
Tel: 35 1750

Honorary consuls
Belgium Honorary Consul
P O Box 160
Gaborone
Tel: 35 2364

Honorary Consul of Finland
P O Box 1904
Gaborone
Tel: 30 1500 Fax: 30 1966

Honorary Consul of Italy
P O Box 451
Gaborone
Tel: 35 2882 Fax: 37 5045

Honorary Consul of Ireland
P/Bag 00347
Gaborone
Tel: 30 3333

Honorary Consul of Netherlands
P O Box 457
Gaborone
Tel: 30 2194 Fax: 35 1200

Honorary Consul of Spain
P O Box 495
Gaborone
Tel: 31 2641 Fax: 37 3441

International organisations based in Botswana

United Nations Development Programme
Tel 35 2121. Fax 35 6093

Commission of the European Communities
Tel 31 4455. Fax 31 3626

United Nations High Commissioner for Refugees
Tel 35 6917. Fax 37 5131

World Health Organisation
Tel 37 1505/6. Fax 35 9483

World Food Programme
Tel 35 2121. Fax 35 6093

South African Development Community
Tel 35 1863. Fax 37 2848

United Nations Children's Fund
Tel 35 2752/35 1909. Fax 35 1233

SERVICE ORGANISATIONS AND SOCIETIES

Alliance Française
Plot 2939, Pudulogo Crescent, P O Box 1817, Gaborone. Tel & Fax 35 1650

American Women's International Association
Meets every second Wednesday of the month, Gaborone. Tel 30 9033

Botswana Bird Club
National Museum, Independence Ave, P O Box 71, Gaborone. Tel 35 1500. Fax 35 9321

Botswana Orientation Centre
Plot 2930, Pudulogo Crescent, P O Box 1482, Gaborone. Tel & Fax 35 1711

Botswana Red Cross Society
Red Cross Building, Plot 135 Independence Ave, P O Box 485, Gaborone. Tel 35 2465. Fax 31 2351

The Botswana Society
National Museum, P O Box 71, Gaborone. Tel 35 1500. Fax 35 9321

The Women's Corona Society
Meets monthly, Gaborone. Tel 30 2610/37 4671

Kalahari Conservation Society
Independence Ave, P O Box 859, Gaborone. Tel 37 4557. Fax 31 4259

Lions Region 5
Clubs at: Francistown, P O Box 412, Francistown; Gaborone, P O Box 618, Gaborone; Gaborone West, P O Box 401759, Gaborone; Jwaneng, P/Bag 18, Jwaneng; Lobatse, P O Box 118, Lobatse; Maun, P/Bag 01, Maun; Orapa Boteti, P O Box 84, Orapa; Palapye, P/Bag 0031; Selebi-Phikwe, P O Box 59, Selebi-Phikwe; Serowe, P/Bag 087, Serowe. The Gaborone club meets every fourth Tuesday of the month at 7 pm at the Gaborone Sun and has a bookstall in the Mall each Saturday morning. Additional information can be acquired by writing to club secretaries. Guest Lions welcome.

Rotary
Francistown meets every Tuesday lunchtime at the Marang Hotel. Tel
21 4412. Gaborone meets every Friday except public holidays, 12.30 pm,
Gaborone Sun Hotel. Tel 31 2718. Tirelo meets every Monday 7.30 pm
Grand Palm Hotel, Gaborone. Tel 31 2718. Lobatse meets every Monday
evening at the Golf Club, 7pm. Tel 33 2185. Selebi-Phikwe meets every
Wednesday lunchtime, Bosele Hotel. Tel 81 1141.

Round Table
Gaborone No 26 meets at 7 pm on the 4th Thursday of the month at the
Round Table Clubhouse at the Cricket Club. P O Box 372, Gaborone.
Gaborone No 64 meets at 7 pm every 3rd Thursday of the month at the
Round Table Clubhouse at the Kalahari Flying Club. P O Box 282,
Gaborone. Francistown No 47: P O Box 76, Francistown. Selebi-Phikwe
No 52: P O Box 158, Selebi-Phikwe. Lobatse No 56: P O Box 270, Lobatse.
Orapa No 61: P/Bag 1, Orapa. Jwaneng No 62: P O Box 461, Jwaneng.

Photographic Society
Meets 2nd Wednesday of the month, National Museum 7.30 pm,
Gaborone.

REFERENCE MATERIAL

It has often been said that Botswana must be one of the most researched
countries in Africa. Whether this is true or not, a great deal has certainly
been written about it.

Alec Campbell, former curator of the National Museum and Art Gallery and a resident of some 35 years' standing, has an encyclopaedic
knowledge of Botswana. His outstanding *Guide to Botswana* and the book-
let *Sites of Historic and National Interest in and around Gaborone* are highly
recommended, although now difficult to find.

Other recommended titles are:

Okavango by Johnson and Bannister
The Bushmen by Johnson and Bannister
Chobe Elephants by Bruce Aiken
Cry of the Kalahari by Mark and Delia Owens
Okavango from the Air by Herman Potgieter and Clive Walker
Guide to Kalahari Gemsbok National Park by Gus Mills
Birds of Botswana by Kenneth Newman
Birds of Southern Africa by Kenneth Newman
Roberts' Birds of Southern Africa by Gordon Maclean
Sasol Birds of Southern Africa by Ian Sinclair

Botswana Bird Atlas by Huw Penry
Kalahari: Life's Variety in Dune and Delta by Mike Main
The Shell Field Guide to the Common Trees of Okavango Delta and Moremi Game Reserve by Veronica Roodt
The Shell Map of Moremi Game Reserve by Veronica Roodt
The Shell Map of Chobe National Park by Veronica Roodt
Wild About the Okavango by Duncan Butchart
Traveller's Guide to Botswana by Peter Comley & Salome Meyer
Any handbook of snakes and reptiles of southern Africa, such as *The Dangerous Snakes of Africa* by Stephen Spawls and Bill Branch.
Guides to mammals of southern Africa, such as *Land Mammals of Southern Africa — a field guide* by Reay Smithers
A Field Guide to the Mammals of Botswana by Peter Comley & Salome Meyer
A Field Guide to the Tracks & Signs of Southern & East African Wildlife by Chris & Tilde Stuart
Wild Ways by Peter Apps.

Published by and obtainable from the Botswana Society, at the National Museum, Gaborone, are several of their outstanding works, including:

Botswana Notes and Records — the Society's annual journal.
Settlement in Botswana — proceedings of a symposium on population, history and land use planning, including problems of migration and urbanisation.
Drought in Botswana — proceedings of a symposium on the ecological consequences and strategic responses to drought, including recognition and prediction of drought conditions.
The Okavango Delta — which looks at the economy and ecology of one of the world's major wetlands.
The Management of Botswana's Environment — a look at the government's national conservation strategy in relation to development planning.

For the serious researcher the National Archives in Gaborone is an excellent source of material and, in this regard, another Botswana Society publication, *The Bibliography of Botswana* by Karala Jones, is an indispensable source of information.

For those with a less serious interest, there are national lending libraries in all the larger towns.

Route maps

USING THE ROUTE MAPS

This edition of the *Visitors Guide to Botswana* is innovative in several ways. Among them is the inclusion of GPS reference points and route maps. It is important for users to be quite clear about the role of these maps. I assume that everybody who uses this guide will either be well acquainted with the main road network in Botswana or will have with them a standard national road map of some sort.

For this reason, few of the main roads are included on the maps here. Those maps that are included are mostly of remote, off-road sections that are not featured on ordinary maps, or at least not in sufficient detail. The maps are mostly schematic; they are not to scale. North is always shown (but it may not point to the top of the page, as convention demands, due to the need to fit the route into a prescribed paper size — you can, of course, always rotate the book!). They have been tested by a number of users who have found them satisfactory and I believe you will have no difficulty with them either.

Key to the route maps

Xaka	Place with water (often)		▲	Campsite
	River		⬭	Pan
- - - - -	Cut-line		Ⓐ	GPS reference point
▬▬▬	Roads & tracks		=	Gate
▬·▬·▬	Vet Fence		)(	Bridge
▬▬▬	Reserve boundary		🏠	Lodge
▬··▬··▬	International boundary		🏠	Village
6,2	Distances in kilometres		✗✦	Border post
			?	Unknown route

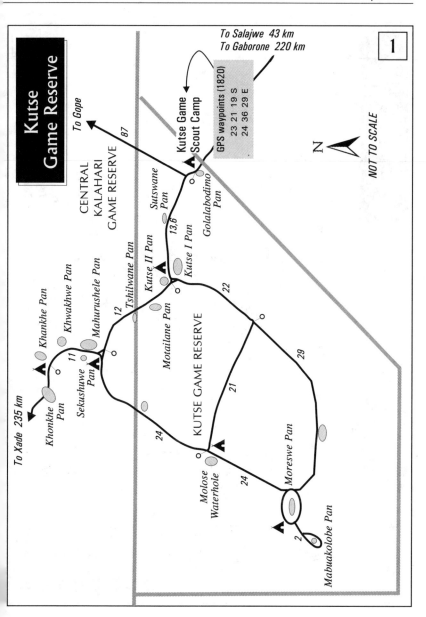

Kutse Game Reserve

To Salajwe 43 km
To Gaborone 220 km

Kutse Game Scout Camp

GPS waypoints (1820)
23 21 19 S
24 36 29 E

1

To Gope

CENTRAL KALAHARI GAME RESERVE

87

Suiswane Pan

13,6

Golalabodimo Pan

Kuse I Pan

Khankhe Pan

Khwakhwe Pan

Mahurushele Pan

Tshilwane Pan

Kutse II Pan

12

Motailane Pan

22

KUTSE GAME RESERVE

To Xade 235 km

Khonkhe Pan

Sekushuwe Pan

11

29

21

24

Molose Waterhole

24

Moreswe Pan

2

Mabuakolobe Pan

N

NOT TO SCALE

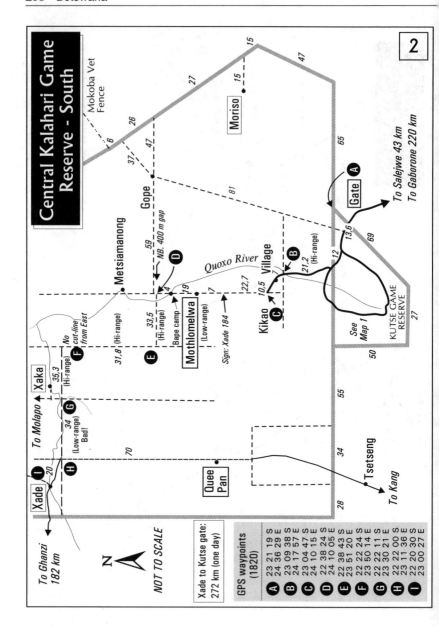

Central Kalahari Game Reserve - South

2

Mokoba Vet Fence

Moriso

Gope

NB. 400 m gap

Quoxo River

Metsiamanong

To Salejwe 43 km
To Gaborone 220 km

Gate A

B (Hi-range)

Village

Kikao C

See Map 1

KUTSE GAME RESERVE

D

Bape camp

Mothlomelwa (Low-range)

Sign: Xade 184

E (Hi-range)

(Hi-range)

No cut-line from East

Xaka

F (Hi-range)

G (Low-range) Bad!

To Molapo

Xade I

H

Quee Pan

Tsetseng

To Kang

To Ghanzi 182 km

N

NOT TO SCALE

Xade to Kutse gate: 272 km (one day)

GPS waypoints (1820)

A 23 21 19 S
   24 36 29 E
B 23 09 38 S
   24 17 57 E
C 23 04 47 S
   24 10 15 E
D 22 38 24 S
   24 10 05 E
E 22 38 43 S
   23 51 20 E
F 22 22 24 S
   23 50 14 E
G 22 22 11 S
   23 30 21 E
H 22 22 00 S
   23 11 36 S
I 22 20 30 S
   23 00 27 E

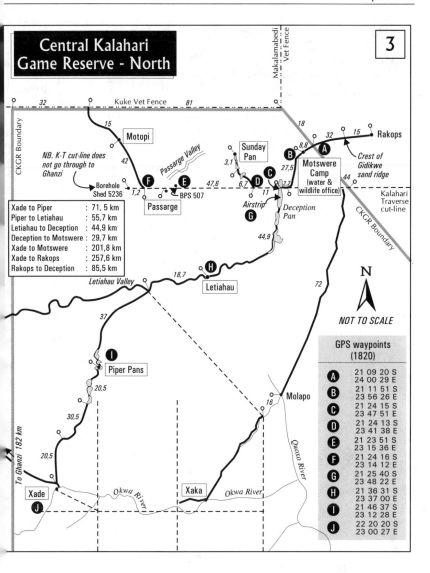

**Central Kalahari
Game Reserve - North**

3

Makalamabedi Vet Fence

CKGR Boundary

Kuke Vet Fence

32

81

15

Motopi

18

8,8

32

15

Rakops

NB. K-T cut-line does
not go through to
Ghanzi

42

Passarge Valley

Sunday
Pan

3,1

27,5

B

A

Motswere
Camp
(water &
wildlife office)

Crest of
Gidikwe
sand ridge

44

Kalahari
Traverse
cut-line

F

E

47,6

6,7

D

C

2,2

Borehole
Shed 5236

1,2

BPS 507

11

CKGR Boundary

Passarge

Airstrip

Deception
Pan

G

Xade to Piper	: 71, 5 km
Piper to Letiahau	: 55,7 km
Letiahau to Deception	: 44,9 km
Deception to Motswere	: 29,7 km
Xade to Motswere	: 201,8 km
Xade to Rakops	: 257,6 km
Rakops to Deception	: 85,5 km

44,9

18,7

H

N

Letiahau Valley

Letiahau

37

72

NOT TO SCALE

**GPS waypoints
(1820)**

I

Piper Pans

20,5

Molapo

16

30,5

Quoxo River

To Ghanzi 182 km

20,5

Xade

J

Okwa River

Xaka

Okwa River

A	21 09 20 S 24 00 29 E
B	21 11 51 S 23 56 26 E
C	21 24 15 S 23 47 51 E
D	21 24 13 S 23 41 38 E
E	21 23 51 S 23 15 36 E
F	21 24 16 S 23 14 12 E
G	21 25 40 S 23 48 22 E
H	21 36 31 S 23 37 00 E
I	21 46 37 S 23 12 28 E
J	22 20 20 S 23 00 27 E

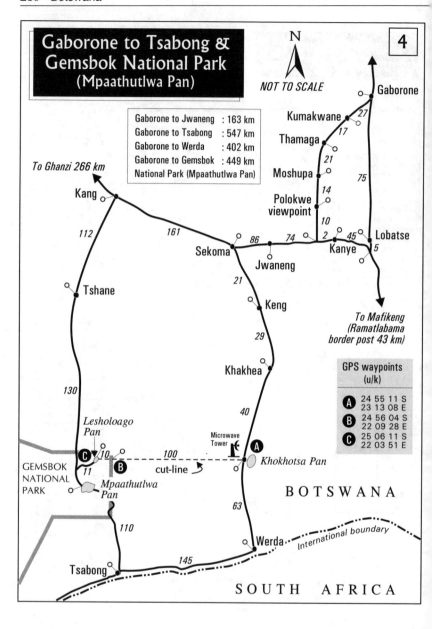

Gaborone to Tsabong & Gemsbok National Park
(Mpaathutlwa Pan)

N

NOT TO SCALE

4

Gaborone to Jwaneng : 163 km
Gaborone to Tsabong : 547 km
Gaborone to Werda : 402 km
Gaborone to Gemsbok : 449 km
National Park (Mpaathutlwa Pan)

To Ghanzi 266 km

Kang

Gaborone

Kumakwane 27
Thamaga 17
21
Moshupa 75
14
Polokwe viewpoint
10
2 45 Lobatse
Kanye 5

112   161   86   74

Sekoma

Jwaneng

Tshane

21

Keng

29

*To Mafikeng
(Ramatlabama
border post 43 km)*

130

Khakhea

40

**GPS waypoints
(u/k)**

(A) 24 55 11 S
    23 13 08 E
(B) 24 56 04 S
    22 09 28 E
(C) 25 06 11 S
    22 03 51 E

*Lesholoago
Pan*

Microwave
Tower

(A)

(C) 10
11 (B)   100
    cut-line

Khokhotsa Pan

**GEMSBOK
NATIONAL
PARK**

*Mpaathutlwa
Pan*

B O T S W A N A

110

63

Werda   *International boundary*

145

Tsabong

S O U T H   A F R I C A

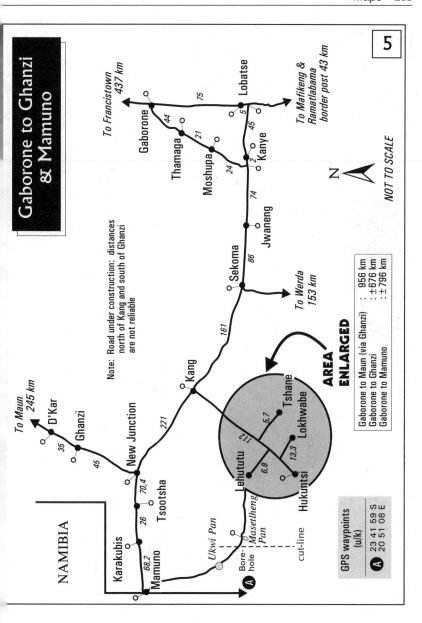

Gaborone to Ghanzi & Mamuno

5

To Francistown 437 km

Gaborone

Thamaga

Moshupa

Kanye

Lobatse

To Mafikeng &
Ramatlabama
border post 43 km

N

NOT TO SCALE

Note: Road under construction: distances
north of Kang and south of Ghanzi
are not reliable

Jwaneng

Sekoma

To Werda
153 km

AREA
ENLARGED

Tshane

Lokhwabe

Lehututu

Hukuntsi

Kang

New Junction

Tsootsha

Ghanzi

D'Kar

To Maun
245 km

Karakubis

Mamuno

NAMIBIA

Ukwi Pan

*Masetlheng
Pan*

Bore-
hole

cut-line

GPS waypoints
(u/k)

A 23 41 59 S
   20 51 08 E

Gaborone to Maun (via Ghanzi)	: 956 km
Gaborone to Ghanzi	: ±676 km
Gaborone to Mamuno	: ±796 km

44 21 24 75 5 45 2 74 86 161 221 70.4 26 68.2 35 45 5.7 112 6.8 13.3

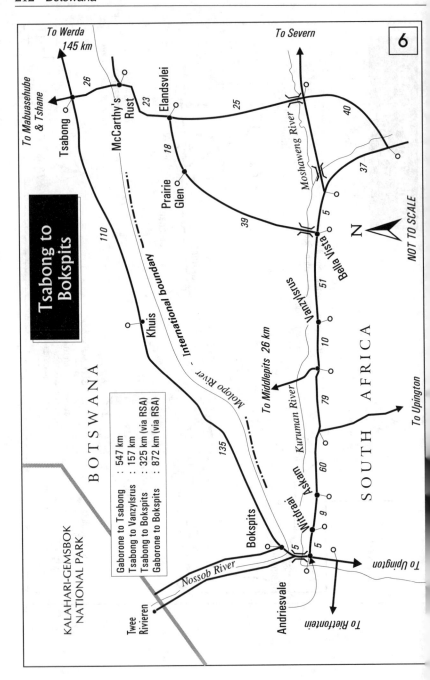

Tsabong to Bokspits

6

To Werda
145 km

To Severn

To Mabuasehube & Tshane

To Tsabong

26

McCarthy's Rust

23

Elandsvlei

25

40

Moshaweng River

37

18

Prairie Glen

39

Bella Vista

5

N

NOT TO SCALE

110

Khuis

51

Molopo River - International boundary

Vanzylsrus

To Middlepits 26 km

10

Kuruman River

79

60

Askam

135

9

Witdraai

5

Bokspits

5

5

To Upington

KALAHARI-GEMSBOK NATIONAL PARK

BOTSWANA

SOUTH AFRICA

To Upington

Nossob River

Twee Rivieren

Andriesvale

To Rietfontein

Gaborone to Tsabong   : 547 km
Tsabong to Vanzylsrus   : 157 km
Tsabong to Bokspits   : 325 km (via RSA)
Gaborone to Bokspits   : 872 km (via RSA)

Serowe to Mopipi

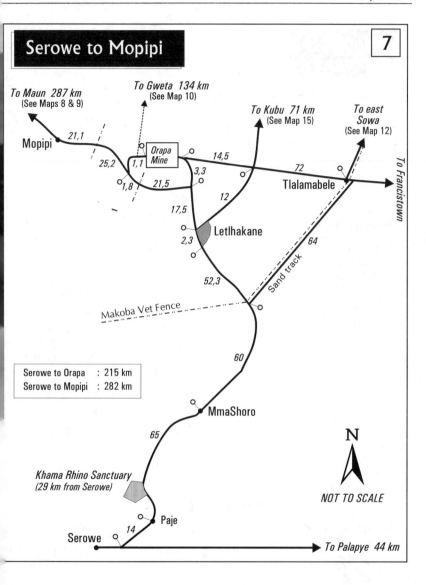

7

To Maun 287 km
(See Maps 8 & 9)

To Gweta 134 km
(See Map 10)

To Kubu 71 km
(See Map 15)

To east
Sowa
(See Map 12)

To Francistown

Mopipi

21,1

25,2

1,1

Orapa
Mine

14,5

3,3

1,8

21,5

72

Tlalamabele

12

17,5

Letlhakane

2,3

64

52,3

Sand track

Makoba Vet Fence

60

| Serowe to Orapa | : 215 km |
| Serowe to Mopipi | : 282 km |

MmaShoro

65

N

Khama Rhino Sanctuary
(29 km from Serowe)

NOT TO SCALE

Paje

Serowe

14

To Palapye 44 km

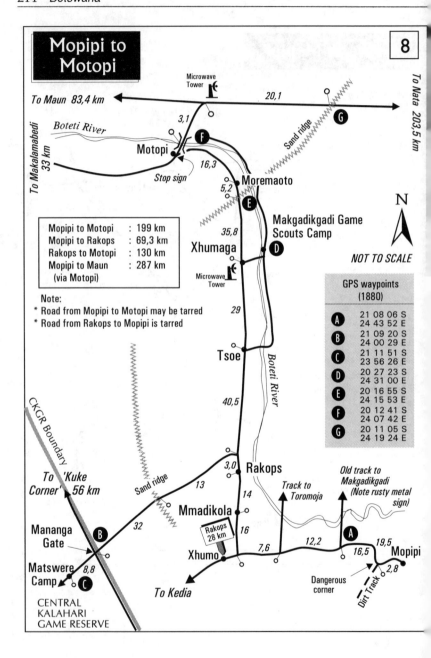

Mopipi to Motopi

8

To Maun 83,4 km

To Nata 203,5 km

Microwave Tower

20,1

3,1

Boteti River

To Makalamabedi 33 km

Motopi

F

Sand ridge

G

Stop sign

16,3

Moremaoto

5,2

E

Makgadikgadi Game Scouts Camp

35,8

Xhumaga

D

N

NOT TO SCALE

Microwave Tower

Mopipi to Motopi	: 199 km
Mopipi to Rakops	: 69,3 km
Rakops to Motopi	: 130 km
Mopipi to Maun (via Motopi)	: 287 km

Note:
* Road from Mopipi to Motopi may be tarred
* Road from Rakops to Mopipi is tarred

29

Tsoe

Boteti River

40,5

Sand ridge

GPS waypoints (1880)	
A	21 08 06 S 24 43 52 E
B	21 09 20 S 24 00 29 E
C	21 11 51 S 23 56 26 E
D	20 27 23 S 24 31 00 E
E	20 16 55 S 24 15 53 E
F	20 12 41 S 24 07 42 E
G	20 11 05 S 24 19 24 E

CKGR Boundary

3,0

Rakops

Track to Toromoja

Old track to Makgadikgadi (Note rusty metal sign)

To 'Kuke Corner 56 km

13

Sand ridge

14

Mmadikola

A

19,5

Mopipi

Mananga Gate

B

32

Rakops 28 km

16

12,2

16,5

2,8

Matswere Camp

C

8,8

Xhumo

7,6

Dangerous corner

Dirt Track

To Kedia

CENTRAL KALAHARI GAME RESERVE

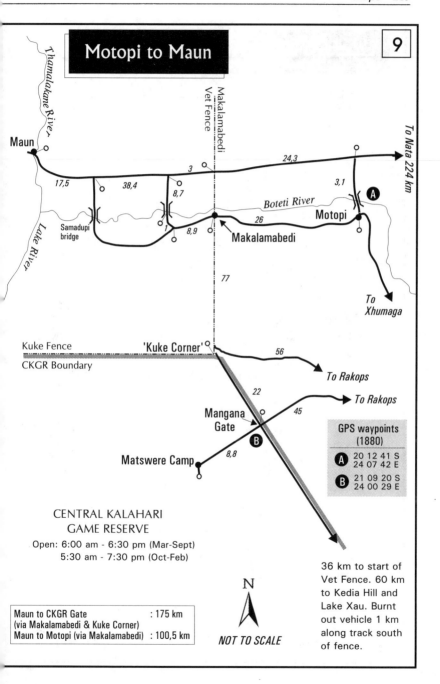

Motopi to Maun

9

Thamalakane River

Maun

Makalamabedi Vet Fence

To Nata 224 km

17,5

38,4

3

24,3

3,1

A

8,7

Boteti River

26

Motopi

1

8,9

Samadupi bridge

Makalamabedi

To Xhumaga

77

Kuke Fence

CKGR Boundary

'Kuke Corner'

56

To Rakops

22

To Rakops

45

Mangana Gate

B

Matswere Camp

8,8

GPS waypoints (1880)

A 20 12 41 S
24 07 42 E

B 21 09 20 S
24 00 29 E

CENTRAL KALAHARI
GAME RESERVE

Open: 6:00 am - 6:30 pm (Mar-Sept)
5:30 am - 7:30 pm (Oct-Feb)

N

NOT TO SCALE

Maun to CKGR Gate	: 175 km
(via Makalamabedi & Kuke Corner)	
Maun to Motopi (via Makalamabedi)	: 100,5 km

36 km to start of
Vet Fence. 60 km
to Kedia Hill and
Lake Xau. Burnt
out vehicle 1 km
along track south
of fence.

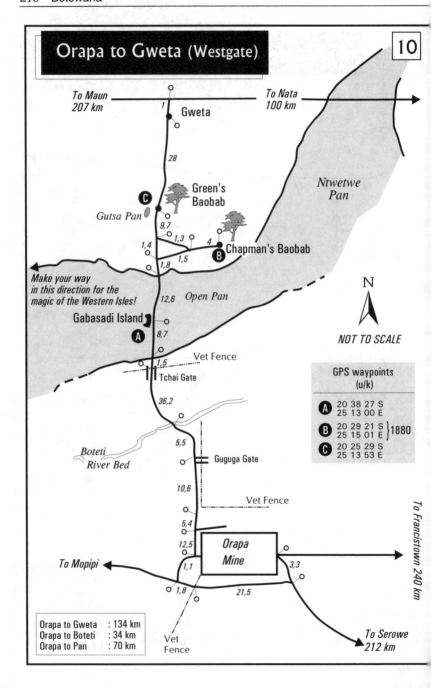

Orapa to Gweta (Westgate)

10

To Maun
207 km

To Nata
100 km

Gweta

1

28

Green's
Baobab

C

Gutsa Pan

9,7

1,3

1,4

1,8

1,5

4

Chapman's Baobab

B

*Ntwetwe
Pan*

*Make your way
in this direction for the
magic of the Western Isles!*

12,6

Open Pan

Gabasadi Island

A

8,7

1,5

Vet Fence

Tchai Gate

36,2

N

NOT TO SCALE

**GPS waypoints
(u/k)**

A 20 38 27 S
25 13 00 E

B 20 29 21 S
25 15 01 E }1880

C 20 25 29 S
25 13 53 E

5,5

Guguga Gate

*Boteti
River Bed*

10,6

Vet Fence

5,4

12,5

*Orapa
Mine*

To Mopipi

1,1

3,3

1,8

21,5

To Francistown 240 km

Orapa to Gweta	: 134 km
Orapa to Boteti	: 34 km
Orapa to Pan	: 70 km

Vet
Fence

To Serowe
212 km

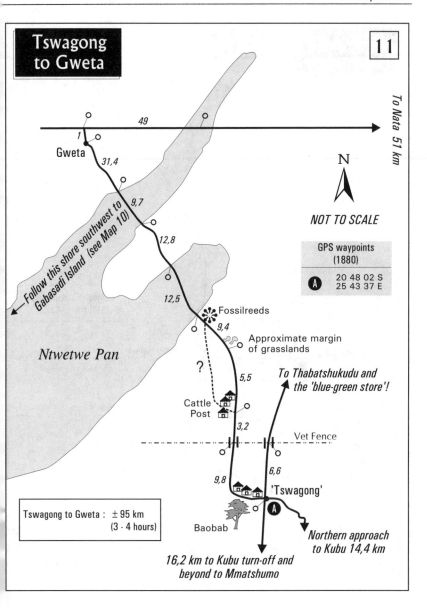

Tswagong to Gweta

11

To Nata 51 km

Gweta

49

1

31,4

9,7

12,8

12,5

Follow this shore southwest to Gabasadi Island (see Map 10)

Ntwetwe Pan

N

NOT TO SCALE

GPS waypoints (1880)

Ⓐ 20 48 02 S
25 43 37 E

Fossilreeds

9,4

Approximate margin of grasslands

?

5,5

To Thabatshukudu and the 'blue-green store'!

Cattle Post

3,2

Vet Fence

9,8

6,6

'Tswagong'

Ⓐ

Baobab

Northern approach to Kubu 14,4 km

Tswagong to Gweta : ± 95 km (3 - 4 hours)

16,2 km to Kubu turn-off and beyond to Mmatshumo

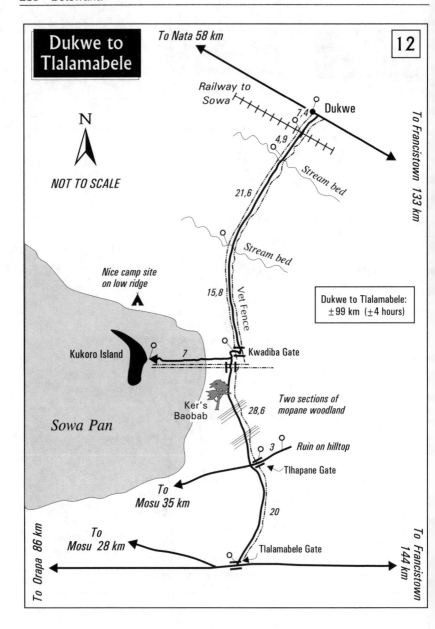

Dukwe to Tlalamabele

12

To Nata 58 km

Railway to Sowa

Dukwe

7,4

4,9

Stream bed

21,6

Stream bed

N

NOT TO SCALE

To Francistown 133 km

Nice camp site on low ridge

15,8

Vet Fence

Kukoro Island

7

Kwadiba Gate

Dukwe to Tlalamabele: ±99 km (±4 hours)

Ker's Baobab

28,6

Two sections of mopane woodland

Sowa Pan

3

Ruin on hilltop

Tlhapane Gate

To Mosu 35 km

20

To Mosu 28 km

Tlalamabele Gate

To Orapa 86 km

To Francistown 144 km

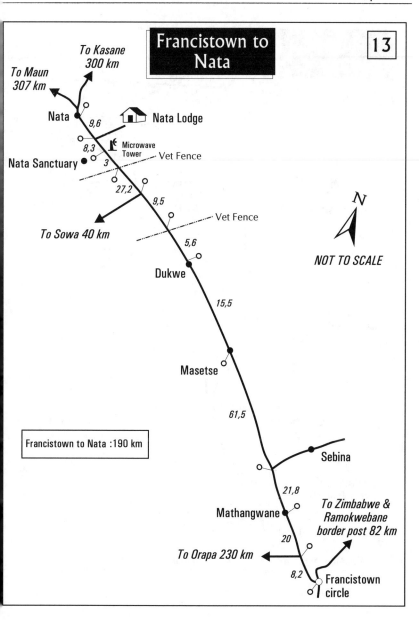

Francistown to Nata

13

To Kasane 300 km

To Maun 307 km

Nata — 9,6 — Nata Lodge

8,3

Microwave Tower — Vet Fence

Nata Sanctuary — 3

27,2

9,5

Vet Fence

To Sowa 40 km

5,6

N

NOT TO SCALE

Dukwe

15,5

Masetse

61,5

Francistown to Nata : 190 km

Sebina

21,8

Mathangwane

To Zimbabwe & Ramokwebane border post 82 km

20

To Orapa 230 km

8,2

Francistown circle

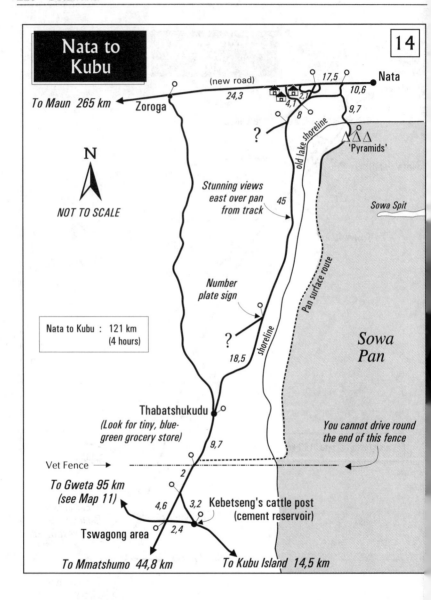

Nata to Kubu

14

(new road)

To Maun 265 km ← Zoroga

Nata

17,5

24,3

10,6

2,7

4,1

9,7

8

?

'Pyramids'

old lake shoreline

N

NOT TO SCALE

Stunning views east over pan from track

45

Sowa Spit

Number plate sign

?

18,5

shoreline

Pan surface route

Sowa Pan

Nata to Kubu : 121 km
              (4 hours)

Thabatshukudu

(Look for tiny, blue-green grocery store)

9,7

You cannot drive round the end of this fence

Vet Fence →

2

To Gweta 95 km
(see Map 11)

4,6

3,2 Kebetseng's cattle post
     (cement reservoir)

Tswagong area

2,4

To Mmatshumo 44,8 km

To Kubu Island 14,5 km

Letlhakane to Kubu

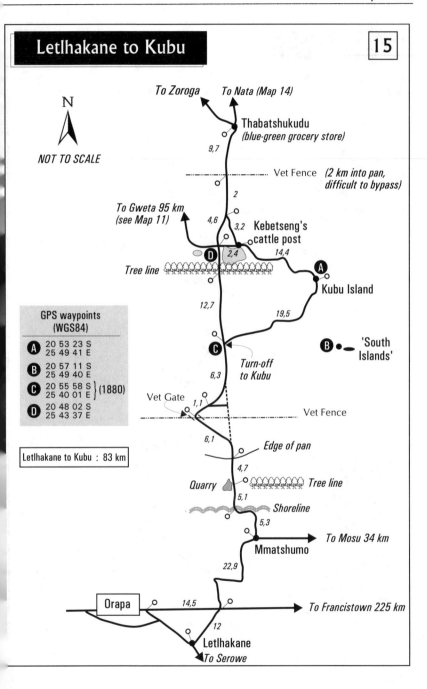

15

To Zoroga

To Nata (Map 14)

Thabatshukudu
(blue-green grocery store)

N

NOT TO SCALE

9,7

Vet Fence *(2 km into pan, difficult to bypass)*

2

To Gweta 95 km
(see Map 11)

4,6

3,2

Kebetseng's
cattle post

14,4

D 2,4

A

Tree line

Kubu Island

12,7

19,5

**GPS waypoints
(WGS84)**

A 20 53 23 S
25 49 41 E

B 20 57 11 S
25 49 40 E

C 20 55 58 S
25 40 01 E } (1880)

D 20 48 02 S
25 43 37 E

C

*Turn-off
to Kubu*

6,3

B •— 'South
Islands'

Letlhakane to Kubu : 83 km

Vet Gate

1,1

Vet Fence

6,1

Edge of pan

4,7

Quarry

Tree line

5,1

Shoreline

5,3

To Mosu 34 km

Mmatshumo

22,9

Orapa

14,5

To Francistown 225 km

12

Letlhakane

To Serowe

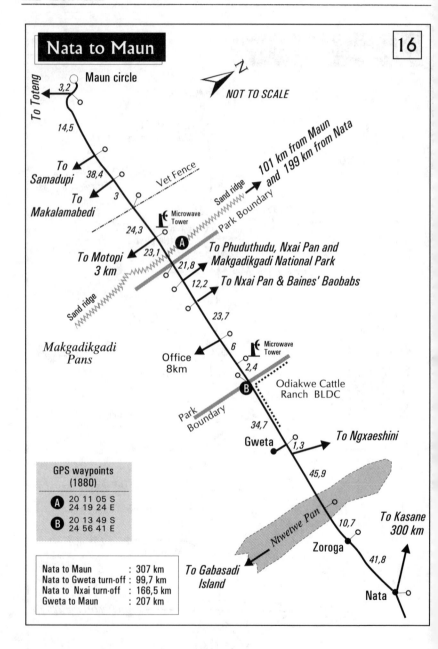

Nata to Maun

16

NOT TO SCALE

To Toteng

3,2 Maun circle

14,5

To Samadupi 38,4

To Makalamabedi 3

Vet Fence

Sand ridge 101 km from Maun and 199 km from Nata

Park Boundary

Microwave Tower

24,3

A 23,1

To Motopi 3 km

21,8

To Phuduthudu, Nxai Pan and Makgadikgadi National Park

12,2 To Nxai Pan & Baines' Baobabs

Sand ridge

23,7

Makgadikgadi Pans

6

Office 8km

Microwave Tower

2,4

B Odiakwe Cattle Ranch BLDC

Park Boundary

34,7

Gweta 1,3 To Ngxaeshini

GPS waypoints (1880)

A 20 11 05 S
    24 19 24 E

B 20 13 49 S
    24 56 41 E

45,9

Ntwetwe Pan

10,7 To Kasane 300 km

Zoroga

41,8

Nata

Nata to Maun	: 307 km
Nata to Gweta turn-off	: 99,7 km
Nata to Nxai turn-off	: 166,5 km
Gweta to Maun	: 207 km

To Gabasadi Island

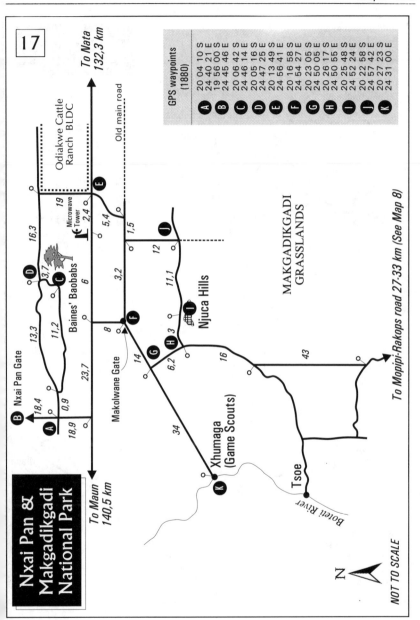

17

Nxai Pan & Makgadikgadi National Park

To Nata 132,3 km

To Maun 140,5 km

GPS waypoints (1880)

A	20 04 10 S	24 40 21 E
B	19 56 00 S	24 45 46 E
C	20 06 42 S	24 46 14 E
D	20 05 16 S	24 47 25 E
E	20 13 49 S	24 56 41 E
F	20 16 58 S	24 54 27 E
G	20 23 05 S	24 50 05 E
H	20 26 17 S	24 50 55 E
I	20 25 48 S	24 52 24 E
J	20 22 58 S	24 57 42 E
K	20 27 23 S	24 31 00 E

Odiakwe Cattle Ranch BLDC

Old main road

Microwave Tower

Baines' Baobabs

Nxai Pan Gate

Makolwane Gate

Njuca Hills

MAKGADIKGADI GRASSLANDS

Xhumaga (Game Scouts)

Tsoe

Boteti River

To Mopipi-Rakops road 27-33 km (See Map 8)

N

NOT TO SCALE

18,4 0,9 18,9 23,7 13,3 11,2 3,7 6 16,3 19 2,4 5,4 1,5 12 3,2 11,1 8 14 6,2 3 16 43 34

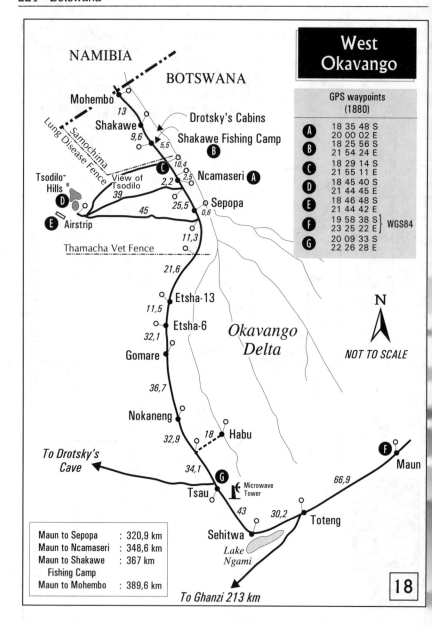

NAMIBIA

BOTSWANA

West Okavango

Mohembo

13

Shakawe

9,6

Drotsky's Cabins

Shakawe Fishing Camp **B**

5,5

10,4

C

Ncamaseri **A**

2,5

Tsodilo Hills

View of Tsodilo

2,2

39

25,5

Sepopa

45

0,6

D

E Airstrip

11,3

Lung Disease Fence

Samochima

Thamacha Vet Fence

21,6

Etsha-13

11,5

Etsha-6

32,1

Gomare

Okavango Delta

36,7

Nokaneng

32,9

18 Habu

To Drotsky's Cave

34,1

G

Tsau

Microwave Tower

43

30,2

F Maun

66,9

Toteng

Sehitwa

Lake Ngami

To Ghanzi 213 km

N

NOT TO SCALE

GPS waypoints (1880)		
A	18 35 48 S	
	20 00 02 E	
B	18 25 56 S	
	21 54 24 E	
C	18 29 14 S	
	21 55 11 E	
D	18 45 40 S	
	21 44 45 E	
E	18 46 48 S	
	21 44 42 E	
F	19 58 38 S	WGS84
	23 25 22 E	
G	20 09 33 S	
	22 26 28 E	

Maun to Sepopa : 320,9 km
Maun to Ncamaseri : 348,6 km
Maun to Shakawe : 367 km
  Fishing Camp
Maun to Mohembo : 389,6 km

18

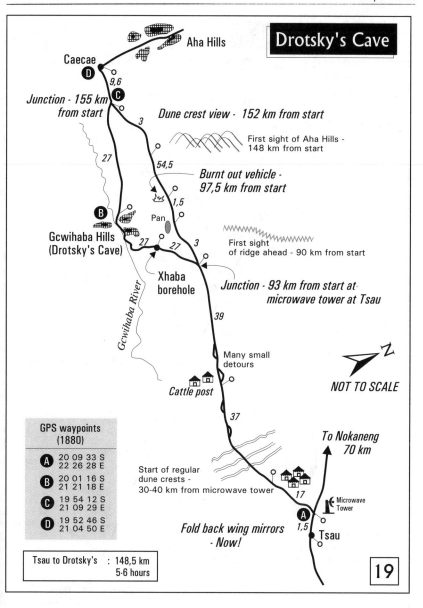

Drotsky's Cave

Aha Hills

Caecae **D**

9,6

Junction - 155 km
from start **C**

3

Dune crest view - 152 km from start

First sight of Aha Hills -
148 km from start

27

54,5

Burnt out vehicle -
97,5 km from start

B

1,5

Pan

Gcwihaba Hills
(Drotsky's Cave)

27   27   3

First sight
of ridge ahead - 90 km from start

Xhaba
borehole

Junction - 93 km from start at
microwave tower at Tsau

Gcwihaba River

39

Many small
detours

Cattle post

**GPS waypoints
(1880)**

A 20 09 33 S
22 26 28 E

B 20 01 16 S
21 21 18 E

C 19 54 12 S
21 09 29 E

D 19 52 46 S
21 04 50 E

37

To Nokaneng
70 km

Start of regular
dune crests -
30-40 km from microwave tower

17

Microwave
Tower

A

1,5

N

NOT TO SCALE

Fold back wing mirrors
- Now!

Tsau

Tsau to Drotsky's : 148,5 km
5-6 hours

19

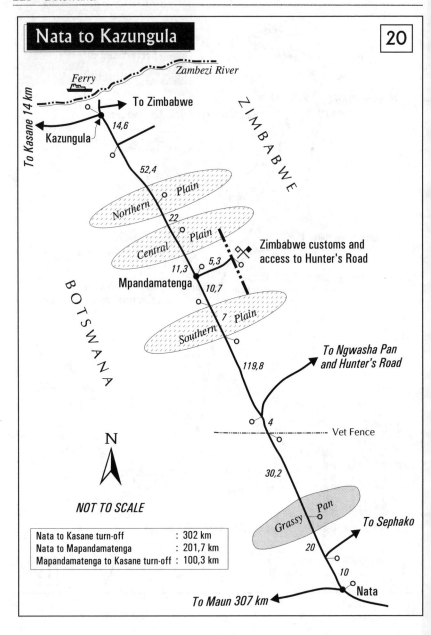

Nata to Kazungula

20

Zambezi River

Ferry

To Kasane 14 km

To Zimbabwe

Kazungula

14,6

52,4

ZIMBABWE

Northern Plain

22

Central Plain

11,3 5,3

Mpandamatenga

10,7

Zimbabwe customs and access to Hunter's Road

Southern 7 Plain

119,8

To Ngwasha Pan and Hunter's Road

4

Vet Fence

30,2

BOTSWANA

N

NOT TO SCALE

Grassy Pan

To Sephako

20

10

Nata

To Maun 307 km

Nata to Kasane turn-off	: 302 km
Nata to Mapandamatenga	: 201,7 km
Mapandamatenga to Kasane turn-off	: 100,3 km

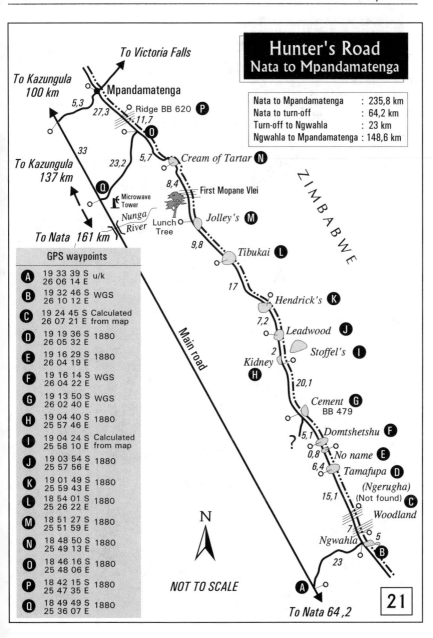

Hunter's Road
Nata to Mpandamatenga

Nata to Mpandamatenga	: 235,8 km
Nata to turn-off	: 64,2 km
Turn-off to Ngwahla	: 23 km
Ngwahla to Mpandamatenga	: 148,6 km

To Victoria Falls

To Kazungula 100 km

Mpandamatenga

Ridge BB 620 **P**

5,3
27,3
11,7
O

To Kazungula 137 km

33

23,2

5,7

Q

Microwave Tower

Nunga River

Lunch Tree

To Nata 161 km

5,7

Cream of Tartar **N**

8,4

First Mopane Vlei

Jolley's **M**

9,8

Tibukai **L**

17

Hendrick's **K**

7,2

Leadwood **J**

2

Stoffel's **I**

Kidney **H**

20,1

Cement **G**
BB 479

5,1

Domtshetshu **F**

0,8

No name **E**

6,4

Tamafupa **D**

(Ngerugha)
(Not found) **C**

15,1

Woodland

Ngwahla 5

B

7

23

A

To Nata 64,2

ZIMBABWE

Main road

N

NOT TO SCALE

21

GPS waypoints

A	19 33 39 S 26 06 14 E	u/k
B	19 32 46 S 26 10 12 E	WGS
C	19 24 45 S 26 07 21 E	Calculated from map
D	19 19 36 S 26 05 32 E	1880
E	19 16 29 S 26 04 19 E	1880
F	19 16 14 S 26 04 22 E	WGS
G	19 13 50 S 26 02 40 E	WGS
H	19 04 40 S 25 57 46 E	1880
I	19 04 24 S 25 58 10 E	Calculated from map
J	19 03 54 S 25 57 56 E	1880
K	19 01 49 S 25 59 43 E	1880
L	18 54 01 S 25 26 22 E	1880
M	18 51 27 S 25 51 59 E	1880
N	18 48 50 S 25 49 13 E	1880
O	18 46 16 S 25 48 06 E	1880
P	18 42 15 S 25 47 35 E	1880
Q	18 49 49 S 25 36 07 E	1880

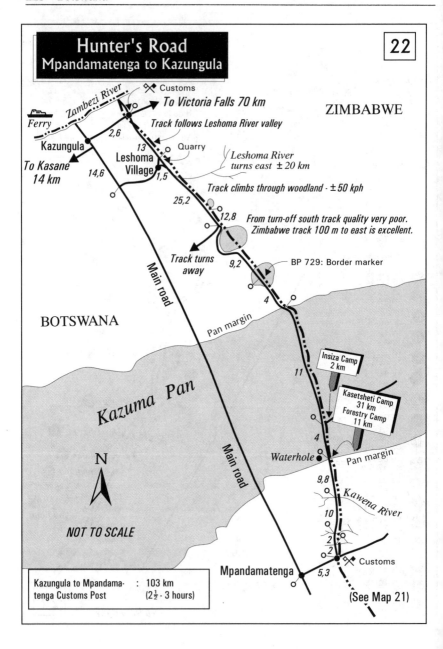

Hunter's Road
Mpandamatenga to Kazungula

22

Customs
To Victoria Falls 70 km
ZIMBABWE

Zambezi River

Ferry
Track follows Leshoma River valley

2,6
Kazungula
13 Quarry
To Kasane   Leshoma
14 km   Village
14,6   1,5

Leshoma River turns east ± 20 km

25,2

Track climbs through woodland · ± 50 kph

12,8 *From turn-off south track quality very poor.*
      Zimbabwe track 100 m to east is excellent.

Track turns
away   9,2   BP 729: Border marker

BOTSWANA   4

Pan margin

Kazuma Pan

Main road

Insiza Camp
2 km

11

Kasetsheti Camp
31 km
Forestry Camp
11 km

N

4

Waterhole   Pan margin

9,8

NOT TO SCALE
10   *Kawena River*

2
2
Customs

Mpandamatenga   5,3

Kazungula to Mpandama-tenga Customs Post	: 103 km (2½ - 3 hours)

(See Map 21)

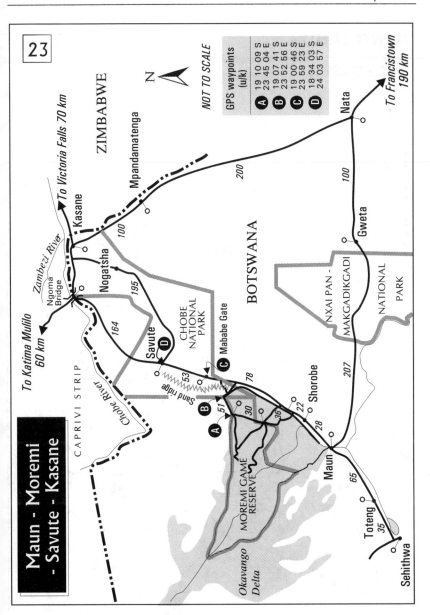

23

To Victoria Falls 70 km

ZIMBABWE

Mpandamatenga

NOT TO SCALE

GPS waypoints
(u/k)
A 19 10 09 S
    23 45 04 E
B 19 07 41 S
    23 52 56 E
C 19 00 46 S
    23 59 23 E
D 18 34 03 S
    24 03 57 E

N

Kasane

Zambezi River

Ngoma
Bridge

Nogatsha

To Katima Mulilo
60 km

CAPRIVI STRIP

Chobe River

Savute

D

CHOBE
NATIONAL
PARK

Mababe Gate

C

Sand ridge

B

A

164

195

100

200

100

Nata

To Francistown
190 km

BOTSWANA

NXAI PAN -
MAKGADIKGADI

NATIONAL
PARK

Gweta

53

78

51

30

36

22

Shorobe

28

207

Maun

65

Toteng

35

Sehithwa

MOREMI GAME
RESERVE

Okavango
Delta

Maun - Moremi
- Savute - Kasane

Town maps

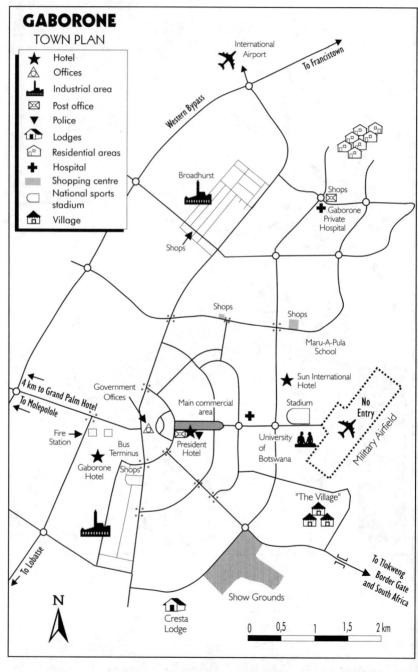

GABORONE
TOWN PLAN

★	Hotel
⌂	Offices
⌂	Industrial area
⊠	Post office
▼	Police
⌂	Lodges
⌂	Residential areas
✚	Hospital
▨	Shopping centre
▭	National sports stadium
⌂	Village

International Airport

To Francistown

Western Bypass

Broadhurst

Shops

Gaborone Private Hospital

Shops

Shops

Shops

Maru-A-Pula School

4 km to Grand Palm Hotel

To Molepolole

Government Offices

Main commercial area

Sun International Hotel

Stadium

No Entry

Military Airfield

Fire Station

Bus Terminus

President Hotel

University of Botswana

Gaborone Hotel

Shops

"The Village"

To Lobatse

To Tlokweng Border Gate and South Africa

Show Grounds

N

Cresta Lodge

0   0,5   1   1,5   2 km

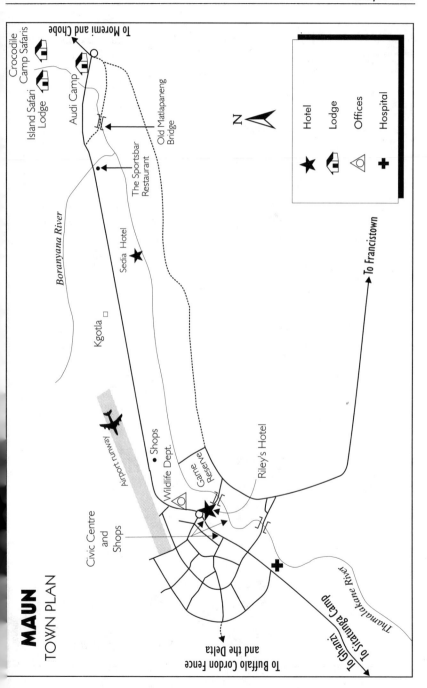

MAUN
TOWN PLAN

To Moremi and Chobe

Crocodile Camp Safaris
Island Safari Lodge
Audi Camp

Old Matlapaneng Bridge

The Sportsbar Restaurant

Boranyana River

Sedia Hotel

Kgotla

Civic Centre and Shops

Airport runway

Shops
Wildlife Dept.
Game Reserve

Riley's Hotel

To Buffalo Cordon Fence and the Delta

Thamalakane River

To Ghanzi
To Sitatunga Camp

To Francistown

N

Hotel
Lodge
Offices
Hospital

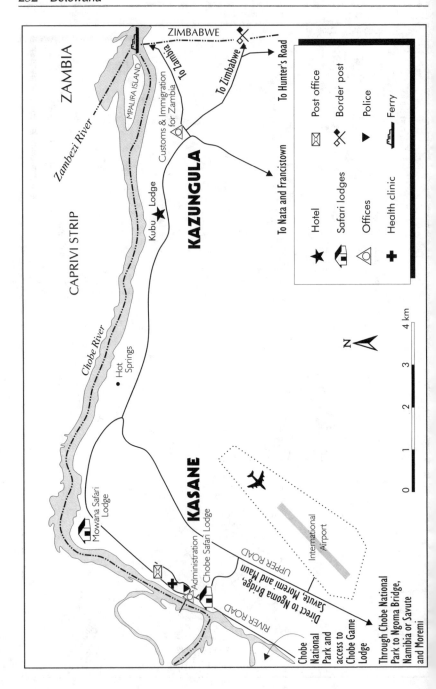

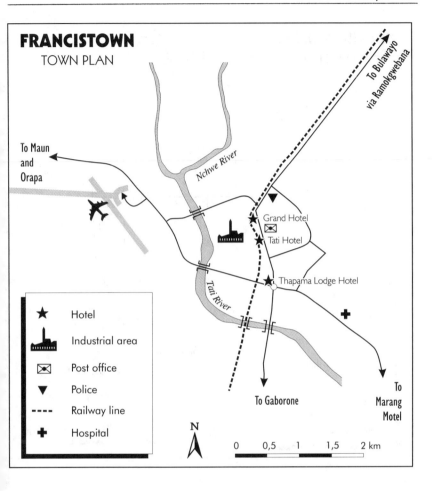

FRANCISTOWN
TOWN PLAN

To Bulawayo
via Ramokgwebana

To Maun
and
Orapa

Nchwe River

Grand Hotel

Tati Hotel

Thapama Lodge Hotel

Tati River

★ Hotel

🏭 Industrial area

✉ Post office

▼ Police

---- Railway line

✚ Hospital

To Gaborone

To
Marang
Motel

N

0   0,5   1   1,5   2 km

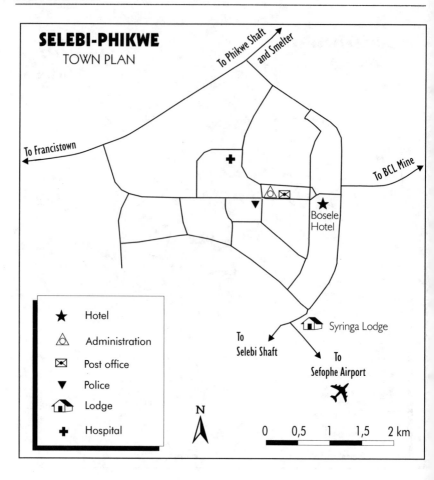

SELEBI-PHIKWE
TOWN PLAN

To Phikwe Shaft and Smelter

To Francistown

To BCL Mine

Bosele Hotel

To Selebi Shaft

Syringa Lodge

To Sefophe Airport

★ Hotel

△ Administration

✉ Post office

▼ Police

🏠 Lodge

✚ Hospital

N

0   0,5   1   1,5   2 km

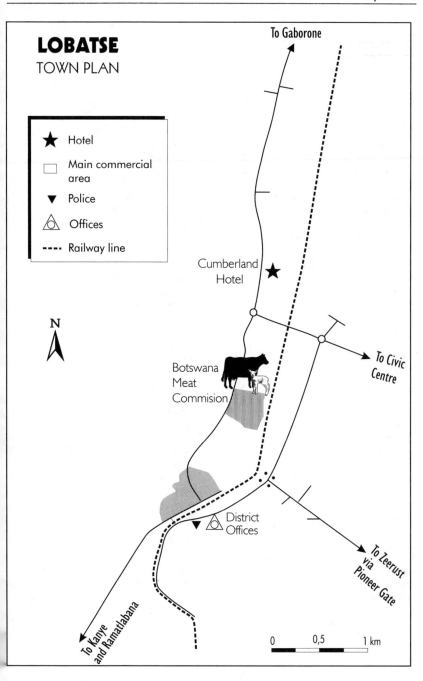

LOBATSE
TOWN PLAN

To Gaborone

Hotel
Main commercial area
Police
Offices
Railway line

N

Cumberland Hotel

To Civic Centre

Botswana Meat Commision

District Offices

To Zeerust via Pioneer Gate

To Kanye and Ramatlabana

0   0,5   1 km

INDEX

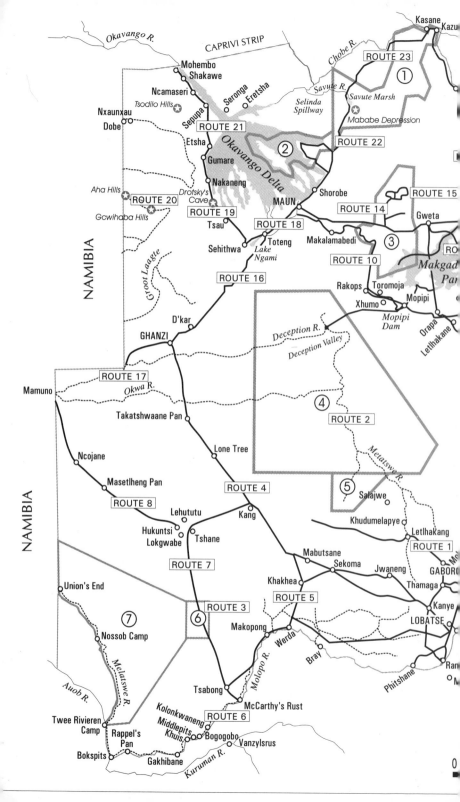